JACQUES CHESSEX: CALVINISM AND THE TEXT

Despite an impressive body of poems, novels, short stories, and literary criticism; high praise for his writing by French and Swiss critics; and a collection of honours that includes the prestigious Prix Goncourt, awarded for his novel L'Ogrein 1973, Jacques Chessex is relatively unknown outside France and Switzerland. With this book, David J. Bond provides the first comprehensive study of his work in any language - a study that reveals Chessex's deep ambivalence towards his Calvinist heritage and his efforts to resolve this dilemma through his texts.

Born in 1934 in Payerne, in the region of French-speaking Switzerland known as the Vaud, Chessex grew up amid the pervasive influence of the Calvinist church. His writing, which tells of Vaud society and the hypocrisy of many of its leading members, reveals his preoccupation with a rigid morality, sin, remorse, and death. Bond shows that while Chessex uses his texts to escape this heritage and affirm alternate values, particularly sexual pleasure and enjoyment of life, his writing reveals a deep nostalgia for the stability and security of a strict religious system in a world that he finds unstable and even absurd without it. Chessex looks to the text as a univocal organizing principle that might impose order and sense. Bond sees in Chessex's writing an attempt to find unity in opposing values, to establish contact with others, and to overcome an obsession with death and the passing of time.

DAVID J. BOND is Professor of French at the University of Saskatchewan.

DAVID J. BOND

Jacques Chessex:
Calvinism and the Text

UNIVERSITY OF TORONTO PRESS
Toronto Buffalo London

© University of Toronto Press Incorporated 1994
Toronto Buffalo London
Reprinted in paperback 2014

ISBN 978-0-8020-0555-7 (cloth)
ISBN 978-1-4426-5208-8 (paper)

Printed on acid-free paper

University of Toronto Romance Series

Canadian Cataloguing in Publication Data

Bond, David J.
  Jacques Chessex : Calvinism and the text

  (University of Toronto romance series)
  Includes bibliographical references and index.
  ISBN 978-0-8020-0555-7 (bound) ISBN 978-1-4426-5208-8 (pbk.)

  1. Chessex, Jacques – Criticism and interpretation.
  2. Chessex, Jacques – Knowledge – Calvinism.
  3. Calvinism in literature.   I. Title.   II. Series.

  PQ2663.H396Z64 1994   848'.91409   C94-930322-4

Photograph of Jacques Chessex, frontispiece, copyright
Philippe Pache, Lausanne.

University of Toronto Press acknowledges the financial
assistance to its publishing program of the Canada Council
and the Ontario Arts Council.

This book has been published with the help of a grant from
the Canadian Federation for the Humanities, using funds provided by
the Social Sciences and Humanities Research Council of Canada.

Contents

ACKNOWLEDGMENTS vii

1
Introduction: Some Preliminary Considerations 3

2
The Calvinist Heritage 18

3
The Nature of Calvinism 25

4
The Ambiguities of a Calvinist 40

5
The Valley of the Shadow 50

6
Les Justes 65

7
The Affirmation of Life 78

8
The Flight from Calvinism 97

9
Division and Unity 104

10
The Text as Unity 116

11
The Text, the World, and Others 133

12
Death, Memory, and the Text 147

13
Conclusion: Religion and the Text 164

NOTES 177

BIBLIOGRAPHY 187

INDEX 195

Acknowledgments

Part of this book was written while I was the recipient of a grant from the Social Sciences and Humanities Research Council of Canada. I would like to thank the Council for its support.

JACQUES CHESSEX: CALVINISM AND THE TEXT

1
Introduction: Some Preliminary Considerations

Since Jacques Chessex is scarcely known outside of Switzerland and France, it is as well to begin with some biographical facts. He was born in 1934, in Payerne, a town in the region of French-speaking Switzerland known as the Vaud. His father, Pierre Chessex, was a teacher, a writer of historical fiction, a keen amateur historian, and an etymologist, who was deeply attached to the Vaud, its history, and its people. Although Jacques Chessex seems not to have had an especially religious upbringing, he grew up, like all Vaudois of his generation, amid the all-pervasive influence of the Calvinist Church.

In 1943, Chessex's father became principal of the Collège Scientifique de Lausanne. The family moved to Lausanne, and, shortly after, to Pully. Jacques attended the Collège Classique at Lausanne until the age of seventeen, when he went to Fribourg to study at the Collège Saint-Michel. In this Catholic city, attending an institution run by priests, Chessex was introduced to a more humane and meditative religion than the Calvinism of his earlier years. Having lost by then his belief in God, he never turned to Catholicism as an antidote to Calvinism, but he has always retained a great affection for his teachers in Fribourg, and for their faith. In 1952, he returned to Lausanne to study literature and the history of art at the university. His first published work, a collection of poems called *Le Jour proche*, appeared in 1954. Meanwhile, his father was undergoing a period of personal crisis that led to his suicide in 1956.

Chessex was, at this time, writing a *mémoire* on Francis Ponge for his *licence*. Ponge's poetry and his ideas on language and literature naturally had repercussions on Chessex's own texts. He was writing and publishing more poetry, and he also began to spend periods in

Paris, where he became a friend of Marcel Arland, Yves Berger, and Georges Lambrichs, all of whom encouraged him to continue writing. He had also become friendly with François Nourissier, who gave him encouragement and help. In 1962, Gallimard published his first work in prose, *La Tête ouverte*.[1]

Since that time, while pursuing a career as a teacher of French literature at the Gymnase in Lausanne, Jacques Chessex has continued to create an impressive *oeuvre* that includes poetry, novels, volumes of short stories, and articles of literary criticism. He has acquired a reputation as one of French Switzerland's foremost writers, and his talents have been recognized in France as well as in his own country. This recognition is perhaps best indicated by the fact that he obtained the Prix Goncourt in 1973 for his novel *L'Ogre*. He has also been awarded the Prix Schiller for *La Tête ouverte* in 1963, the Prix Alpes-Jura in 1972, the Diplôme d'honneur Hans-Christian Anderson in 1982, and the Grand Prix du rayonnement français, awarded by the Académie Française in 1983.

The respect for Chessex's texts that these prizes indicate is shared by many critics, who have been unstinting in their praise of his writing. He has been called 'un écrivain de la meilleure trempe,' 'un écrivain de premier ordre,' and 'peut-être le plus doué des jeunes écrivains romands.'[2] His technical mastery of the text has been singled out for comment, and it has been said of him: 'Chessex joue en artiste maître de ses moyens.'[3] Others have remarked on the poetic nature of his style, whether he is writing in prose or in verse. It has been stated, for example, that his novel *L'Ogre* 'éclate de santé, de naturel et de poésie.'[4] The ability of Chessex to capture and convey life and vitality in his texts has been noticed by several critics, who say his work has 'l'épaisseur des choses vécues, des émotions, des sentiments lentement recuits,' 'une palpitation cachée ... Si l'on veut, l'animisme immanent de la poésie,' and 'de nombreuses pages gonflées de tendresse, d'odeurs, de visions d'enfance et de précieuse sensualité.'[5] He has even been compared to Zola, Baudelaire, Kafka, Flaubert, Constant, and Supervielle.[6]

As well as being the subject of such flattering critical commentaries, Chessex is himself an author of critical articles and books who has also been a teacher of literature. His writings show a distinct preference for a certain type of literature and literary criticism, a preference that carries with it an intense dislike of another kind of modern literature and criticism. He attacks very harshly what he believes to be a modern critical approach that is too dry and theoretical. Semiotics, structuralism, post-structuralism – all those critical methodologies that emphasize theory – are condemned by him because he believes they overintellectualize the art of writing and criticizing. In a diatribe that is also an excellent example of Chessex in full spate, he says that there are 'assez de poètes lacanisants, de sémioticiens, de saussuriens, de jakobseniens, de patoisants derridiens ne déridant plus personne, de kristéviens extatiques, d'agités de la structure et de la révolution culturelle, de bredouilleurs fanatiques du clivage et du schème-niveau, de théoriciens du bafouillage initiatique et du brouillon préremptoire, de petits maîtres fous de leur embaumement du pauvre Ponge et de sentencieux béjaunes à la mine de gardiens du Temple!' (*Carabas*, 135).

This kind of criticism, according to Chessex, is unable to appreciate texts that are not themselves highly theoretical and full of jargon. Hence, when something strikingly original appears, practitioners of such critical methodology cannot come to grips with it: 'Lorsqu'apparaît une oeuvre qui ne jargonne pas, qui ne se paie pas de mots, personne n'en parle.'[7] He points to the way that critics have ignored or vilified Philippe Jaccottet's work because 'ce n'est pas dans le vent, parce que ce n'est pas accroché à un clan, ou à l'Ecole Normale, ou au Collège de France' (Garcin, 157). Michel Tournier's work, which Chessex considers to be 'une des oeuvres vraiment importantes de ces dix dernières années' (Garcin, 156), is likewise misrepresented or ignored by critics of this sort.

The type of literature that such critics prefer is described by Chessex in another lengthy diatribe as: 'Oeuvrettes habiles, romans d'intellectuels rompus aux techniques, à la mode, tristes canevas de laboratoire, schémas de géomètres exténués, pavés professoraux à degrés indigestes et pédants, contorsions savantissimes à la syntaxe vacillante, fausses parodies, faux monologues, petites trouvailles de précieuses ridicules telquellisantes, coquetteries marxisantes de sabots littéraires cachant leur médiocrité sous les désopilants échafaudages derridiens' (*Carabas*, 131). Among such academic exercises he counts, as one might expect, the *nouveau roman*. While admitting that this type of novel had its importance because 'les recherches sur la prose qu'il nous a proposées étaient nécessaires' (*Cingria*, 75), he sees it as part of an intellectualizing trend that has impoverished the novel. It was produced, he says, by intellectuals who had little interest in life or in the problems and pleasures of life. They were 'des hommes qui avaient sans doute la passion de la littérature et des idées, mais qui n'étaient que des intellectuels: ils n'avaient absolument aucune forme d'expérience de la cicatrice, du drame, de l'horreur, ou de la folie comme l'ont vécus Céline, ou Cendrars ou le premier Sartre' (Garcin, 151).

The result of this overintellectualizing of literature, of this excessive emphasis on theory, Chessex argues, is that French literature is no longer the dynamic force that it once was, and that 'la littérature française contemporaine est appauvrie et que surtout le roman n'a plus grand chose dans les veines' (Garcin, 156). In place of this kind of text, Chessex would like to see ones that attempt to convey the presence of the world around the writer, that are based on the writer's experience of the world. 'Moi, je rêve d'une littérature pleine de sang et farouche, d'une littérature puissamment nourrie et se foutant pas mal des modes et des conventions de l'intelligensia' is how he expresses his wish (*Carabas*, 131).

Chessex's dismissal of theory and of the intellectualizing of literature cannot be allowed to pass without comment. It is, of course, impossible to produce literary texts or to write about them without adopting a theoretical stance. The attempt to eschew all theory is itself one such stance, and what may be presented as a 'non-theoretical' attitude to writing is based on a definite conception of the text and of the role of both reader and writer. As Catherine Belsey says: 'But there is no practice without theory, however much the theory is suppressed, unformulated or perceived as "obvious"'[8] By attacking critics who are too 'intellectual' and 'theoretical,' Chessex is attempting to 'naturalize' and present his own theoretical standpoint as the common-sense one.

The point is that Chessex adopts an approach to writing that is the product of a specific society and of the language used by that society to express itself. When he writes, he uses a medium that carries with it a whole series of attitudes and assumptions. The discourse used by a group to express and to construct itself contains certain assumptions shared by members of that group. Attitudes, ways of thought, shared views are inscribed in that discourse, but they are often so intimate a part of the group's experience that they are felt as 'natural' and 'normal' rather than as just one set of possible assumptions.

Chessex's discourse is that of a particular religious and social milieu. Having been born and brought up in a society imbued with a certain kind of Calvinism, he uses a language, references, images, and a whole discourse that are coloured by the vision of life represented by that religion. This applies even to his view of writing and of the text, for, as will become apparent in the course of this study, he has an essentially logocentric view of the text. The Calvinism that forms his vision represents God and His Word as a central organizing presence. Although Chessex's texts constitute an attempt to escape this Calvinism, they remain firmly within the Judaeo-Christian logocentrism of which Calvinism is just one (albeit extreme) expression. Because his attitudes are dependent on the idea of a central authority that gives sense to existence, once he rejects the idea of a God who stands at the centre of that existence, he experiences the world around him as chaotic. Consequently, when the Calvinist organizing principle is removed, he has recourse to another such principle. The text becomes the equivalent of the Word – a power that welds the chaos around it into meaningful patterns.

In this view of things, the author is seen as he who stands at the centre of the text, a presence that imposes itself on the text and uses it, as God uses His Word, to create order. This attitude is seen particularly in Chessex's avowed admiration for writers who dominate their texts to such a degree that one can, in his opinion, almost feel their physical presence in them. He says that, in these texts, one is aware of the writer's mind at work, but there is not just an intellectual power here, for one can also sense the author's presence in the world, and his link to that world through mind *and* body. He particularly loves the work of Flaubert and Maupassant because, in their texts, 'leur présence physique est énorme' (*Carabas*, 128). Body and mind are both at work as organizing principles in the texts of such writers as Bernard Noël, Annie Leclerc, Marguerite Duras, and Anne Philippe (Garcin, 165–6).

This logocentric view of the text flies in the face of much contemporary linguistic and literary theory of the kind that Chessex ridicules in *Carabas*. There is no room here to discuss at length the objections that would be raised by structuralists, deconstructionists, and many other theoreticians to Chessex's practice of the text and to his views on literature. However, these objections must be evoked briefly because they do have some relevance to this study, and particularly to the last four chapters, in which I examine the solutions proposed by Chessex to the problems created by his Calvinist heritage. Chapters 10 to 13 reveal a conception of the text on Chessex's part that runs counter to current theory. Although the reader will be reminded in these four chapters that this is the case, in order to avoid needless repetition, the main thrust of the objections to Chessex's views will be presented here.

Chessex adopts the assumptions of mimetic literature, which sees language as an instrument for referring to or reflecting the world outside the text. The writer is able to use language to seize the world around him, to organize it into meaningful patterns, and to communicate these patterns directly to a reader. Most contemporary theory would deny these assumptions. It starts from Saussure's contention that language is not a transparent medium, each signifier within it corresponding to some signified outside of language. In any given language, the speaker has become accustomed to associating a particular signifier with a specific signified. However, this association is the result of convention within a linguistic community, and it is purely arbitrary. In Saussure's famous phrase, 'le lien unissant le signifiant au signifié est arbitraire.'[9] Modern theory would argue that the claim of mimetic literature to grasp firmly the 'real' world is therefore misleading, and that: 'mimetic or representational notions have been exposed as an "illusion" in the sense of a rhetorical trick designed to mask the arbitrary nature of the literary sign.'[10]

According to Saussure, signs signify because of their difference from other signs within a language. Hence, language is an autonomous system of signs, regulated not by referents outside the system, but by the relation of signs to one another within that system. Many theoreticians would argue that language cannot, therefore, grasp or impose order on nonlinguistic phenomena outside the system. To quote Gérard Genette: 'Le langage ne peut imiter parfaitement que du langage, ou plus précisément, un discours ne peut imiter parfaitement qu'un discours parfaitement identique, bref, un discours ne peut imiter que lui-même.'[11] Some would view language as a totally closed system in which each sign refers back to another one, which refers back to another one, and so on, in a process over which the speaker has little or no control, over which he cannot exercise any real power, and on which he cannot impose himself. Derrida argues that language is an unlimited semiosis in which each signifier refers to some other in an endless chain of differences in which meaning is forever deferred, in a process that he calls 'différance.' It is essentially an unstable, shifting medium in which it is impossible to find some original or final term that might halt the chain and impose some stability. To attempt to stabilize language by imposing a hierarchy of meaning that privileges some central term is to ignore its very nature, for 'aucun mot, aucun concept, aucun énoncé majeur ne viennent résumer et commander.'[12]

These theories lead to the conclusion that there can be no single 'meaning' in a text, and the 'realistic' or 'mimetic' writer who proposes a particular view of 'reality' is ignoring the fact that his text has other possible hierarchies in it – or none at all. This constitutes a total rejection of the idea of the writer as a univocal presence who communicates his view of the world to a reader. The communication model of literature – which, as we shall see in chapter 11, is adopted by Chessex – is replaced by one of plural meanings.

To be fair to Chessex, he does not subscribe to a naïve view of language that sees it as a simple mimetic instrument capable of faithfully reflecting the world outside itself. He does not treat it as a system of signs, each of which bears a straightforward and unambiguous relationship to a specific non-linguistic phenomenon. He is aware that language rarely functions in this way, and that its grip on the 'real' world is often tenuous. As will be seen in chapter 11, he knows that language cannot exhaust 'reality' and that even Flaubert, Maupassant, and the naturalists sensed that their project could not always be realized. The world resists language, and the attempt to bring the two together often does not succeed.

There is, however, a considerable difference between Chessex's view that it is a difficult and arduous struggle to match the text to reality outside the text, and theories that deny *any* possibility of correspondence between language and nonlinguistic phenomena. As his own practice of the text, and his own critical commentaries show, Chessex clearly believes that language can come to grips, however imperfectly, with realities exterior to itself. He argues that this has been done, and that it has been done particularly well, by the naturalists. Because of their example, he considers it worth attempting to do so himself, however difficult he may find the task.

Chessex's approach, then, is based on the assumption that there is some link, however tenuous, between signifier and signified. It must be said, in defence of this assumption, that it is one that most of us make most of the time. Although the theories that Chessex rejects stem from Saussure's original contention that the link between signifier and signified is arbitrary, Saussure never denies that such links *do* exist. Howard Felperin argues: 'What Saussurian linguistics does do away with is not signified meaning, but direct, unmediated reference or denotation.'[13] In the practical world, most people assume some link between language and nonlinguistic phenomena, or language would be pointless for communication and for the business of everyday life. The members of any linguistic community treat language as referring to something, since this is the only practical way of living and communicating, however imperfectly, with our fellows.

Chessex assumes that, as readers, we will carry this attitude over into our approach to his texts. In order to appreciate what he writes, we must treat it as conveying something beyond the text itself, something that we recognize from our own lives. As a writer, he assumes that his words will communicate some such correspondence to us. This is the communication model of literary competence that most readers and writers still tend to accept. Robert Scholes points out that 'much of literary competence is based on our ability to connect the worlds of fiction and experience.'[14] In order to understand a text, we naturally seek some consistency between it and the world of our own experience. As another critic points out, commenting on Rifaterre's study of Wordsworth's 'Yew Trees,' 'we have to know what yews, trees, temples, groves and so on are like in the real world in order to understand the poem.'[15]

Chessex's views and practice do not invalidate the theories that have been briefly summarized here. Indeed, in view of his admitted awareness of the difficulties of using language, his attack on critics like Derrida, Kristeva, and the Tel Quel group is regrettable in its harshness (although one may admire and enjoy its humour and vigour). The best of modern criticism, whether it be associated with semiotics, structuralism, deconstruction, or offshoots of these groups, has contributed enormously to our critical apparatus and ability to analyse texts. The theoretical emphasis that has entered criticism has had a salutary effect in forcing critics to review many of their assumptions. It has made them look at literary criticism as a discipline and to 'justify it as a mode of knowledge.'[16] Chessex's attacks on the *nouveau roman* are likewise somewhat unfair. This genre has played a major role in forcing readers and writers to think about certain hitherto unquestioned assumptions in the activities of reading and writing novels. It has made better and more attentive readers, and it has, in its way, contributed to the development of novelistic techniques.

One may also agree with Chessex, however, that some modern

criticism – and this is inevitable in any such attempt to renew – has developed into mindless use of jargon and has served only to obfuscate the activity of criticism. Some critics have adopted an excessively theoretical approach that relies heavily on neologisms and that treats the text exclusively as what Wayne C. Booth calls 'labyrinths, enigmas, or textual puzzles to be deciphered.'[17] As for the *nouveau roman* (and the *nouveau nouveau roman*), it seems to have pushed the novel as far as it can usefully go in a particular direction. An exclusive diet of criticism and novels of this kind does indeed produce an appetite for the sort of unabashed storytelling that Chessex admires and hopes to emulate. After many years of such theorizing in both the novel and criticism of it (which are often difficult to distinguish from each other, anyway), Chessex's approach has its appeal.

The important point is that there is room in any living literature for more than one kind of approach. Both the 'flesh and blood' novel that Chessex advocates and the intellectually stimulating games of the *nouveau roman* have their place and their contribution to make. There is equally a place for a whole range of critical approaches. It makes sense, however, to adopt the critical approach that seems the most likely to be fruitful for any given text, and to avoid applying blindly some methodology that is out of sympathy with the temper and aims of the matter studied. I have, therefore, tried as far as possible to use an approach that is in accord with Chessex's goals and assumptions.[18] While acknowledging that this is not the only possible way to read his texts, I have adopted a traditional interpretive approach that examines themes in the texts. This is based on the assumption that the writer can use language to convey elements of his own existence, and that we can relate them to our experience of the world. I have accepted in particular that one may treat literary characters as being close representations of 'real' people and that one may share, however imperfectly, the experiences of such characters as though they were one's own, while reading the text.

The following study is a close examination of Chessex's texts, and it remains firmly rooted in that corpus. I have treated his fiction on its own terms as a series of stories about characters in whose lives certain anguishing problems occur and who look for solutions to these problems, and I have read the poetry and critical work by Chessex as a commentary on the same problems. Although the objections that may be raised on theoretical grounds to his methods must be borne in mind by the reader, they will not be introduced at any length in the rest of this study.

Whatever one's approach, however, the one element of Chessex's work with which any critic must come to terms is its very personal nature. Chessex writes about himself in some way in nearly all his texts. He has admitted: 'Je suis écrivain, j'écris sur moi, un seul sujet' (*Carabas*, 236). The problems of living (and of dying) that his characters confront, the dilemmas with which they struggle, are Chessex's own. In order to make the lives of his characters 'real' and to convey their physical presence in the world, Chessex frequently uses a first-person narrative. He has said that 'le *je* du conte ... assure au récit une vérité existentielle, une présence, une force plausible qui lui garantissent l'authenticité d'un témoignage' (*Maupassant*, 31). The anguish that Chessex's characters feel, the difficulties they experience, are made to seem even more Chessex's personal ones by this choice of narrative voice.

I am aware, of course, that no writer can be fully identified with the characters he creates, and that 'the lines connecting literary characters and anything that might be called the "real author" are hazy indeed.'[19] Chessex himself points out that, despite the natural tendency of readers to assimilate him to his characters, he is not those characters. A literary character is made up of some elements of the writer's self, but also of the writer's potential selves – those things that the writer would like to be, fears to be, can never really be. 'Le personnage d'un roman est profondément composite,' he says. 'Il est fait de tous les destins qui auraient pu être celui du romancier' (Garcin, 146–7). Thus, although Jean Calmet, the protagonist of *L'Ogre*, is a teacher, like Chessex, and shares many of Chessex's fears, obsessions, and attitudes, he is also made of elements taken from the lives of people whom Chessex has known, and of elements that are pure invention. The borrowed and invented parts are what he calls 'des destins que j'aurais pu vivre' (Garcin, 147). Even Flaubert's famous 'Madame Bovary, c'est moi' is just a striking formula that cannot be taken at face value. Flaubert knew, Chessex argues, that Emma was composed at least partly of his potential selves. The real situation for any novelist is: 'Je ne suis pas mes personnages, ils ne sont pas moi, mais tout se passe comme si j'avais pu être l'un d'entre eux' (Garcin, 147).

Thus, despite the admitted element of confession in such works as *Carabas* and *Portrait des Vaudois*, these should not be read *just* as confessions. Although *L'Ogre* contains many of Chessex's potential selves, it is not a confession either. Chessex says of this text: 'Il est évident qu'il y a toujours une projection inconsciente ou consciente de soi-même dans l'invention romanesque: mais pourquoi serait-elle ou devrait-elle être servile?'[20] It is true that some of him went into the creation of Jean Calmet, but he cannot be fully identified with that character. In *all* of his fiction, Chessex depicts *some* of himself in various characters, presenting us with multiple selves in various disguises. 'Il porte des masques,' one critic says of Chessex in these texts.[21]

I have tried to bear constantly in mind these warnings and not to treat Chessex's characters as though they were straightforward projections, unaltered and complete, of Chessex himself. Nevertheless, the potential selves that he puts in his characters, the obsessions and anguish felt by these selves, are all useful in composing a picture of the problems and dilemmas that he examines and attempts to solve in the text. Certain attitudes and fears recur too frequently from one text to another, and in such a wide variety of characters, for them not to be part of the fundamental problems that Chessex analyses. For example, the fact that the protagonists in *L'Ogre*, *L'Ardent Royaume*, *Judas le transparent*, *Jonas*, *Morgane Madrigal*, and *Les Yeux jaunes*, all link women to sin, death, and evil is surely sufficient reason to see this link as significant in the religious issues that Chessex explores in these books.

Several components of the view of life that I wish to examine in these pages occur not just in the fiction. In essays such as *Carabas* and *Portrait des Vaudois*, in which Chessex speaks in his own name, they are explicitly put forward as part of that view. They also occur with considerable frequency in his poems. Furthermore, many of the opinions and attitudes to which I am referring are openly expressed in interviews in which Chessex is obviously giving his personal views. Finally, the cluster of problems and obsessions in question are the result of a Calvinism that is, Chessex tells us, a cultural phenomenon. Since he is as much a product of that culture as are his characters, one may assume that he is subject to at least some of these problems, too. As Chessex says of another writer in one of his book reviews: 'L'auteur s'y peint en racontant autrui'[22]

Because these elements of a particular view of existence are so consistent from text to text, and because the opinions expressed on Calvinism are equally consistent, I have tended to ignore the usual distinction made between what Booth calls 'the flesh and blood author,' the 'implied author,' and the 'career author,' or between the poet and his 'persona.'[23] It is not that I do not consider these to be useful distinctions. Indeed, in many cases, and from many critical perspectives, they are essential. However, my goal here is to extract from the texts a picture of a certain kind of religion or religious sensibility, and this picture is consistent from the point of view of all of these authors.

I should also point out that I have used mainly Chessex's prose writings in constructing this picture, and I have used certain of the poems as supporting evidence. This is not because I consider his verse in any way less important than or inferior to his fiction and essays, but simply because the prose writings are more explicit and accessible.

In any case, Chessex believes that the distinction between prose and poetry is entirely artificial, and he considers all his work to be in some measure a form of poetry. He says: 'Cette distinction entre prose et poésie me paraît moliéresque. On parle en prose, on parle en poésie, on ne sait pas qu'on le fait' (Garcin, 19). The finest prose passages, such as the one describing Emma Bovary's death, are indistinguishable from poetry. 'Langue de romancier, langue de poète, quelle différence, au fond?' he asks (Garcin, 129). What matters in prose and poetry is the creation of a style, of a form that has truly poetic beauty: 'Il y faut la forme, la langue neuve, cette rigueur neuve qui touche aussitôt notre oreille, la retient' (Cingria, 57). Many critics agree that Chessex has succeeded in his prose work in creating something essentially poetic, and that he is 'un conteur, sans quitter le poète qu'il est.'[24]

Obviously, Chessex attaches considerable importance to style and form. He has said: 'Une fois pour toutes, nous rejetterons l'écriture qui n'est pas *dans sa forme* sa justification et son commentaire' (Cingria, 71; italics in original). His own style has been praised by critics, who have said of his writing that 'tout ... est écrit dans une langue vigoureuse, nette, éclatante de poésie réaliste, accomplie'; that it is written 'dans la verdeur, la fraîcheur cristalline d'une montagne qui sonnaille de sources et de brise fringante'; and that its style 'vous enivre longtemps après, comme une rasade de liqueur forte.'[25]

The attention that Chessex pays to this aspect of his own writings has resulted in certain changes in his style over the years. His early prose works, *La Tête ouverte* and *La Confession du pasteur Burg*, are short pieces written while he still felt the influence of Ponge and Paulhan, and they are in a noticeably sparse, concise style.[26] Critics have been particularly aware of this aspect of *La Confession du pasteur Burg*, and have commented on 'la sobriété du récit et son classicisme'; 'l'accent classique d'une langue où fermeté, nombre et rigueur s'unissent à la pénétration'; 'ce beau récit dépouillé et desséché'; 'une perfection classique, ardente et froide'; and a language that is 'almost classical in its restraint.'[27] The early poems are similarly concise, leading Alain Bosquet to refer to 'ces poèmes âpres, durs, rocailleux, qui débouchent sur un ascétisme bien proclamé.'[28] Even some of the later prose works, particularly the short stories, retain some of this classical concision, and Christiane Baroche refers to *Où vont mourir les oiseaux* as being 'd'une écriture contenue, sobre, *efficace*.'[29]

With the publication of *Portrait des Vaudois* in 1969, Chessex adopted a more 'popular' style that attempts to capture the cadences and idioms of Vaudois speech. He describes it as 'un chant populaire qui essaie de reproduire à travers l'oreille de son auteur les parlers ... les façons de dire d'un peuple' (Garcin, 79). But the major turning-point was *Carabas* (1971). In that work he abandoned restraint, feeling it was time to write 'un livre dans toutes les circulations possibles et imaginables, sans aucune rétention quelconque' (Garcin, 43). The style of this and many subsequent works has struck critics as being at the opposite pole from the early restrained classicism. They have written of 'l'ouverture et parfois la démesure du style'; of 'une plume alerte, colorée qui ne se refusait pas à appeler un chat un chat'; and of 'ivresse, enthousiasme du langage.'[30] Chessex's texts are now marked by a Rabelaisian love of words that leads him to construct extravagant lists and catalogues, such as the ones already quoted in which he attacks a certain kind of literary criticism.[31]

These few comments must suffice as an indication of Chessex's style and the importance that he attaches to form. Although it is one of the preliminary considerations that has to be mentioned, the purpose of this study is not to provide a stylistic analysis of Chessex's texts. It should be borne in mind, however, that Chessex *is* one of the major stylists writing in French today.

The purpose of this study, as will have been gleaned from some of the remarks already made, is to examine certain recurring ideas, attitudes, or obsessions – and *obsession* is by no means too strong a word – in Chessex's texts, and to see how he uses the text to provide possible solutions to them. These recurring elements are all driven by Chessex's background, by the Calvinist upbringing that he projects into the lives of his characters, by the Calvinist influence that he believes has been felt by all those of his generation born in the Vaud. Chapters 2 to 6 examine the various aspects of this Calvinism as they are manifested in the texts. They look at the lives of the characters created by Chessex, at his own comments on Calvinism, and they attempt to reconstruct what is meant by this term and how the influence of this religion is felt. They examine Calvinism as a cultural phenomenon rooted in the Vaud, the very strict and rigorous nature of this belief, its emphasis on sin and divine retribution, and the place of women and nature in this picture.[32] They look at the obsession with death produced by Calvinism, at the social implications of this faith, and at the nature of Calvinist society as it is presented in Chessex's texts. They also point to the strange contradictions within these attitudes, which may also be traced to certain Calvinist influences.

The picture of a particular type of Calvinist conscience that emerges in these chapters has a horrifying fascination. However, while this picture is important for an understanding of Chessex's texts, in chapters 7 and 8 I attempt to study the ways in which Chessex tries to counter the Calvinist influence, and especially the way in which he uses the text as a means of doing this. In these chapters we shall find that, behind the Calvinist obsessions, is a somewhat less evident vision of life that struggles to make itself felt. This other vision is totally opposed to the Calvinist one, for it emphasizes the joy of life and it presents both nature and women in a totally different light. It is a complex, apparently contradictory, view that sees existence in terms of pairs of opposites. Chapter 9 points out that there is an attempt in Chessex's work to look for a fundamental unity behind these opposites. Chapters 10 to 12 study how Chessex uses the text to seek solutions to the difficulties and problems exposed in previous chapters, how he proposes the text as a means of restoring harmony, of imposing order on the chaos of existence, and of overcoming the obsession with death and passing time. The final chapter explores the similarities between religion and Chessex's use of the text.

This study focuses, then, on a series of problems associated with a certain religion, and with rejection of that religion. It chronicles an agonizing and only partially successful attempt to escape the influence of a crushing, all-embracing religious influence, and to use the

Introduction: Some Preliminary Considerations 17

text as a means of doing this. It also shows how Chessex realizes that there can be only a partial victory over Calvinism and over the problems that rejection of this religion produces. My focus on the Calvinist conscience in Chessex's work necessarily excludes certain considerations such as the style and the structure of the texts, some of Chessex's ideas on literature, and some of his exploration of human sexuality. No doubt there are several other aspects of Chessex's writings that other readers would consider just as important as their view of Calvinism. However, to have included all these other considerations would have produced an impossibly long and unfocused study of what is a complex and multifaceted body of writing.

In any case, although this study is 'specialized' in the focus that has been chosen for it, it is inevitably, to some extent, an 'introductory' one. The Calvinist conscience in Chessex's writings is so basic to an understanding of them that any serious examination of his work must begin at that point, or at least incorporate it in some way. Since Chessex is not a well-known writer outside of Switzerland and France, this must also be an introductory study in that it is the first attempt outside of these countries to examine his work as a whole.

It is hoped that, in the spirit of Chessex's own effort to combine and unite, this study will combine the specialist examination of specific elements in Chessex's writing with a satisfactory general introduction to a fascinating work that deserves to be better known.

2
The Calvinist Heritage

Throughout Chessex's texts, from the earliest poems to the most recent verse, from his first *récits* to the longer novels, in short stories, essays, and critical commentary, one may discern the same preoccupation with certain problems. The basic themes of Chessex's works are remarkably consistent through what has been a fairly long and productive literary career. 'Chacun des livres de l'auteur ne laisse pas de revenir aux mêmes interrogations, aux mêmes angoisses,' remarks Jérôme Garcin,[1] and the same critic says to Chessex in his book of interviews: 'J'ai l'impression que chacun de tes livres pose toujours les mêmes questions, interroge toujours les mêmes phénomènes' (Garcin, 63). Chessex, for his part, readily agrees with this assessment of his work. He compares his writing to a ring of mountains, in the centre of which he lives and writes, turning now to one part of the circle for his inspiration, now to the other (Garcin, 46). The result is a body of texts that all form part of that same circle, although perspectives and emphasis often change.

Because perspectives change there *is* variety in Chessex's work. We are not dealing with the monotonous repetition of the same situations or the same characters living the same events. Under these differing situations, however, lie the same basic concerns, and in the lives of various characters are the same preoccupations. As Jérôme Garcin points out in a review of *Le Séjour des morts*, the superficial reader will say that Chessex merely repeats himself, but the discerning one will realize that 's'il est vrai que le centre est toujours le même, les approches en sont chaque fois différentes.'[2] Hence, despite this never-changing core, Alain Bosquet is able to classify Chessex as 'le plus varié des écrivains qui nous soit venu de Suisse.'[3]

The core that lies beneath the variations is of a distinctly sombre, even tragic nature. 'La fascination des matières tragiques me porte,' Chessex has said, and almost every text that he has written bears this out.[4] They all show the same concern for that part of the human spirit that drives man to ask the most basic and elemental questions about life, man's place in the world, the threat of death, and the presence or absence of God. Chessex lists as his major preoccupation 'l'effroi d'être, la mort' (Garcin, 12), and, writing of his studies of other Vaudois writers in *Les Saintes Ecritures*, he says, 'j'ai regardé la part d'ombre' (13). He might say the same of all his texts, which inevitably look towards the darker side of life.

Chessex refers to such preoccupations as being 'metaphysical' in nature, and he argues that he shares them with most writers of French Switzerland, and particularly with those from the Vaud. He says, for example, that 'la poésie romande est le plus souvent métaphysique' (*Saintes*, 161), and he writes of the poets studied in *Les Saintes Ecritures* that 'ces poètes sont des métaphysiciens' (11). He argues that even the engravings of an artist like Etienne Delessert have a 'dimension métaphysique' (*Les Dessins*, 2). Typical of the writers and artists that Chessex has in mind is Ramuz, whose works constantly raise metaphysical questions (*Saintes*, 24).

Often these concerns have a distinctly religious overtone and are expressed in terms of God, evil, and sin. According to Bosquet, in Chessex's writing, 'il s'agit ... de la faute, devant Dieu et devant les hommes, de la peur de la mort, de la lutte que le bien livre au mal, de l'appel à l'ange, de la déchéance, de la rédemption trop différée.'[5] Chessex believes that he shares with all Vaudois a tendency to view life in such terms because they are the heirs to a long tradition of Christian worship and ritual, a tradition that sees and expresses life in Biblical terms and images. He describes how, one day, as he listened to a pastor reading a psalm, he sensed that the whole congregation was seized by the words and by the images that they provoked. At that moment, they were all united in a common vision of life and death expressed in familiar words belonging to a tradition that they all shared. He concludes: 'J'appartenais à la même race qu'eux, moi aussi j'étais pénétré de cette parole, de cette façon de comprendre la précarité de la vie à travers Job, à travers l'Ecclésiaste, à travers les Psaumes' (Garcin, 16). Because of this common heritage, he is able to say of all Vaudois: 'Nous avons, inclues en nous, des vérités qui sont la naissance dans la douleur, l'amour dans la douleur et l'attente de la mort dans la douleur. Et comme il peut être compris chez nous seuls, le repos aussi dans la douleur' (Garcin, 17).

As these words indicate, we are dealing with a dark and unattractive view of life. The religious influence to which Chessex is referring is a particular form of Calvinism, one that has for centuries maintained a stern and uncompromising hold over the Vaud and other Protestant cantons. Chessex's own ancestors lived this religion every moment of their lives, and his great-grandfather would hold communal worship every evening for the whole family, including the servants.[6] Chessex says of his own upbringing: 'J'ai écouté assez de calvinistes dans mon âge tendre, assez de sermonneurs effarouchés, de bas-bleus, de conseillers de paroisse choqués, de vicaires mégalomanes, de suffragants vengeurs et de hoquetants ministres' (*Carabas*, 76). It is so much a part of him that it is almost as though he were a Calvinist from birth. 'Je suis né calviniste, Dieu ne le sait que trop,' he writes (*Carabas*, 194).

Many of Chessex's characters share this upbringing, and bear the mark of Calvinism like a scar. This is true of Alexandre Dumur in *Les Yeux jaunes*, whose parents were itinerant preachers; of Maître Mange in *L'Ardent Royaume*, whose childhood was lived in the shadow of the Calvinist church; of Jean Calmet in *L'Ogre*, who can never throw off the sense of guilt bred in him by this religion; of Benoît Rouvre in *La Trinité*, who studied theology and whose manner still resembles that of a pastor. Most of all, it is true of Jean Burg, the narrator of *La Confession du pasteur Burg*, whose entire childhood centred on Calvin, and who himself becomes a Calvinist minister. 'Calvin me tenaillait l'esprit,' he says, as he looks back on his adolescence. 'Je le prenais pour juge de mes démarches, de mes propos, de mes lectures' (*La Confession*, 22).

It soon becomes apparent to any reader of Chessex's writings that the immense importance of Calvinism in them does not imply a personal belief in these doctrines. What we are dealing with is a cultural phenomenon, an influence that stems from Chessex's Vaudois heritage. He argues that all Vaudois born when he was have undergone this influence, as have the inhabitants of other Protestant cantons. He says: 'Dans les cantons de tradition protestante, il existe une filiation calviniste profonde qui n'est absolument pas le fait d'une fréquentation de l'église ou même d'une pratique de la foi, mais d'une tradition culturelle, d'une tradition je dirais même, psychanalytique. Elle est devenue psychotique, même'.[7] He believes that the women especially have fallen under this influence and perpetuate it in their lives and in the lives of their children. They are imbued with 'la vieille foi huguenote sans faille; une morale plutôt qu'une croyance à l'égard de la vie et des gens' (*Portrait*, 91). The very symbol of the Vaud and its religious heritage is the Calvinist minister, without whom Chessex cannot evoke his native region. In *Portrait des Vaudois*, a chapter is devoted to these 'hommes sombres, ouverts, heureux, malheureux sur leurs chemins de terre entre les haies, à petits pas allant frapper à la porte tiède des dernières fermes où s'use doucement une vieille' (142).

Despite the grip of this religion on the minds and on the lives of Vaudois, including himself, Chessex does not believe in the Calvinist God, or, indeed, in any God. He makes clear in his interview with Garcin that the religious influence on him, while visible in his writing, does not produce a personal faith: 'Je ne suis pas croyant, je ne suis pas chrétien, je suis de culture chrétienne, c'est autre chose' (Garcin, 16). For Chessex, God as a personal deity is dead, and he refers in a poem to 'le ciel de Dieu mort lui aussi' (*Elégie*, 18). In another poem, the poet seeks peace and respite in a life that is described as 'supplice,' but finds himself speaking to a Deity who either does not exist or who simply chooses not to answer, and whom he finally addresses as 'Toi Maître du tout / Toi muet sur la vieille question' (*Le Calviniste*, 107).

The result of this is a literature that is full of God while denying His existence. Chessex's words concerning Flaubert might have been written about himself: 'Il ne croit pas, et ses oeuvres sont pleines de Dieu' (*Flaubert*, 26). Like Flaubert's, his work 's'ingénie à mettre en scène un Dieu qui n'existe pas' (*Flaubert*, 34). Sentence after sentence, page after page, refer to God, and not one of his pieces of fiction omits Him. Here is a case of 'la *non-existence* d'un Dieu figuré par une pure rhétorique paradoxalement *pleine* de Dieu' (*Flaubert*, 75; italics in original).

The particular idea of God that remains in Chessex's case is the one that Calvinism has imposed on the Vaudois. So strong is this influence that Chessex comes to the paradoxical conclusion: 'Dieu n'existe pas / Et il règne' (*Elégie*, 30). The cultural influence of Calvinism, its idea of God, remains as an all-pervading force that it is simply impossible to escape. It becomes a burden that Chessex and many of his characters strive to throw off, but it stays with them all the time. As Alexandre Dumur points out, it is impossible for them to think in categories other than those imposed by Calvinism, however mistaken and sad they consider them to be. 'Mais dans quelles autres catégories penser et vivre? J'étais lié à cette tristesse par ma naissance et par le sang innombrable de ma race,' he laments (*Les Yeux*, 39). Benoît Rouvre likewise sees much of his life through biblical and Calvinist analogies, and he says, 'Encore la sainte analogie. Comment connaître hors d'elle?' (*La Trinité*, 251). It is perhaps the unsilenced and unsilenceable voice of Calvinism that Chessex is referring to when he writes of 'la bouche nocturne qui ne se tait pas' (*Le Calviniste*, 71). Even though Chessex rejects the Calvinist vision of God, even though he casts doubt on the very existence of God and says: 'Et le regretté Dieu dans ses nuages / Ne nous appelle plus, ne nous punit plus' (*Le Calviniste*, 64), he cannot escape that God. While rejecting the God of Calvin, he still prays to Him: 'Mais je suis fidèle à Ta crainte, Dieu des combats / Je finirai mes jours en Te priant dans le mensonge / Je mourrai criant à Toi, en mentant' (*Comme*, 137). The writers whom he studies in *Les Saintes Ecritures*, his fellow Swiss Protestants in most cases, are, like him, 'Des fous de Dieu' (9). They seek to escape God, but cannot: 'Dieu craint, Dieu perdu, Dieu nié: mais il demeure, il taraude, il questionne, il est interrogé, pressé, sommé jusqu'au vertige' (10). Chessex recognizes in these writers his fellow sufferers from a Calvinist vision of life that they must always bear with them: 'J'ai scruté secrètement mon visage en eux' (15).

Imbued with a certain idea of God that they never seem to escape, yet having rejected Calvinism and the very belief in God, Chessex and many other writers of the Vaud find themselves in a world in which nothing makes sense. They exist in what French writers like Malraux, Camus, and Sartre have called the 'absurd.' They need a God to give meaning and order to life, but sickened by the Calvinist view of God and of man, they can no longer believe in any God. 'Rien ne guette ni ne délivre / Rien au vent, dans le soleil, ni au regard / Jamais donne aucun sens aucune loi,' says Chessex in 'La Dernière Elégie' (92). Their work – and, of course, Chessex's is part of it – is 'neé d'une blessure' (*Saintes*, 13).

The result is a literature that is constantly preoccupied with what lies behind appearances, with the 'metaphysical' or 'religious' problems that lurk behind the everyday activities of characters. In this sense, it is a profoundly mystical work that looks for communion with some kind of beyond, that seeks a God it knows does not exist, and that constantly pursues an anguished search. This is why Chessex says that Gustave Roud's work invites us to 'une communion mystique' (*Saintes*, 68), and why he says that Mercanton's writing is the product of 'une aspiration mystique' (*Saintes*, 100). A similar mystical impulse is visible in all his own work and in the lives of his characters. Jean Calmet in *L'Ogre*, Alexandre Dumur in *Les Yeux jaunes*, Maître Mange in *L'Ardent Royaume*, Jean Burg in *La Confession du pasteur Burg*, Benoît Rouvre in *La Trinité*, and even Raphaël Turner, the Judas figure in *Judas le transparent*, all raise these metaphysical questions and pursue their mystic quest. This is why Anne-Marie is able to say to Jonas Carex, 'Tu es un mystique' (*Jonas*, 130).

This is why one may also describe Chessex's work as being mythical in nature. He is preoccupied by the great problems with which religions and myths attempt to deal, and, because of his cultural background, he tends to express and examine these problems in mythical images. His major characters may be likened to mythical heroes engaged in a quest for some divine revelation, but one that they know will never come. Like Matthey and Jaccottet, poets whom he admires greatly and who 'voient ... les dieux, les métamorphoses ou les débris de la part mythique dans la simplicité quotidienne' (*Saintes*, 12), Chessex depicts a preoccupation with the metaphysical in and through the lives of his characters. Because of the particular religious background that is his, he nearly always represents this quest in terms of the Christian myth. He relies 'à la fois sur les grandes figures bibliques et sur les mythes collectifs.'[8] He borrows naturally from a myth and a tradition that still form part of his cultural heritage, and that of most of his readers, whatever his or their personal religious beliefs. 'Je pense simplement que nous vivons quotidiennement, je dirais jour et nuit, les grands mythes judéo-chrétiens,' he explains.[9] Hence, in novels like *Judas le transparent* and *Jonas*, he uses biblical myths and allusions to the lives of biblical figures, and in such essays as 'La Septième Trompette de Jéricho' (*Carabas*, 249–53) and 'L'Ecclésiaste me convoque' (*Carabas*, 75–8), he draws parallels with biblical narratives.

The result of this preoccupation is a body of texts that draws its inspiration and its very being from a particular and very distinct kind of religion practised in a specific area of Switzerland. Yet these texts raise fundamental questions that face all men and women at all times. It is a curiously local literature that could have been produced only in this region, yet it is universal in the questions it raises. What

Robert Kanters says of *L'Ogre* is applicable to most of Chessex's texts: 'Le talent de M. Chessex est de nous obliger à faire le saut de sa simple histoire vaudoise à la plus vieille – à la plus constante – de l'humanité.'[10] As we shall see in subsequent chapters, however, this ability to combine the particular and the universal is just one example of how Chessex uses the text to embrace apparent opposites and, finally, to reconcile them.

3
The Nature of Calvinism

The critic must tread warily when writing of Calvinism in Chessex's texts, for it is a complex and multifaceted phenomenon. Beyond these texts, in the realm of theological debate, and within the practice of the Calvinist Church, it becomes even more complicated. It is important, therefore, to make certain distinctions at this point, before continuing the discussion of Calvinism as Chessex describes it.

First, it must be made clear that there are often differences between what Calvin actually wrote, and the interpretations put on his writings by the Church. It is, of course, inevitable that this should happen when the writings of any theologian, philosopher, or builder of systems fall into the hands of his followers. While it is not necessary for our purposes to examine specifically what these differences are, it should be pointed out that they do exist, and that Chessex is aware of them.[1] He reserves considerable respect for Calvin and his writings, a respect that contrasts strongly with his attitude to Calvinism as he has experienced it in his own life. He realizes that Calvin wrote a series of magnificent texts full of inspired and inspiring messages, and, as a poet, he is particularly sensitive to their wonderful use of language. He praises this writer for the quality of his style, and refers to 'une prose poétique très forte ... un discours sans faille' (Garcin, 34).

Secondly, a distinction must be made between two trends within the Calvinist Church. Again, it is beyond the scope of this study to examine these differences in any detail, so what follows greatly simplifies many interwoven but distinct threads of Calvinist theology. For the sake of fairness, however, it must be pointed out that, beside the harsh Calvinism that Chessex depicts, there is a more 'liberal' tradition within Calvinist theology. This tendency lays stress on Christian charity, on God's love for His Creation, and on the role of Christ as the Saviour of mankind. Instead of emphasizing the vengeful God of the Old Testament, it places Christ at the centre of its discourse. This kind of teaching is apparent from the beginning of Calvinism, and it has been said that 'in early Reformed theology, exemplified by Calvin, Knox and Zanchius ... a consistent focus was evident on Christ as the ground of our knowledge of God, as the subject and object of election.'[2] The Christocentric tendency in Calvinism has endured to this day, and has received considerable new strength in this century through the teaching of Karl Barth: 'More recently, those influenced by Barthian theology of our time wish to show Calvin as drawing forth from the Scripture alone ... a living theology having the immediacy of the Word of God and an emphasis on the Christocentric interpretation of the chief doctrines of the faith.'[3]

Chessex does not refer specifically in his texts to the 'liberal' or Christocentric trends within Calvinism as it is practised today. He does recognize, however, that there is a humane and charitable element within the Calvinist Church. He writes, for example, of ministers in the Church who are caring and worthy Christians, humbly pursuing their calling and living close to the land and to the people who work on it. One whole chapter of *Portrait des Vaudois* is devoted principally to these men, and in it Chessex treats them with great affection.[4] However, he is more conscious of the restrictive, harsh interpretation of Calvin, and the presence of this type of theology in the practice of the Church. This is the Calvinism that we have encountered in the previous chapter, the kind that Chessex sees as his cultural heritage, and the kind that dominates his consciousness. According to Chessex, this interpretation of Calvin's doctrines has influenced the lives of most Vaudois of his generation, and its effects may still be felt in all aspects of life in the Vaud. It is almost exclusively this form of Calvinism that the reader encounters in Chessex's work. Consequently, when the terms 'Calvinist' and 'Calvinism' are used in subsequent pages, it is to the traditional, excessively severe form of the doctrine that reference is being made.

Chessex sees this darker Calvinism as a perversion of the religious spirit, and in his novels, short stories, and poems, we find what François Nourissier has aptly called 'le royaume obscur de la Foi malade et pervertie.'[5] Works like *L'Ogre, Les Yeux jaunes, L'Ardent*

Royaume, and *Jonas* are inspired by hatred of this kind of religion, and constitute attacks on it. They show the effects of a religion that is obsessed with sin and punishment, and of a Church that appears to have forgotten Christian charity. Even *Judas le transparent*, while not depicting a specifically Calvinist sect, shows the horrifying effects of these obsessions in a fundamentalist group that is really a projection of the most severe traits of Calvinism.

It is Jean Burg, the narrator of *La Confession du pasteur Burg*, who best illustrates the excessive form of Calvinism that pushes the desire for purity to the point of the pathological. His calling to the ministry is based on what he calls 'la force et l'austérité de notre foi' and he makes no bones about being 'protestant, profondément et violemment' (12). Certain of the righteousness of his cause, he searches out all traces of sin in his flock, and he takes a very obvious delight in imagining the punishment that God reserves for those who do not cleanse themselves of sin. He evokes with relish the punishments he would like to see inflicted on the old man who was his predecessor in the village. He detests what he considers this man's lack of ardour, his compromises, and his desire not to upset his parishioners. When the old man remonstrates with him about excessive zeal, Burg imagines him burning in the fires of the Counter-Reformation or massacred on Saint Bartholomew's Night. He sees himself as being in a tradition of austere preachers of Calvin's word, and he is proud to be one of 'ces terribles hommes noirs dont la parole et le geste avaient accablé des générations de paroissiens immobiles' (21).

For Chessex, Jean Burg is typical of the kind of Calvinism that he detests and from which he himself never ceases trying to escape. It is based on 'une morale à brodequins' (*Saintes*, 59) that represents God as a vengeful and all-seeing deity from whom it is impossible to hide one's sins (and whose sole interest seems to be to find them out). It is, no doubt, to this God that Chessex writes the lines: 'Je n'ai pas d'abri contre ton souvenir / Pas de rempart contre ton regard / Je suis le fruit que tu ronges / Ver monstrueux' (*Le Calviniste*, 52). Jonas Carex, seeking to flee his Calvinist background, goes back to Fribourg, where he once attended a Catholic school, and which he associates with the first woman he loved. But the God of Calvinism pursues him, and some words from his Calvinist catechism keep coming to his mind: 'L'Eternel regarde au coeur' (*Jonas*, 109).

This God, with His all-pervasive gaze, is represented in *L'Ogre* by

Jean Calmet's father, Dr Calmet. The latter has just died when the novel begins, and Jean is filled with a sense of relief that he can now escape from the crushing influence of a domineering personality who is depicted as a veritable ogre. Dr Calmet is a huge, vital figure who has always stifled his son's attempts to live his own life, and who even stole Jean's first love from him. But the feeling of freedom that floods over Jean when his father dies does not last, for his father's image seems to appear before him at moments when he asserts his freedom, particularly when he makes love to Thérèse, who represents love and liberty in his eyes. At such times, he is rendered impotent, robbed even of his virility by his father. The perfect representation of Dr Calmet is the statue that Jean sees in Berne: an enormous ogre devouring a child while carrying several other children in its pockets.

Because of his Calvinist background, Jean Calmet projects onto his father all the characteristics of the Calvinist God. He is all-powerful, and he crushes Jean beneath his will; he can hold death at bay, since he is a doctor, who brings health and healing; he can even overcome death, for he reappears in Jean's life after he has apparently died. He is such a force in Jean's existence, such a centre of power, that, as a child, Jean watches him at the meal table, with the setting sun on his face, and sees him as 'le père immense' and 'cet autre soleil, infaillible et détestable' (12). But, above all, Dr Calmet is vengeful and all-seeing, for 'son regard implacable se posait sur chacun des siens' (12). Jean instinctively feels guilty as those eyes fall on him, as though this God-like figure can see all his hidden thoughts. He is sure that 'son père connaissait ses désirs de larve' (13), and we are told that 'le docteur savait tout de lui; le docteur lisait en lui parce qu'il était le maître, et le maître demeurait épais, massif, impénétrable dans sa force serrée et rubiconde au soleil du soir' (13).[6] Not surprisingly, the epigraph to the novel is taken from the Book of Job, in which Job addresses God: 'Quand cesseras-tu de me regarder?'

Jean Calmet's reaction to his father's gaze points to one of the principal characteristics of Calvinism as Chessex describes it: its insistence on man's guilt, on the evil within him, and especially on the sins of the flesh. It gives man no credit for finer emotions or abilities, and seems to ignore any capacity for good in him. Its sole concern is to root out evil, and this is why Jean trembles before his father's eyes, as does the Calvinist in the sight of God. 'Mais à la chair s'attache la malédiction mortelle, c'est l'héritage calviniste,' writes Chessex (*Saintes*, 49). It is equally his own inheritance, and is just as visible in his work. In *L'Ogre*, it is precisely when Jean is about to make love to Thérèse that his father's image appears and renders him impotent. Alexandre Dumur in *Les Yeux jaunes* feels the presence of unclean desires of the flesh all around him. Because his parents were Calvinist preachers who instilled in him the idea that sexual desire is evil, he sees the body as 'un lieu de la pire espèce, un cloaque que Dieu méprise et punit' (17). He never fully rids himself of the lingering belief that the devil is behind sexual pleasure, and he says: 'Le désir est son oeuvre. Tout ce qui plaît, tout ce qui attire, tout ce qui nourrit le sexe et le regard: son oeuvre' (84). In *Jonas*, the devil in the form of the serpent, familiar from the Garden of Eden myth, is linked explicitly to sexual activity. Just as Jonas and Anne-Marie are about to make love in a clearing in the woods, Anne-Marie is bitten by a viper.

References to the devil are commonplace in Calvinism, for this is a religion that posits a literal belief in Satan. Indeed, he is frequently seen as being the inspiration of man's acts. Chessex even says that many of his own acts, ones of which he is not proud, are apparently inspired by the devil: 'C'est le diable qui m'effare, m'agite comme un grelot, m'étrille comme l'idiot du village, me lance sur la route, me jette au slip des coquines, remplit mon verre au Café Romand' (*Carabas*, 196). Although he may be speaking figuratively here, and naming the devil as a convenient shorthand form of all the unsavoury impulses that control his behaviour, it is a significant choice. The Calvinist conscience that he is never able fully to escape spontaneously provides such terms. For characters like le père Krieg in 'Le Mage,' there is no question of borrowing language or using imagery: for him the devil is a living presence against whom he must make war every day. (The combat is symbolized by his very name.) He sees the devil behind every human action: 'Partout où l'on regarde, partout où l'on pense, donc partout où l'on parle, le père ne cesse de dénoncer ses ruses' (*Où*, 90). In *Jonas*, the main character carries on a dialogue with the devil, in which he informs his tempter that he knows his ruses perfectly. The devil's tactics are familiar to him because his Calvinist background has taught him to recognize them. This awareness is 'sang de la race, lait de ma mère' (208). As for the devil himself, he can only agree that he inspires human behaviour: 'Je guette, je repère, je me glisse dans la conscience et dans le coeur de mes victimes, je leur parle, je les convaincs' (207).

For the Calvinist who still lies within Chessex, God and the devil are everywhere: 'J'ai de la peine à imaginer un paysage sans Dieu derrière les pentes et sans le diable et même sans les anges ravisseurs et punisseurs. J'ai tiré à la mamelle calviniste; il y a un sévère lait à boire au bord du Léman solaire et dans les douces campagnes au fond des terres' (*Carabas*, 179). But it is the devil whose presence seems the more apparent. He haunts every aspect of the Calvinist's life, is concealed in every corner of the world around him, and lies behind his every thought and act. 'Le diable me saute dessus à tout bout de champ,' says Chessex (*Carabas*, 166). The fear of the devil that he imagines in the immigrant Italian farm-hand is surely a projection of this Calvinist belief: 'Diable, tu souffles sous la porte ... Tu cries la nuit dans le bois. Tu ricanes dans le cimetière' (*Reste*, 47). Alexandre Dumur is clearly drawing on the teachings of his Calvinist parents when he sees the devil behind everything in his life. He remembers his mother ensuring that every particle of his clothing and every inch of his body were kept clean. He recalls her reason for this: 'C'est le diable qui se cache dans ces plis, disait ma mère, il n'y a qu'à l'écouter! Et je l'écoute, quarante ans après' (*Les Yeux*, 29). Many years after consciously rejecting his parents' teaching, Alexandre Dumur cannot fully free himself of the belief that the devil lies hidden in so much that attracts him in life: 'Tu vois, le Malin s'incarne! Il a le velouté des fruits défendus, la robe des vins exquis, le cri des trop belles bêtes, le corps des filles. Tout ce qui séduit lui appartient' (84).

But, although he is everywhere, it is especially nature that is the devil's favourite abode. In *Carabas*, Chessex pictures himself in the Swiss village of Sépey, looking at a lake that is praised for its beauty in guide books and tourist publicity, but to him it is a sinister place that hides the devil, 'un bloc luisant d'eau satanique' (108). Raphaël Turner in *Judas le transparent* looks at the green and smiling countryside, but instead of peace and beauty, he sees the work of the devil: murder, suicide, violent crimes, and fear. The poet imagines himself in 'Revenant du val adorable' (*Comme*, 57-8) climbing up from an alpine valley, when suddenly the cries of crows and the presence of swarms of black flies remind him of the evil behind the beauty of nature. In the folklore of the Vaud, the devil in nature appears in the form of a mythical creature called the Dari, who haunts the woods and dark places of the night, kills the poultry, poisons the springs and wells, and shrieks terrifyingly at night (*Portrait*, 51-60).

Chessex's tales are full of representations and representatives of the devil: characters, animals, sicknesses, and disorders that are merely forms taken by Satan. The most obvious character to identify as the devil's representative is Raphaël Turner in *Judas le transparent*. Turner is a former adherent of a fundamentalist sect called Les Témoins de la Nouvelle Résurrection, led by a singularly cruel and strict patriarch named Aschenbach. Turner owns an old farm, where he lives with his two sons, Pierre and Paul, and part of which he rents to Aschenbach. He uses his proximity to the latter to spy on the sect, and especially on its meetings, during which sessions of ritual punishment are held. Turner plans to betray the sect and his former master to the police, who have already received complaints about the punishments from disaffected members.

Turner sees himself as Judas, as the man destined to betray the leader. He believes his reason for doing this is the same as Judas' for the betrayal of Christ: the devil has taken control of him. He begins the novel by saying: 'Je ne sais pas comment le diable est entré en moi' (13), recalling the biblical explanation of the betrayal of Christ: 'Then entered Satan into Judas surnamed Iscariot' (Luke 22: 3). The parallel between Turner and Judas is pursued throughout the novel, which is set at Easter, and has a 'last supper' scene in which Aschenbach gathers twelve followers (including Turner) in an upper room, and warns them of his impending betrayal. The novel culminates in this betrayal and the arrest of Aschenbach, after which Turner hangs himself. Turner is even described as being red-haired, as Judas is traditionally depicted, and, like Judas, he has charge of the sect's finances. Because he is linked to Judas, he becomes the devil's representative in this novel, an incarnation of what he calls 'la part du diable' (172).

Another character who may be seen as the devil's representative is Louis in *Les Yeux jaunes*. Alexandre Dumur, the narrator of the novel, is a writer whose marriage to Anne has produced no children. They decide to adopt a child, Louis. Before long, Louis disrupts the calm of their lives, destroys their marriage, and prevents Alexandre from writing. He is a corrupting influence who seduces Anne and leads her to abandon Alexandre, to move in with her lover, to share that lover with him, and to engage in voyeuristic games. Alexandre, too, is corrupted by Louis' presence and sinks into voyeurism. Louis seems to excite sexual desire, to inspire perversion, and to destroy the calm and order that Alexandre needs in order to write. He is a principle of disorder, and he eventually drives Alexandre to suicide. One might say that his crowning achievement is to seduce his piano teacher, who is also the pastor's wife. The victim is well chosen, for the devil, by destroying this man's marriage and causing his wife's suicide, strikes at God's representative.

Louis is more than once shown as the devil's tool. Alexandre declares: 'Car dès que Louis fut installé chez nous, il me sembla que le diable s'était installé avec lui' (10), and he refers to '[le] caractère infernal de Louis' (98). When Louis awakens Alexandre's interest in his furtive sexual adventures, Alexandre comments: 'Le diable montrait le bout de l'oreille,' and he sees Louis 'auréolé d'un collier de soufre' (99). Jérôme Garcin rightly describes Alexandre's adopted son as 'diabolique Louis, envoyé du mal, messager d'une raison obscure, ambassadeur de la tentation et du péché au pays de la raison calviniste.'[7]

Louis naturally attacks Alexandre and the pastor through their wives, for woman is seen as the temptress who leads man astray. Jean Burg notices the ravages that women cause in the lives of even the saintliest of men, including one of his teachers at the seminary, and this leads him to flee their presence. Gaspar Hahan in 'L'Oeuf' is a respectable scholar who becomes obsessed with Paula, his assistant. Convinced she is the devil's handmaiden, he addresses her in his mind: 'Paula, tu es marquée, tu es perdue, on devrait te coller sur le ventre l'araignée du diable pour que tout le monde voie ta saloperie' (*Le Séjour*, 208). For Aschenbach, all women are representatives of the devil, and the punishment sessions of his sect concentrate almost entirely on women, because, as Turner explains to the police: 'Elles ont le mal en elles, elles doivent se purifier devant nous' (*Judas*, 128). A line from a poem by Chessex sums up the role of women in the lives of many of his male characters: 'Je te blâme, sexe des filles de Sion' (*Comme*, 92).

Often women are assimilated to witches and other such traditional assistants of the devil. Hence Turner's son Paul says of Aschenbach's daughter: 'C'était le mal qui m'attirait en Virginia ... C'est une sorcière. Je touche Satan dans sa peau' (*Judas*, 49). The pinball machine in the café where Pierre, Turner's other son, goes to drink, bears the word *Seawitch* and the image of a naked woman, a serpent between her legs. This image reminds him strongly of Aschenbach's second daughter, Johanna. The woman who bewitches the narrator of *Morgane Madrigal* is called Morgane – yet another witchlike creature who, in the Arthur myth, is an instrument of evil. As this man thinks of her body, he is irresistibly assailed by images of 'scènes et pratiques de sorcellerie, souffle de la grotte' (*Morgane*, 127).

The devil in nature is usually represented by animals. Naturally, because of the Garden of Eden myth, the snake frequently plays this role. Hence Anne-Marie is bitten by a snake as she is about to sin with Jonas, and a huge stuffed snake in a pharmacist's window faces God's house across the cathedral square in *Jonas*. The owl, the bird of night that haunts the poet's dreams and leads him, like Dante's Virgil, through the spectacle of hell, is treated as 'L'Oiseau-Diable' (*Reste*, 96). The wolf, although it disappeared from the Swiss countryside a hundred years ago, still seems, like the devil, to haunt it. Its image appears in many a child's tale and in folklore, lingering in human memory like the trace of the devil: 'C'est lui, en nous, pour toujours, le loup des histoires' (*Reste*, 44). The cat that Thérèse draws for Jean Calmet, with its eyes that seem to see right into his soul, is 'chat maléfique' (*L'Ogre*, 156).

But of all the animals in Chessex's work, it is the fox that is most consistently linked to the devil. Like the devil, the fox is a cunning, patient destroyer. The narrator of *La Tête ouverte* compares himself to a fox, waiting calmly for the right moment to strike, lulling others into a false sense of security. In *L'Ardent Royaume*, the policeman who carefully collects evidence against Monna and destroys Mange's idyll with her, has red hair, yellow eyes, and is actually called Inspector Renard. For the Vaudois, the fox is evil and death in the natural world: 'Frère onirique de l'inquiet et du cruel, il déteste et fréquente la mort, choie la peur, hante les songes et le clair obscur des forêts comme un démon rieur et furtif' (*Reste*, 78).

In *Les Yeux jaunes*, Chessex weaves a complex symbolic web linking the fox, Louis, and an outbreak of rabies to the devil. Louis is himself foxlike: he has red hair, a reddish complexion, a furtive and oblique way of moving, sharp teeth, and yellow eyes. Alexandre, when he first sees Louis, notices 'une ressemblance animale qui me choqua' (15). Louis is ill at ease in the house, and seems happy only in the open. Patiently and cunningly, he destroys Alexandre, who nevertheless continues to love him, and who calls him 'petite bête vicieuse et chérie' (105). The pastor, who is, of course, practised in seeking out the devil, immediately recognizes Louis for what he is, and describes him as 'une sale bête! Une bête dangereuse!' (55).

At the time when Louis arrives in Alexandre's home, there is also an outbreak of rabies that affects foxes in particular. This disease symbolizes evil, death, and the devil in nature, and, of course, Louis carries this evil, like a fox carrying rabies. The pastor warns Alexandre: 'Votre fils est enragé, monsieur' (61), and one of the first things that Louis does on his arrival is to bite Anne, infecting her with the disease of evil. As Alexandre puts it, describing the advent of disorder in his life: 'Tout est venu à la fois et de très loin, comme chez ceux qui ont été mordus par une bête folle' (16). He later describes his adopted son as 'Louis Dumur, le renard enragé' (62).

The devil and evil are everywhere in this Calvinist vision of things: in human acts, in men's thoughts, and in nature itself. The world is seen as a theatre in which good and evil, God and the devil, confront each other. For the Calvinist, the world is a place of endless struggle between these two forces. As one critic says, in Chessex's work 'Dieu et le Diable seraient les acteurs invisibles, mais de première importance.'[8] Chessex has captured this struggle as clearly as Chappaz and Ramuz, whose work depicts a world that Chessex describes as 'un champ de bataille où s'affrontent Dieu et Satan' (*Saintes*, 11).

What first strikes the reader of Chessex's work, however, is not the presence of God in this struggle, but the emphasis placed on the devil and his role in human affairs, on the necessity of seeking him out and discovering his hand behind so much human activity. This Calvinist insistence on the presence of evil produces a sense of guilt and remorse that hangs like a black pall over nearly all that he has written. According to Henri-Charles Tauxe, Chessex has captured the feeling of guilt and failure that is typical of the Calvinist conscience and that still reigns in parts of Switzerland. He conveys 'la fatalité de la névrose calviniste, [le] totalitarisme d'une révélation divine imposée et vécue comme un jugement condamnant l'homme à l'indignité et à la défaite.'[9] Another critic says that it is as though the very act of living is a sin, and 'le simple fait d'être au monde ... une agression à la pureté, une souillure que l'on ne peut effacer.'[10] According to Chessex himself, the Calvinist conscience of the Vaud is marked by 'le sentiment du péché, le remords, la solitude, la macération dans la faute, le sentiment très fort de la chute originelle, le sentiment de ne pas honorer Dieu, de ne pas faire assez pour célébrer sa Création ou pour la mériter' (Bevan, 58–9). Most writers of French Switzerland are marked by these feelings, Chessex argues. Crisinel, for example, is 'assiégé, traqué, torturé par un sentiment de remords qui l'obsédait et l'affolait' (*Saintes*, 55). Likewise, Georges Nicole's work is marked by 'l'inquiétude, le regret, l'obsession du péché' (*Saintes*, 80), and Velan's characters are possessed by 'les remords, la peur égarante' (*Saintes*, 131).

Chessex's own creation, Jean Burg, is well aware of the sense of guilt that assails all those who have a Calvinist background, and he uses this 'sentiment si vivace du mal et du péché qui couve au fond de chaque protestant' (*La Confession*, 21). He attacks his parishioners for their sins, knowing that, however much they resent his words, there is still a residual feeling of guilt within them that responds to him. He says: 'Je sais trop bien qu'à travers moi s'exprimaient tous ces siècles de contrition et de repentir, toutes ces voix pastorales qui avaient flétri la chair, le gain, l'orgueil' (21). Not surprisingly, when his own love for Geneviève results in her death in childbirth, he sees this as punishment from God.

Jean Calmet's father is able to maintain a grip on Jean's mind from beyond the grave precisely because Jean is also afflicted with remorse. His sense of liberation when his father dies is mingled with guilt for feeling free, and it is in part this guilt that resurrects the image of Dr Calmet. The voice of self-reproach is also represented by the cathedral bells, which toll when he is feeling particularly happy and remind him he is a sinner and has no reason to feel happy. In the presence of the principal of the school where he teaches (another father-figure who assumes the attributes of God), Jean is assailed by remorse. 'Toujours ce sentiment d'être pris en faute, d'être coupable,' he thinks when he remembers this (*L'Ogre*, 71).

In the case of Alexandre Dumur, Calvinist remorse may be traced to the influence of his parents, who were itinerant preachers. As he sinks further into disorder and sexual excess, his one comfort is that his parents did not live to see it: 'Ah! Mes parents sont morts, Dieu merci, ils n'auront pas souffert de la tache suiffeuse et nauséabonde que je suis sur la Création' (*Les Yeux*, 30). He becomes obsessed with dirt, the unclean, the evil-smelling, believing these things to be his natural element. He neglects himself to the point that he becomes filthy, and then he sees this as confirmation of what his parents had predicted.

Several characters in *Judas le transparent* labour under a burden of guilt. Paul Turner is a student of theology who sees his conduct as unworthy of a man of God. His awareness of sin in others serves to heighten his own feelings of guilt, forcing him to admit: 'C'est facile de voir le mal chez les autres, tartuffe, quand on est soi-même tout gluant de saleté' (48). Pierre, his brother, has similar feelings, and he blames himself for debauching Johanna. But it is in the sect led by Aschenbach that self-accusation reaches a paroxysm. The ceremonies of flogging and violent punishment are fuelled by a conviction among the participants that they are guilty in the eyes of God. Overcome by remorse produced in these sessions, Johanna takes literally the evangelist's injunction 'and if thine eye offend thee, pluck it out' (Matthew 18: 9). She punishes herself for the evil she has witnessed by blinding herself in one eye.

Jonas Carex's feelings of guilt pursue him to Fribourg, even though he associates this city with a more humane form of Christianity and with his love for Anne-Marie. But he seizes on those aspects of Catholic doctrine that appeal to his Calvinist sense of being a sinner. He adopts as his own motto the words 'Indignus sum qui orem' (*Jonas*, 77), he continues to see life through a Calvinist haze of self-accusation, and he blames himself for leaving Anne-Marie and for his son's death. Because of his name, he frequently compares himself to the biblical Jonah, and he gives many symbolic interpretations to the sea monster that swallowed the prophet. On one of its many levels, this monster represents Jonas' guilt, the all-embracing feeling of sin that engulfs him. 'La baleine est le cilice de mon esprit et de mon coeur. Elle m'emplit de doute et de désespoir,' he cries (59).

Chessex argues that such feelings are typical of the remorse that Calvinists of the Vaud have lived for centuries. When the Reformation and Calvinism were brought to this region and imposed by Berne, the Vaudois had to forsake his Catholic faith and a certain pleasure in life. In its place, 'il apprend le remords et l'inquiétude avec la terrible nouvelle foi' (*Portrait*, 131). Since Chessex too is a Vaudois, he shares these feelings, and has projected them onto many of his characters and texts. *Carabas* is in many ways his confession of this remorse – an avowal, like the *Confessions* of his fellow countryman Jean-Jacques Rousseau, of his many sins and evil deeds. It runs the gamut of his sexual excesses, his drunken sprees, his violent acts, and his betrayals, and behind a certain flaunting of these unsavoury aspects of himself lurks a distinct feeling of guilt. He thinks of the woman who conceived his child, and whom he persuaded to have an abortion, and he is flooded with shame; he remembers when he first deceived a woman with whom he was living, and he realizes that his pleasure was tempered with guilt; he fears that any child he might father will be dreadfully deformed, as punishment for his sins.

In *Portrait des Vaudois*, he even remembers his father's death and he is submerged by regret that he did not show more love for this man when he was alive. Like Jean Calmet, he is 'hanté par un poids de culpabilité épouvantable' when he thinks of his father (*Portrait*, 257). In such poems as 'Se Défaire,' 'A Ton Silence,' 'La Lumière de l'air,' 'Plainte du mort,' and 'Je suis un mensonge' (all from *Comme l'os*) his sense of guilt seeps from every line. When he reads a writer like Giono, whose enjoyment of nature was unalloyed by this Calvinist regret, the contrast with his own experience strikes him immediately. There is an almost inexpressible longing when he says: 'Le drame solaire ne connaissait pas l'angoisse manichéiste des Vaudois, et je m'attachais d'autant plus à Giono qu'il nous ressemblait et qu'il s'était délivré de nos remords.'[11]

Giono's freedom from remorse is all the more striking because he is a writer. To the Calvinist conscience, the act of writing itself can be seen as a sin. The writer, by creating, usurps a function that properly belongs to God alone. His work is therefore a blasphemy. Alexandre Dumur, for example, knows that his parents would have viewed his writing as a grave sin. The subjects that he chooses are particularly evil, and his life may be summed up as 'ecrire le mal ... le penser, le faire, le dire' (*Les Yeux*, 104). Because he has offended God by creating, he is fittingly punished: he is unable to father children. However, he attempts to circumvent that punishment by adopting a child. He thus renders his sin even graver, and he realizes this, for he says: 'J'avoue que l'arrivée de [Louis] me troublait comme une faute' (11). He is punished once more when Louis wreaks havoc in his home, and creates a disorder that prevents him from writing. He realizes at once that his mother would have seen this artistic sterility as evidence of God's displeasure, and he himself comes to believe that Louis is 'l'envoyé d'une raison obscure pour me punir dans ma seule activité un peu louable' (45). He grimly accepts that there is a poetic (not to mention divine) justice in this, and he quotes: 'Le méchant sera puni dans ses oeuvres' (92). When he does eventually manage to write a book, it is an inferior piece of work that his publisher rejects.[12]

It is interesting to compare this idea of writing as sin to the attitude that Chessex detects in the work of his fellow Swiss writer Yves Velan. For Velan, whose Calvinist upbringing is as powerful an influence on him as on Chessex, writing itself becomes the punishment. It is viewed as a cause of suffering, as a burden with which the author struggles, as something to be approached with 'la résolution ascétique de lui sacrifier chaque instant' (*Saintes*, 125). Velan believes that writing is an escape from political and social activity, and that it must therefore not be treated as an enjoyable activity, but as a punishment for rejecting certain responsibilities. It is easy to recognize behind this social conscience the old Calvinist belief that enjoyment of any kind is a sin. For those who inherit such an attitude, writing and art are treated with suspicion as frivolous entertainment that detracts from more important concerns. Hence, when Chessex evokes in *Carabas* the image of a vengeful Deity who inspires this attitude to life, he chooses to depict Savonarola turning Florence into a pyre on which all the beauty created by that city – but especially its books – is consumed.

The Calvinist as Chessex depicts him is obsessed by the idea of punishment. Naturally, then, Alexandre Dumur sees his own decline, the destruction of his marriage, and his inability to write as divine retribution, and he admits: 'Je ne peux m'empêcher de penser que j'ai été puni par cette fameuse justice, si chère à mes parents' (*Les Yeux*, 137). It is as though some black fatality hangs over human beings, whose inescapable lot is punishment for sin. When Alexandre witnesses the shooting of a rabid fox by a gendarme, he sees this as symbolic of the inevitable destiny of the human race: punishment by death for sin, represented here by the rabies. He sums up the situation: 'Car une fatalité pesait, détruisait, vengeait de Dieu savait quelle injure, de Dieu savait quelle faute suant ses conséquences comme une abominable plaie' (149).

It is a cruel and unjust God who metes out such punishment for crimes of which the sinner is often unaware. Jean Calmet is unable to understand why, for example, a young girl in his class dies of cancer. He is sure that God is punishing the innocent, and he sees the girl as 'petite martyre bourrelée par l'Auschwitz de Dieu' (*L'Ogre*, 24). He is forced to conclude that 'Dieu est un salaud' (25). When he himself loses Thérèse to one of his pupils, he immediately sees this as punishment by an unjust God, and he wonders: 'Mon Dieu, qu'ai-je fait pour que Tu me retires tout?' (170). Chessex says that when he thinks back to his father's death, the word that springs to his mind is 'injustice' (*Bréviaire*, 70). Sarah, the Jewish woman in *La Trinité*, points to the appalling history of injustice suffered by her people, and says: 'Je déteste Dieu parce qu'il nous a proscrits. Le peuple élu! Laissez-moi rire' (103). Addressing God directly in one of his poems,

Chessex says: 'Ah Dieu, tu n'es pas digne de ce jeu sans gloire' (*Le Calviniste*, 134).

It is a sad, sorry religion that oppresses and pursues Chessex's characters. As he listens to Schubert's 'Unfinished Symphony,' Alexandre Dumur is struck by the utter sadness of the religion that could inspire such music, by the darkness of Christianity in general and of its basic tenets. 'Triste pensée occidentale,' he thinks, 'où la révélation et le salut ne passent que par l'humiliation, les clous, le suaire, le tombeau. Triste méditation sur la souffrance qui rachète ... Triste foi. Triste Occident. Triste héritage' (*Les Yeux*, 39). Calvinism has taken these elements of Christianity and made them its foundation. The unutterable melancholy of this religion is at least partially conveyed in a verse from one of Chessex's poems:

> O tristesse de la faute mortelle
> Cicatrice d'être homme
> Parmi les spectres des aimés, les rêves des vivants
> Le passage des fauves ailés de la nuit
> Qui se hâtent comme notre sommeil désarmé vers toute fin
> (*Le Calviniste*, 31)

The images of this religion are the owl that haunts the night, the fox that lies in wait, the sickness in nature that destroys the animals, the black and bottomless lake that swallows the unsuspecting, and the night itself. To convey what Calvinism means to him, Chessex uses images of decay and decomposition, as when Jonas imagines his dead son, taken from him by an unjust God: 'Tu te dissous, tu coules, tu t'affaises dans tes liquides, tu baignes dans tes humeurs comme un poisson dans une eau saumâtre' (*Jonas*, 149). He uses images of flames that suggest the Last Judgment, flames that consume Jean Calmet's father when he is cremated, but that Jonas immediately links in his mind to the flames of the Inquisition and the ovens of Auschwitz. But the most fitting and haunting symbol of this religion and of its effects is Krieg in 'Le Mage': a madman driven to insanity by the vision of a jealous and vengeful God and by the constant struggle against the devil.

4
The Ambiguities of a Calvinist

Chessex paints a dark and despairing picture of Calvinism and its effects on the psyche. It is shown as a cruel, life-destroying force that concentrates exclusively on man as a sinner. It is also a force that, once it has been felt, leaves its mark. Characters like Alexandre Dumur, Jean Calmet, Benoît Rouvre, and Jonas Carex spend their lives attempting unsuccessfully to run from it. From Chessex's own comments on Calvinism, from the way it pervades his texts, and from the way he depicts men and women struggling against it, one has evidence to assume that he himself has never fully escaped its influence.

Yet, although Chessex relentlessly attacks Calvinism and exposes its deleterious effects, there is often, behind these attacks, a nostalgia for religious belief. He mourns the loss of religious faith provoked by the excesses of Calvinism, and he looks at religion with a sense of exile from something of which he would like to be a part. Many of the poems in *Comme l'os* may be interpreted as the fruit of this feeling of Paradise lost, especially the one entitled, significantly enough, 'Car j'ai été chassé.' In this poem, he contemplates the beauty of the world around him, and he wonders why he is still filled with a feeling of loss. 'Dites-moi l'énigme de ma faute,' he implores, and asks: 'Quelle passerelle à tendre sur cette crevasse?' (*Comme*, 74). It is as though the beauty of nature is a reminder of some Eden he once knew, or, as he puts it in a poem dedicated to Gustave Roud: 'Et la splendeur du paradis terrestre où nous nous défaisons / Reflète le jardin de la première nostalgie.'[1] In another such poem he writes: 'J'ai perdu le Jardin, gagné l'heure et la Loi' (*Comme*, 85).

Loss of belief produces no sense of freedom, for the feeling of guilt and sin remains. The problem is that he can no longer assuage the guilt since he no longer believes in God and cannot ask forgiveness. Paradoxically, he addresses that God and complains of his loss: 'Oui, j'ai tout perdu, Maître de l'esprit et des choses / Et mon âme enfuie achève de se dissiper dans le néant' (*Comme*, 133). This sense of loss and of frustration, mingled with guilt, casts a melancholy air over much of what Chessex writes, and particularly over his poetry. Chessex, sensitive as always to his own obsessions when reading the work of others, might be commenting on his own writing when he says of Anne Perrier's *Le Temps est mort*: 'La nostalgie de Dieu suscite ... une mélancolie légère.'[2]

As one might expect, many of the characters in Chessex's fiction share this nostalgic sense of loss. Jonas Carex looks back on his happy childhood with regret at having lost that particular paradise. Most of us grieve at some time or another for the loss of childhood, but in Carex's case the grief is heightened by the fact that his childhood was lived under the influence of Calvin, and his subsequent repudiation of Calvinism represents a loss of his childhood religion. When he says, 'j'ai passé mon adolescence dans un jardin dont j'ai été expulsé,' he is referring partly to that religion (*Jonas*, 20). Pierre Turner also says, 'j'ai été chassé du jardin' (*Judas*, 47), but he is referring to his expulsion from the Faculty of Theology. In his case, it is even more clearly the Paradise of religion from which he is ejected. The death of his mother, and his attendant discovery that religious faith cannot make such horrors easier to accept, constitute another expulsion from Paradise. Without his mother, his faith, his God, he finds himself forced to wander in a world that has itself become hell: 'L'enfer retrouvait ses droits d'un seul coup, j'allais y reprendre l'insupportable errance' (88).

The nostalgia for religious belief extends in some cases to the Calvinist extreme of such belief. Indeed, because of its unbending severity, Calvinism is sometimes regarded with yearning. It is seen as a stable system that provides certainty and protection for its adherents, while those excluded from it have no such reassurance. Jean Burg openly admits that Calvin's writings provide him with a sense of rigour and order in his life. 'Et je *veux* l'ordre,' he explains (*La Confession*, 40–1; italics in original). His vocation in the Church is born of this need: 'J'ai toujours eu le sentiment que Dieu m'avait choisi comme instrument à cause de mon goût extrême pour la rigueur' (41). God for him is synonymous with order, and he even sees authoritarian states and political systems as having something of the divine in them. 'Dieu triomphe dans ces systèmes purs,' he contends (41). For Burg, the necessity, even the beauty, of order is axiomatic: 'On ne discute pas la nécessité de l'ordre' (79).

Whereas Jean Burg never hides this love of authoritarian systems, a character like Jean Calmet is somewhat more ambiguous in his attitude. Jean welcomes the freedom represented by his father's death, but the influence exercised by Dr Calmet from beyond the grave shows that Jean still respects his father's authority. This respect extends also to the principal of the school where he teaches, who is a 'symbole autoritaire' (*L'Ogre*, 140) for whom he cannot help feeling a grudging admiration. Even watching a theology student reading a Bible causes Jean to sense the presence of order and stability that emanates from the man's faith.

Jonas Carex, too, is a character who longs for security. In this context, the sea monster assumes another of its symbolic meanings. Jonas often evokes this monster as an image of return to the security and warmth of the womb. He admits longing for such security when he says, 'je rêvais depuis toujours d'un ventre où retourner, où me tapir, où me loger pour l'éternité' (*Jonas*, 29), and the belly of the monster assumes womblike characteristics. He refers at one point, for example, to 'ma Mère-Baleine' (40). He imagines himself as the biblical Jonah throwing himself back into the monster's mouth and finding again the security of its inside. Even the café in which he seeks refuge from the cold night evokes the monster's warm interior. 'Déjà je sentais, je voyais les parois de la salle rouge m'emprisonner et me contenir comme un ventre,' he says (46).

While seeking a return to the security of the womb, Jonas is also looking for the protection of a religion that he associates with his mother and with his native region. His very name, a biblical name of the kind that Calvinists often gave to their children, links him to the Calvinist religion. His name and its biblical connotations lead him to see the sea monster as a representation of security. Calvinism and security are linked in his mind, and he more than once points out that the monster is referred to in the Bible as a 'fish,' and the fish was a symbol that the early Christians used for Christ. It is, therefore, the protection of Christ and Christianity that Jonas seeks, and beyond that, the security offered by God. He concludes that 'il fallait donc entrer dans le sein de Dieu pour connaître la paix' (86).

Chessex's portraits of Jean Burg, Jean Calmet, and Jonas Carex provide a fascinating glimpse into the Calvinist mind. He has surely captured in these characters an essential element of that mind: the love of rigour, order, and security. As Pierre Hugli points out, Calvinism is historically linked in the Vaud to the imposition of order by the armies of Berne on a society in disorder and close to collapse. It was a means of bringing security, even if in a brutal manner, and this association with safety and order persists in the Calvinist mind, including Chessex's.[3] But there is also at work here the appeal of order represented by *any* religion. Although Calvinism, because of its austerity and severity, appeals especially as representing order, any system of faith has a similar basis. Jonas Carex sees in the Roman Catholic ritual the same sense of harmonious arrangement that he once knew in Calvinism. As he listens to Catholic services, he realizes that the rites of any religion, by their fixed and repetitious nature, provide a form of stability. All the trappings and ceremony of religion are 'des hymnes, des litanies, des espaces peints, des formes sculptées, à jamais pareils' (*Jonas*, 211).

To the religious mind, which longs for the protection of stability, any activity that might lead to disorder is seen as sin. In fact, this kind of mind – and particularly the Calvinist one – might define sin as that which causes disorder. Hence, when Maître Mange becomes obsessed with Monna, his ordered life begins to disintegrate: he neglects his law practice, he brings Monna to work with him, he offends his clients, and he is expelled from the bar. He is even driven from the Masonic lodge, which represents the summit of ordered respectability and ritual. It is no wonder that he is fascinated by an exhibition of paintings by Louis Soutter, riveted by their disorganized mixture of symbolic images, fantastic scenes, and provocative situations: these all reflect the growing disorder in his own life. Unable to escape the Calvinist teachings of his childhood, he cannot help but see his love for Monna as a sin that provokes disorder, destroys his marriage, and causes his daughter's death.

In the case of Alexandre Dumur, disorder is even more obviously linked to sin, since it is provoked by Louis, the devil's representative. Even before Louis arrives in his house, Alexandre is upset by the idea of his arrival, and he is unable to write. As his marriage falls apart under Louis' influence, he begins to drink, to wander around the more sordid areas of the city, and to resort to voyeurism. Louis causes trouble at school by provoking fights, and he destroys the pastor's marriage. He causes disorder in Anne's life, too, pushing her into the arms of lovers, and robbing Alexandre of someone he sees as 'ma joie, ma sécurité' (*Les Yeux*, 37). Everywhere Louis goes, he causes havoc. In the end, Alexandre sums up the result of Louis' actions as 'plus de tranquille pensée. Plus d'enfant. Plus de poème' (73). Alexandre is finally pushed to the greatest of sins: suicide.

Since sin causes disorder, the Calvinist believes it must be controlled by a severe and unbending religious code. Chessex's characters never seem to succeed in escaping from this view, but Chessex himself points out that there is another way of looking at this excessively severe religion. He argues that Calvinism is not always the antidote to chaos and disorder, to sexual and other excesses. On the contrary, an overstrict application of Calvinist doctrine can actually produce these disorders. Jean Burg is an excellent illustration of this point. He is horrified by what he calls 'la tyrannie du désir' (*La Confession*, 76), but the very tone of his condemnations of excess, the way he dwells on the evils of the flesh, the severity of his attacks on sin, all betray a certain fascination with these things. When he falls in love with Geneviève, his ardent Calvinism takes a new direction: it is transferred to Geneviève. He now idolizes her, centres his whole life on her, and confuses her with his religion. When she dies, he has nothing left, and he has to fall back on self-accusation: he decides that her death is his fault. As Chessex says, this novel illustrates 'l'érotisme ressenti dans une chair calviniste' (Garcin, 36).

Geneviève first comes to Jean's notice because she is the daughter of a man who is celebrated in the region for his sexual excesses and his flouting of Calvinist morality. Jean decides to punish this man by seducing his daughter, but this cynical plan fails when he falls in love with her. Some critics have found Jean's choice of punishment rather unlikely on the part of a strait-laced Calvinist, but there is actually a logic in his decision.[4] Obsessed by sins of the flesh, determined to punish a man for precisely these sins, he naturally chooses, in an Old Testament spirit of finding a fitting punishment, to strike at the man where he sins. Unfortunately for him, the excessive streak in his nature takes him beyond this coldly calculated plan and propels him into falling in love with Geneviève.

In *L'Ardent Royaume*, Mange is called on to defend a Calvinist who is accused of sexual crimes. Mange, who shares his client's Calvinist background and his sexual obsessions, realizes that the strict nature of Calvinism has fostered the man's appetites rather than restraining them. He sees his client as 'le type même de calviniste dérouté qui compensait dans ses fausses audaces et ses singeries amoureuses, les envies qui le rongeaient' (*Ardent*, 158). Even more obviously, the strictness of Aschenbach's sect in *Judas le transparent* leads to sexual disorders. The floggings meted out to penitent women have obvious sexual undertones and provoke a keen sexual excitement in the sect member who inflicts them. Violence, cruelty, self-immolation are seen here as a direct result of the strictness of a group that is obsessed with sin and punishment. Virginia Aschenbach at least is able to see this, for she comments, 'dès qu'il y a Dieu, il y a méchanceté, on dirait' (*Judas*, 41).

Chessex argues that, behind the traditional picture of a Switzerland strictly governed by Calvinist morality, upright and respectable, is another reality. The very severity of the religion has produced a society that hides violence and excess, all kinds of dark crimes, behind its bland exterior. He addresses these respectable Calvinists: 'Vos mouflets se soûlent au L. S. D., le fils du Juge donne des sauteries au hachisch, la fille de la conseillère de paroisse voyage à l'éther, à chaque poste de douane on alpague une brochette de fils à papa à la peau plus séringuée et plus piqueé que dé à coudre' (*Carabas*, 198). The society that projects such a strict image for the outside world is rotten within: 'Je ne sais pas si nous vivons dans Sodome ou dans Jéricho, mais je vois que vos murs ne sont plus très fermes et que vous pourrissez de l'intéreur comme des gangrenés' (198).

The hypocrisy of this society is likewise a product of Calvinism, and the duplicity of Jean Burg again provides a fine illustration. Determined to punish his parishioners, he pretends to listen to their criticisms of him, to moderate his demands on them, and to 'fit in.' But all the while, he is merely looking for an opportunity to strike. So sure is he of the righteousness of his cause, that the hypocrisy of his methods never seems to strike him. Instead, he delights to see how easily he dupes people, and he savours in advance their discomfiture when they are finally punished. 'Je tirais de ces pensées un plaisir vif et sans tache,' he says (*La Confession*, 33). There is, in this attitude, no small measure of pride and self-righteousness, for Burg is sure that he is right and that God is on his side. He sees himself as God's instrument, and he believes that 'la punition que je préparais ferait de moi son justicier et son bras droit' (58). Calvinism has here produced the kind of refusal to accept criticism that Jean Burg also admires in authoritarian régimes.

Although Jean Burg never flinches in his belief in a strict order, most of Chessex's characters display an ambivalent attitude to religion, and even to its Calvinist version. They hate it, flee it, condemn it, yet they cannot escape it. They see the cruelty and excess for which it is responsible, yet they feel nostalgia for it as a protective system. Chessex's comment on one of his novels is equally true of them all: 'J'ai écrit *La Confession du pasteur Burg* sous l'influence de Calvin' (Garcin, 34). Yet these novels are also attacks on Calvinism, since they show the disastrous effects of a Calvinist upbringing. *La Confession du pasteur Burg*, for example, has been described as 'le procès des désordres de la foi,' 'un témoignage terrible sur les ravages qu'une foi intransigeante peut causer chez un être,' and an assault on 'l'inviolable Calvin, père des âmes de ce pays, gendarme des esprits, et maître de l'inconscient collectif.'[5] *Portrait des Vaudois* has likewise been seen as evidence of the 'ressentiment que l'auteur nourrit naturellement à l'égard de l'austérité calviniste,' *Les Yeux jaunes* as 'révolte contre une théologie,' *L'Ogre* as 'le procès d'une éducation calviniste,' and *L'Ardent Royaume* as 'sa croisade contre le puritanisme protestant.'[6] Like Cingria, Chessex 'vitupère la tradition calviniste' (*Cingria*, 25).

These descriptions of Chessex's work are perfectly accurate. He does attack the Calvinist tradition and the Calvinist view of God. But the attacks are due in some measure to the belief that Calvinism has deformed and perverted the idea of God. There is still, in Chessex's writings, a longing for a living God who cares for mankind – the God that Jean Burg glimpses and almost comes to believe in under the influence of his love for Geneviève. Happy in this love, Burg begins to see God as a merciful deity. This is particularly true as he celebrates Christmas, which he now realizes is the commemoration of God's love for man, and which he describes with a verse from the Gospel of Luke: 'Les entrailles de la miséricorde de notre Dieu se sont émues' (Luke 1: 78; *La Confession*, 108). He now reads the Bible in a new light: 'Auparavant, j'y découvrais les hontes et les punitions, les paroles menaçantes d'un Dieu jaloux, les guerres, les destructions. J'y trouvais maintenant l'accord, la passion des corps et des âmes, la bonté du blé, la chaleur du pain, l'eau fraîche aux lèvres assoiffées' (84–5). He finally sees the possibility of 'notre bonheur sous le regard du Dieu bon' (102).

Chessex indicates that, although he does not believe in God, he is attracted by the idea of a loving, charitable Deity. This is the God of Father Emonet, one of the priests who taught him at Fribourg. It is in some measure because of this man's influence that Chessex still has 'un insatiable appétit de foi' (*Carabas*, 194). He writes in *Carabas* of a moment in his life when he sank as low as he could in sexual excess, drunken debauchery, and betrayal of the ideals of love. Disgusted with himself, sickened by his behaviour, he suddenly felt uplifted, pulled, as it were, towards the ideal of God, the kind of God he had learned of from Father Emonet. At this, and at certain other moments, he has felt the attraction of an ideal, an absolute of goodness and mercy that, in many versions of religion, is represented by God. At these times, he says: 'Je cède. Je subis et je m'exalte. Dieu, ou l'absolu, ou l'éclair, la totalité de la vie et de la mort, l'extrême, l'inimaginable' (*Carabas*, 211). It is of this God that Chessex has said, 'j'aime Dieu; c'est pourquoi, sans doute, je l'engueule.'[7]

And *engueuler* is not too strong a word. Chessex is unable to rid himself of the Calvinist view of God, unable to replace it with a gentler, happier vision. Consequently, much of his work is an attack on the Calvinist God, while the idea of a more charitable God of whom he was taught in Fribourg remains as an unfulfilled longing. Like Jonas Carex, Chessex left Fribourg and went back to the Vaud – a symbolic return to a Calvinist God whose influence is all-pervasive. When he returned to the Vaud, he found: 'La méfiance. Le doute de soi. Le regard des autres vrillé en moi' (*Carabas*, 197). Chessex is tied, as though by an umbilical cord, to his native region, which is the source of his being and provides the nourishment and inspiration for his writing. But the Calvinist God is also part of that region, and Chessex cannot draw inspiration from the one and escape the influence of the other. He rejects this God, proclaims that he does not believe in Him, yet the vestige of that belief remains. 'Je ne crois pas et je crois,' he says (*Carabas*, 213). The God of Calvin remains in his mind, in his memory, and in his writing, as it does in the writings of most Vaudois authors. His work, like theirs, bears the imprint of 'Dieu craint, Dieu perdu, Dieu nié.' But, Chessex adds: 'Mais il demeure, il taraude, il questionne, il est interrogé, pressé, sommé jusqu'au vertige, jusqu'à l'extase frénétique' (*Saintes*, 10). In the end, Chessex's work inevitably falls under the influence of a God of whom he writes: 'Dieu punisseur, Dieu extatique, Dieu violent comme un fer dans la chair brûlée et le regard exaspéré, ce sont les seuls que je connaisse et que j'admire' (*Carabas*, 213–14).

Chessex's use of the word *admire* says a great deal about his attitude to this God. He hates Him, yet there is a sneaking admiration for His severity. Jean Calmet, one of Chessex's most complex characters, exemplifies this ambiguous behaviour.[8] Jean fears and hates his father, the avatar of the Calvinist God, and he feels liberated when Dr Calmet dies. But he also admires and loves his father. He admires his father's energy and strength, and, when his father makes fun of him, he wants to weep: 'Car Jean Calmet aimait son père' (*L'Ogre*, 13). When his father reprimands him, 'Il aurait voulu lui crier qu'il se trompait. Qu'il l'aimait' (58). Jean secretly longs to be like his father, for there is part of him that also wants to be harsh and to exercise authority. Although he likes teaching because it brings him in contact with young people, who are open and free from restraint, he is also attracted to it because it enables him to impose his authority. The school represents a system of rules and order within which he finds protection from his father: 'Les classes où il a pénétré, et où il entrera désormais, sont des refuges contre l'autorité de ce père' (43). But it affords protection by enabling him to become like his father and to exercise power over others. In one scene, we see him marking some work done by Marc, the pupil who has replaced him in Thérèse's affections. Convinced that the work is badly done because of Marc's fatigue after his sexual excesses, he corrects the work severely. He is here using his authority and 'correcting' someone whose conduct displeases him.

The most odious form of authoritarianism in *L'Ogre* is represented by Mollendruz, a neo-Nazi whose absurd beliefs repel Jean, while also exercising a strange attraction. He sits in Mollendruz' apartment, surrounded by Nazi memorabilia, and he admits: 'Je suis médusé' (190). At one point, he even gives in to the temptation represented by Naziism when he meets a Jewish friend in the street, and, to his own horror, greets him: 'Sale Juif!' (204). There is obviously something inside Jean Calmet to which the idea of excessive and cruel authority appeals. There is, as it were, an ogre inside him to whom the ogre represented by his father and by Mollendruz (and also by God) speaks most eloquently. He is aware of this side of himself, for he describes himself as: 'Four-ogre ... Mengele-ogre. Mollendruz chauve-souris-ogre. Vampire mou. Jean Calmet-ogre' (212).

The symbol of the ogre's power is the razor that his father would use to shave himself, and with which he would pretend to cut Jean's throat.[9] Jean loved the delicious fear that this game would produce, and he loved his father all the more for provoking it. Indeed, Jean generally loves suffering and is a willing martyr: 'Je souffre, se répétait Jean Calmet avec bonheur, et quelque chose inondait son sang d'un feu noir qu'il n'oublierait plus' (20). He tells himself: 'Je dois résister à la peur, je dois aimer cette souffrance' (21). As an adult, he perpetuates this love of suffering. He buys a razor like his father's, and he often goes to a barber who shaves him with a similar razor. He is also, in another part of himself, horrified by his love of suffering, by his admiration of strength, and by the ogre inside himself. When he finally commits suicide, it is not just to escape the recurring memory of his dead father, but to escape the temptation of becoming like that father. Yet, even in his death, his attitude is ambiguous, since he kills himself with the razor that he associates with his father. This may be seen as his final surrender to his father and to the principle of authority and power whose attraction he cannot escape.

Jean Calmet epitomizes the dilemmas and ambiguities of Chessex's characters. He rejects the Calvinist God, but is unable to escape Him; he seeks freedom, but secretly longs for a system of order and authority; he loves the God who persecutes him, while also hating Him; he fears punishment, yet seeks it; he suffers but cannot do without that suffering. Jean Calmet is the perfect representation of the Calvinist who would escape his Calvinism, but who cannot.

5

The Valley of the Shadow

Death plays a privileged and determining role in Chessex's texts. A glance at the titles of some of his fiction reveals just how important a role this is: *Le Séjour des morts, Où vont mourir les oiseaux,* 'La Mamelle des morts' (*Où*, 117–20), 'La Fosse' (*Où*, 227–35). Many of his poems also refer to death in their titles, poems such as 'Plainte du mort,' 'L'Air des morts,' 'Passé l'ombre' (*Comme l'os*); 'Histoire d'une mort,' 'Cimetière de Ropraz,' 'Mort de Gustave Roud,' and 'J'ai trouvé un crâne de renard' (*Le Calviniste*). Other works, like *Une Voix la nuit* and *L'Ouvert obscur*, refer, through their titles, to the darkness and night associated with the demise of the individual. In fact, death casts a shadow over most of Chessex's writing, and he has said, 'la mort est au centre de mon oeuvre, elle a toujours été au centre de moi' (Garcin, 112).

This obsession is, of course, linked to Chessex's Calvinist background, for Calvinism is a death-centred religion that views man as a sinner who is doomed to death and damnation. It directs the efforts of its adherents away from living and towards preparation for the end of life, and instills fear of what that end may bring. Chessex's definition of Calvinism neatly sums up this aspect of the religion: 'La cosmologie calviniste est simple: l'homme en proie à la mort dans une nature belle, mais pleine d'embûches et de menaces.'[1] Indeed, death looms so large in the Calvinist cosmology that it becomes the centre of life for the likes of Jean Burg, who says: 'La mort m'avait toujours paru meilleure que la vie' (*La Confession*, 90).

Death may, at times, seem better than life, but it is more often a cause of fear. It is presented as the fruit of sin, and as God's punishment to the sinner. Chessex describes the admonition that is always present in the Calvinist's mind in these words: 'Ce même Dieu veut ma blessure et ma mort ... Souviens-toi de mourir puisque Dieu existe et qu'il a voulu ton malheur. Souviens-toi de la pourriture' (*Carabas*, 214). Alexandre Dumur believes that his wife will die for her sins because 'il y a une justice' (*Les Yeux*, 161). Jean Burg, convinced that he has sinned by loving Geneviève, preaches his Christmas sermon crushed by the burden of guilt. Suddenly, the faces of his congregation turn into leering skulls, 'une assemblée de morts ricanants, accourus à l'ordre de Dieu pour me presser et me juger' (*La Confession*, 131). In 'Le matin vient et la nuit aussi' (*Le Séjour*, 21–5), the young man and woman who ask the pastor to marry them are told that death and damnation await them for their sins, and that although they are young and happy, they must not forget the night that is to come.

Chessex is particularly sensitive to the idea of death as punishment when he meets it in the works of other writers and artists. He points out that Etienne Delessert frequently represents death in the midst of erotic scenes, and that 'comme les Egyptiens de Montaigne qui faisaient apporter une momie au milieu de leurs festins, Etienne Delessert installe son horreur de la mort dans la chair fascinante' (*Les Dessins*, 13). He sees the same obsession in several Swiss writers who share his background. Crisinel, for example, appears to view the demise of a young friend as 'l'effet d'une punition brutale, atroce' (*Saintes*, 59), and Ramuz displays in his writing 'le gouffre toujours ouvert de l'enfer et de la vengeance' (*Saintes*, 19).

Because of the emphasis that it places on death, Calvinism destroys all joy in life. When it was imposed on the Vaud, it transformed the spirit of a people, turning their thoughts away from life. According to Chessex: 'Tout l'esprit sévère de la Réforme pratiquement s'installe et passe un grand coup de noir sur l'esprit et le coeur d'une nation' (*Portrait*, 130). Death has become an obsession with them, fascinating and repelling them, often pushing them to suicide and crimes of violence. 'Salut squelette laboureur,' he says. 'Tu n'es pas fatigué n'est-ce pas de tailler dans le peuple vaudois! Il te voue une crainte merveilleuse' (*Portrait*, 233). In a chapter of *Portrait des Vaudois* entitled 'Pendu et content' (61–7), Chessex provides an amazing and horrifying list of men and women, ranging from his mother's uncle to his grandmother's brother, from numerous friends to old people in institutions, whom he knows to have taken their own lives. In 'Voir sa mort' (253–67), he lists the Swiss writers who have committed suicide, many of them his personal friends, and he wonders: 'Quel poison avait donc sécrété ce Canton pour que les meilleurs crèvent?' (*Portrait*, 262). Of course, he knows the answer to this question: the poison is the Calvinism that he shares with them.

Chessex writes with envy of the joyous Catholicism of a Cingria, which leads that writer to accept death as just another step in life. For Cingria, death is, as it was for the first Christians, 'un pas allègre et glorieux' (*Cingria*, 55). A similar sense of longing can be felt in his description of happy saints' day processions that were part of the Vaudois way of life before Calvinism (*Portrait*, 131). Jonas Carex is drawn by the same possibility of a happier religion when he moves to Fribourg, but he is unable to escape his Calvinism. Chessex, too, continues to carry the burden of a death-centred religion, and he describes how, listening to a minister read from the Psalms, he was gripped, like the others in the congregation, by its grim words about death. He looked at the faces around him, and concluded: 'J'ai compris que depuis toujours, comme enfant, comme adolescent, comme homme, comme amant, comme écrivain, comme fils, comme frère, j'avais été lié à la mort' (Garcin, 16).

Chessex's father was one of those Vaudois who, at least partly because of the importance of death in his cultural heritage, took his own life. This event, too, served to focus Chessex's attention on death, and particularly on suicide. His father was a deeply loved influence in his life, a man who taught his son to love the Vaud, its past, its natural beauty, and its language. He is so identified with the Vaud in Chessex's mind that he has said: 'Mon père est devenu le pays' (*Portrait*, 254). His father and his native region thus combine in his mind, and, since both are associated with Calvinism and death, they tend to deepen the influence of the latter on him. The particularly strong obsession with suicide that is due to these two forces in his life is reflected in the number of characters in his works who take their own lives: Jean Calmet, Alexandre Dumur, Julien Court in 'La Voie abandonnée' (*Le Séjour*, 39–41), Mange's daughter, Jonas Carex's father, Raphaël Turner. These suicides, as François Nourissier points out, are not just a convenient way of disposing of characters and bringing a novel to an end, but are the result of memories and past influences, for 'c'est contre un souvenir qu'il se débat.'[2]

The result of these combined influences is a hypersensitivity to the same obsession with death when Chessex encounters it in other writers. He sees it, for example, in Alice Rivaz' *Comptez vos jours*, of which he says: 'Tout le récit se cabre sous le regard de la mort' (*Saintes*, 191); in Chappaz' *Thomas l'incrédule*, which is 'fasciné par la mort' (*Saintes*, 11), and in the works of most other Vaudois writers, who are 'livrés à l'incohérence des choses, à l'arbitraire des arrêts de mort' (*Saintes*, 12). He is equally aware of this element in such French masters as Maupassant, and he entitles one chapter of *Maupassant et les autres*: 'Maupassant, ou dites plutôt que c'est la mort' (13). He also appreciates Henri Calet, whose works demonstrate that everything ends in 'la boue, ou dans le sang, ou dans un four' (*Maupassant*, 178).

Naturally, Chessex's own texts, like Delessert's drawings, demonstrate an 'aptitude à la réflexion sur la mort' (*Les Dessins*, 9). One might sum up this aspect of his work by mentioning the nightmarish scene described in *Reste avec nous*: Death's army, led by a grinning skeleton dressed in black, a huge scythe over his shoulder, parades through a Swiss valley. Chessex's writings, like those of Jean Cuttat, show that 'la mort ... a pris forme et figure, elle ricane, elle agrippe' (*Saintes*, 164). Sometimes death comes in violent and bloody form, as when a felled tree crushes a man (*Le Séjour*, 46), or when a man hacks to death with an axe a woman to whom he has just made love (*Où*, 203); sometimes it is slow and lingering, like the cancer that takes Jean Calmet's pupil, Isabelle, and Benjamin Gousenberg in *La Trinité*; sometimes it is timely and peaceful, like the death of Antoine Bulle, who is 'doucement foudroyé' (*Où*, 80). Certain works begin and end with death, like *L'Ogre*, which opens when Dr Calmet has just died, and concludes with Jean's suicide. The characters in such tales are, of course, constantly aware of death. Jean Calmet, for example, meticulously copies from a medical text the clinical signs of death, imagines the process of decay in a corpse, and meditates on the death of martyrs in the flames of the Inquisition. The narrator of *La Tête ouverte* constantly thinks of his own demise, imagines his burial, and thinks of himself as 'prisonnier ... dans le brouillard des morts' (54). Stéphane in 'La Mamelle des morts' (*Où*, 117–20) claims that when he was a baby, his mother would lay him on the tombs in the cemetery to change his diapers, and that, since that time the dead have been his constant companions. One could multiply these examples many times, for they may be found in nearly all that Chessex has written.

Since Calvinism tends to stress predestination and the idea that man has little choice in his fate, it is precisely the inevitability of man's demise that is emphasized in Chessex's texts, the realization that 'tout destin penche vers la mort' (*Saintes*, 68). Chessex is always aware that 'nous [sommes] tous embarqués dans une espèce d'abominable wagon à bestiaux, pour une destination qui est inéluctablement la tombe' (Garcin, 112). This is not just an abstract awareness, a vague recognition of a principle, but is based on a lifelong scrutiny of death as it has struck others. The deaths of Chessex's father, of many friends and fellow-writers, have shown him what he must expect himself. As he puts it: 'Je comprends que l'horreur ce n'est pas de mourir ou de se savoir mortel soi-même, mais de se reconnaître mortel dans l'autre. Et de se reconnaître mortel parce que l'autre est mort' (Garcin, 112).

The truth that lies behind so much of Chessex's work, the guiding principle of his fiction and poetry, is that all men die. He tends to see men and women as future corpses, as what Céline calls 'de la pourriture en suspens.'[3] For Chessex, 'nous sommes déjà poussière de notre mort' (*Le Calviniste*, 64). Jean Calmet, when he visits his mother, notices above all the signs of age in her, the declining vitality, the evidence of approaching death. This is the fate of all human beings, and, according to Chessex, it is the only thing of which we can be sure: 'Mors certa, hora incerta' (*Carabas*, 215). Chessex's credo is, therefore, based on this one sure and certain fact of existence: 'Cousez mon mémorial dans mon linceul: je crois dans la sainte horreur universelle de la mort. Je crois dans le pire destin au monde. J'ai la preuve, heure par heure, de l'injustice, de la misère, de la faiblesse de ma condition' (*Carabas*, 217). More succinctly, he writes in one poem: 'Je serais revenu à cette idée à peu près simple / Que je suis fait pour mourir' (*Le Calviniste*, 89).

Death is a law of nature. It affects all that lives, and the Calvinist finds reminders of this in nature:

Je vais mourir dit l'oiseau
Je tue le temps dit la brume
Je fonds dit la grappe
Je me défais dit le fruit tombé dans l'herbe rousse
Je passe dit le soleil de poudre dans le bleu fixe
Je vais mourir dis-je comme le fruit comme l'oiseau comme la brume
(*Elégie*, 90)

Chessex, who loves the natural world, especially in the Vaud, who constantly observes it, delights in it, and describes it, is nevertheless aware that death is part of it. This idea is conveyed in *L'Ardent Royaume* by the naïve painting seen by Raymond Mange in a country inn: a group of harvesters stand around a bird's nest that they have just destroyed with their scythes. The same image of death as the Grim Reaper is found in *Reste avec nous*, in which Chessex evokes 'l'allégorie si puissante du squelette avançant dans le champ d'hommes-blés' (43).

Chessex and his characters frequently look back at the natural world and see in it the presence of death. Benoît sits looking out of his house at the lake, the mountains of Savoy, the sweep of the bay, but what strikes him is 'une apparence unique, parfaite, du réel inéluctablement en marche vers sa mort' (*La Trinité*, 20); in 'Le Génie du lieu' (*Où*, 77–80), Antoine Bull sees images of his own demise in the stream that wears down even the hardest rock; Alexandre Dumur finds similar reminders of death in the rabies that strikes the wildlife where he lives. But it is above all the seasons and the passage of time represented by them that constitute the most constant reminder of death. Winter especially is seen as the season of cold and death, and the silence that it imposes on the world is described as 'silence injuriant' (*Le Jeûne*, 13). Even the snow that covers the countryside is a blanket of death, and one poem says: 'La blancheur soude le traité compact / Noeuds pour la mort' (*Ouvert*, 13). Autumn, when it appears in Chessex's work, is a prelude to winter, and is the season when 'tout vire à la cendre et au sable' (*Le Calviniste*, 21). As for summer, it cannot halt the approach of death, and it is seen as a mask that temporarily hides the menace that awaits. In a section of *Elégie soleil du regret* called 'L'été, le masque,' Chessex writes of 'l'été totalement trompeur / Totalement menteur' (51).

There are many other reminders of death in Chessex's writing. The most obvious of these is the cemeteries that seem to exercise a curious attraction for his characters. Jean-Paul Dallut in 'Une Fête-Dieu qui finit mal' (*Le Séjour*, 93–9) frequents cemeteries, as does David Seligmann in 'Te Deum' (*Le Séjour*, 177–85); the narrator of 'Le Séjour des morts' (*Le Séjour*, 255–66), knowing that his own end is approaching, spends much of his time in cemeteries, lying on tombs and imagining his future grave; Jean Calmet evokes the visit to a graveyard made by his dying pupil, and he dreams of skeletons lying in their tombs; the narrator of *La Tête ouverte* daydreams of the cemetery in which he will be buried. It is no surprise to learn that

Chessex, too, is fascinated by tombs and graveyards, and that he had a house built close to one (Garcin, 56–7, 62).

Burials and funeral ceremonies occur with similar frequency. Hence, 'Repose en paix' (*Le Séjour*, 51–3) is a description of a funeral; 'Le Fort' (*Le Séjour*, 213–24) contains another such description; *L'Ogre* evokes Isabelle's funeral; Mange goes to his daughter's burial and Benoît goes to Benjamin's; one chapter of *Feux d'orée* ('La Halte en février') is the description of yet another funeral. One chapter of *Reste avec nous* ('Reste avec nous') gives a detailed account of a wake, and in the centre of the scene is the coffin and the body it contains. Naturally, when writing of Maupassant and the naturalists, Chessex points out the importance of cemeteries and funerals in their work (*Maupassant*, 26, 27).

Mention must also be made of hospitals and hospital wards, which are seen as antechambers of death. *Portrait des Vaudois* contains a chapter entitled 'Mourir à l'hôpital' in which Chessex speaks of his horror of these places and his memory of his mother's life in one such hospital. In a scene worthy of Bosch, he describes the sick, demented, deformed and dying patients, concluding: 'L'hôpital, c'est peut-être la vraie église, le lieu le plus fraternel où lire notre destin et notre détresse dans chaque plaie, chaque regard' (234). In *La Trinité*, the private clinic in which Benjamin Gousenberg is dying is the scene of much of the action. It dominates the novel, focusing Benoît's attention on the suffering and death that it contains within its walls, occupying the centre of his thoughts. The hospital is seen in both these works as a microcosm of our everyday world, with its suffering and inevitable end.

Cemeteries, funerals, hospitals – these are obvious reminders of death, but there are several other, less obvious ones. Chessex sees death everywhere, and is constantly reminded of its presence, for 'la mort a gravé les signes entre tous reconnaissables de son effet et de son passage' (*La Trinité*, 211). He is like those characters in 'Juke-Box ou le contrôle des terres,' who sit in a café, unable to enjoy themselves because one customer persists in talking of his job – which is to shave corpses. Such reminders are unwelcome, but they are inescapable. One character says: 'Derrière la scène ... il y a l'imagination du pire' (*Le Séjour*, 231). Maître Mange, too, is hyperconscious of death, and, as he looks at a picture of his daughter when she was alive, he can see the presence of death already there, threatening her. In the poem 'Absent nuage,' the poet imagines a man walking in the street, assailed suddenly by thoughts of his demise (*Batailles*, 51). The dead themselves seem to intrude into the poet's mind: 'Et nos morts, nos visages, nos chères ombres / Ne cessent de parler derrière les surfaces' (*Elégie*, 68). In such works, as in those of other Swiss writers like Crisinel, Roud, and Nicole, 'La mort guette, profère ses présages, distille sa nuit dans le jour blanc' (*Saintes*, 83).

One aspect of our existence that has frequently been linked in the minds of men and women to death is sexual activity. It is no surprise to find that, in Chessex's writing too, the erotic provokes thoughts of death. Few texts illustrate as well as these Georges Bataille's contention that 'l'érotisme a, d'une manière fondamentale, le sens de la mort.'[4] Chessex says, in fact, that *Le Séjour des morts* was inspired by the realization that 'la mort est liée au sexe' (Garcin, 58). This idea is illustrated in 'Cul et chemise' (*Le Séjour*, 155–8), in which two lovers are buried one on top of the other in the same grave. Also in this volume is the story in which a dying man watches from a cemetery as a woman undresses in front of her window ('Le Séjour des morts'). In 'Clairière' (*Où*, 201–5), a man kills a woman with an axe, after having made love to her. *L'Ogre* contains a scene worthy of Pieyre de Mandiargues in which Jean Calmet's dying pupil makes love on a tomb, and Jean himself, lying in bed while Geneviève makes love to him, compares himself to the stone figure of a knight lying on a tomb. In one instance, the psychological link between death and sex finds an outlet in necrophilia. The tale that bears the humorous but grisly title 'Les Restes de la nuit' (*Où*, 255–62), describes in gruesome detail the exploits of a man who disinters recently buried young women in order to make love to them. It is in *La Trinité*, however, that the link between sex and death is pursued the most consistently. The dying Benjamin invites Benoît to become his wife's lover, and then, as he lies dying, he imagines their lovemaking. They, in their turn, think constantly of him as they make love. In Benoît's words, his activities with Sarah consist of 'la caresser, l'écouter gémir, la pénétrer quasiment sur le cadavre de son époux' (43).

The link between eroticism and death seems to reinforce the one between women and death that Chessex inherits from the Calvinist tradition. Woman is seen as inextricably bound to death because she represents sin, and sin for the Calvinist is usually sexual in nature. Little wonder that Chessex appreciates the drawings of Delessert that show a death's head on a voluptuous female body, or a skeleton with a woman's sex organs (*Les Dessins*, 13). He says of his own attitude to women: 'Je n'ai jamais tenu un seul corps embrassé sans imaginer les os qu'il sera dans la tombe et son rire déchu dans la fosse' (*Carabas*, 147). Maître Mange looks at Monna's naked body, thinks of it as it will be after death, and remembers Baudelaire's poem 'Une Charogne.'

In the popular imagination, the sex act itself is often considered to resemble death because of the sense of loss of self that it provokes. (Hence, the French refer to orgasm as 'la petite mort.') Chessex takes up this idea, especially in *Morgane Madrigal*. The narrator of this story writes to Morgane, describing his sexual experiences with her in these terms: 'Fondre, me noyer, me dissoudre en vous, me perdre en vous, mourir en vous, disparaître en vous, m'anéantir' (151). He says that he has always associated her with death: 'J'ai toujours respiré et absorbé la mort sur votre chair, dans votre bouche, dans vos cheveux, sur toute votre peau' (228). Because he thinks of her as linked to death, and because he likes to watch her intently, he refers to her as Méduse. This word, in French, refers not just to the figure of myth who destroyed all men who looked on her, but also to a dangerous kind of jellyfish that can destroy, too. His attitude to her is best summed up in the verses that he writes to her: 'Plonger, nager en toi, méduse / Dans ton odeur de ténèbre / Et d'eau de mer, nager sans ruse / Dans ton puits solaire et funèbre' (167).

The consequences of this never-failing consciousness of death are several. The most evident one is that life is felt as fleeting and precarious, a mere interlude before the final passing. There often appears to be a desire to get life over as soon as possible, since it will not last anyway. 'Que le vent vienne et nous efface,' says a line in a poem (*Le Calviniste*, 45), and the quotation from Georges Perros that serves as an epigraph to *La Tête ouverte* refers to 'l'inutilité d'entreprendre quoi que ce soit puisqu'on viendra nous chercher d'un moment à l'autre.' The brevity of life and its pointlessness in the face of death are accepted by the woman in *Reste avec nous* when her husband dies. 'La vie est comme une fumée, nous passons,' she says (138).

The pages of Chessex's work show an acute awareness of the passing of time and the realization that 'rien jamais ne demeure de notre espace pourrissant' (*Les Dessins*, 31). What Chessex says about Jean Cayrol's writing applies equally to his own: 'L'obsession du temps nourrit ces livres et les porte.'[5] His poems in particular are filled with the sense that life does not last and that the individual is borne helplessly forward towards his demise. The poet looks at the sky and exclaims: 'Les nuages s'en vont blancs / Dans le vent, pareils à nos vies' (*Une Voix*, 32). However much the poet tries to enjoy the warmth of summer, he knows that 'cet été s'enfuit trop semblable à ma vie' (*Le Jour*, 21). He realizes that man has no power against this 'effrayant travail des jours,'[6] for time seems almost to eat up man, and is described as 'le temps, vielle mâchoire / qui détruit un jour après l'autre' (*Chant*, 35).

Mingled with the horror caused by the passing of time is a deep-seated fear of old age and decay. Chessex's characters display that 'intuition aiguë de l'usure, de l'érosion des corps, du vieillissment' that he discerns in the writings of Alice Rivaz (*Saintes*, 188). Jean Calmet, Maître Mange, and Alexandre Dumur all imagine the women they love as they will appear in old age, while the narrator of 'Allons, allons' (*Le Séjour*, 141–4), meeting his ex-wife by chance, is struck by her ageing face, the deepening lines around her eyes, the hesitation in her step. As he thinks of the approach of old age in the woman to whom he addresses one of his poems, Chessex, unlike Ronsard, does not see in this an incentive to live now, but simply a foretaste of horror to come: 'Toi quand tu seras vieille, horreur de toi / Vieille, je crie de peur' (*Le Jeûne*, 65).

Chessex admits to an almost obsessive preoccupation with age, sickness, and physical decay. He has said: 'Je suis hanté par le vieillissement, la détérioration, les ruses de la maladie. Tout meurt. Les visages de mes morts luisent dans la pénombre, ils m'appellent au fond de leurs niches' (*Portrait*, 264). He frequently dwells in morbid fascination on the decay that accompanies age, on 'l'horreur et la fascination de la chair vouée à la pourriture' (*Maupassant*, 176). Characters often imagine the decaying bodies of the dead: Jean Calmet thinks of the dead Isabelle, Mange imagines his daughter's body, Jonas evokes the body of his son in the grave, and Alexandre shares with them this 'hantise de la chair détruite' (*Les Yeux*, 124). These characters also dwell on their own decay, before and after death. The poem called 'Car ma chair est vraiment viande' sums up their attitude: 'Et comme tes créatures je me défais sur place / Fibre déjà puante et infâme / Avant de pourrir une bonne fois dans le trou démocratique de ma commune' (*Le Calviniste*, 131).

Such obsessions as these, lying as they do at the heart of so much that Chessex has written, produce a constant feeling of menace. Behind the often excessive pleasures that he describes, behind the joyful descriptions of nature and its beauty, behind the happier moments in his characters' lives, lies an unease that sometimes breaks into outright fear. Writing of Queneau's work, Chessex gives the reader some advice that might be borne in mind when reading the latter's texts, too: 'Il faut se méfier. Ici le rire a quelque chose du grelot des lazarets, la plaisanterie débouche sur l'angoisse, le calembour ouvre sur la mort, la pourriture, le squelette rongé dans la terre.'[7] Behind Jean Calmet's attempts to live happily and freely are the fears that take almost palpable form in the recurring image of his father. Mange's love of Monna is a shield against his vulnerability, which is pierced by his daughter's death, his own thoughts of death, and Monna's dark past. Alexandre's biting humour and his love for both Anne and Louis do not prevent the disintegration of his life and his suicide. Almost all the stories in *Où vont mourir les oiseaux*, with their apparently innocent details of everyday life, suddenly reveal fear and horror, as, to quote one critic, 'le quotidien se transforme en sommeil de la raison, qui engendre des monstres.'[8]

In *Carabas*, Chessex describes his many sexual excesses, his lust for life and for the enjoyment that it offers, then he speaks of the fear that lies behind all this, and he says that all his excesses can never really banish it from his awareness. He talks of 'l'affolement de l'être devant le vide. La terreur de la solitude. L'effroi des maladies, du vieillissement, des déchéances' (148). It is easy to see why he loves the work of Maupassant, who was haunted by similar fears, and whose tales suddenly reveal death beneath the placid narration of unremarkable events. What Chessex immediately seizes on in the writings of Jean Paulhan is the sense of disorder and impending destruction behind apparent order, the 'infimes failles qui se sont ouvertes dans la réalité la plus banale.'[9]

Chessex believes that all Vaudois are inhabited by a sense of unease produced by the awareness of the dark side of reality. They share a feeling that, in the words of a critic, 'les tire vers l'inquiétude, la mort, l'ouvert obscur.'[10] Chessex himself describes this feeling as 'une plaie' (*Saintes*, 9), and he finds typical examples of it in such writers as Jaccottet, who 'se découvre précaire, menacé' (141) and Cuttat, whose revolt against the presence of death remains 'celle d'un inquiet' (165).

The feeling of unease can sometimes reach a pitch of anguish, a kind of metaphysical *angst* that Chessex describes as 'l'angoisse qui serre la gorge à la fin de l'automne, quand le brouillard monte des vallons, noie les lampes, gagne tout le grand plateau désolé qu'il enveloppe dans son linceul' (*Saintes*, 69). Such anguish seems to cover everything, to colour the writer's vision of the world around him, and to make life unbearable. He describes in *Bréviaire* how his view of the Vaud, his appreciation of its beauty, his sense of solidarity with its people are all underlaid by anguish. There are times when he cannot look at the countryside without feeling this, when even a thunderstorm, with all its sudden violence, cannot drive it from his mind. 'L'orage éclate,' he writes, 'mais les trombes d'eau ni le tonnerre ne chassent l'angoisse' (48). Everywhere, he is conscious of 'l'effroi dans la fibre qui se sait mortelle' (48), and of 'cette angoisse, cette panique de l'être précipité dans le monde hostile et qui le blesse de toute part' (*Saintes*, 196). It is this anguish that breaks into the consciousness of the narrator of 'Un Coq à Esculape,' a man who has always shown stoical fortitude, but who, one day, feels 'cette saloperie de poison qui me tue le sang. L'irrémédiable' (*Le Séjour*, 30). It is this fear that M. Hahn tries to hide behind a bland exterior, but that forces him to admit to himself: 'Moi aussi, j'ai l'air calme et clair, et la morsure est camouflée à l'intérieur' (*Le Séjour*, 203). One might say of such texts as these, as Chessex has said of René Pons's work, that they are 'le théâtre même de l'angoisse.'[11]

They are also texts that are, not surprisingly, filled with ineffable sadness, by that 'poudre de la mélancolie' that Chessex refers to in a poem (*Comme*, 51). As the poet looks at the world around him, he cannot shake off his sadness at the shortness of life and the insignificance of man. 'Et la tristesse ici s'installe comme la mort gagne un corps défait de ses forces,' he writes (51). This sadness is incarnated by the narrator of 'Dans l'oreille d'un sourd' (*Le Séjour*, 11–18), a man weighed down by grief and who bears the name of that prophet most associated with lamentation: Jérémie. Jean Calmet, Alexandre Dumur, and Jean Burg are also stricken by moments of grief as they contemplate a life in which suffering is never far away. Any one of them might be speaking in the poem that ends: 'La fosse est pleine de la pluie de cette nuit / Je vois cette tristesse, je ne peux plus rien' (*Le Jeûne*, 34).

Perhaps the saddest characters in Chessex's fiction are those who have lost loved ones. The death of others leaves the individual overwhelmed by a feeling of solitude. Hence, Mange almost feels abandoned when his daughter dies, and Jean Burg is thrown back into solitude by the demise of Geneviève. As for those who die, they often do so in loneliness and isolation. Gustave Roud, for example, is imagined dying in solitude, cut off from others by his approaching end, and confronted by his 'solitude à la mâchoire nocturne' (*Le Calviniste*, 79). The dead and dying are represented symbolically by the little girl in 'Paroles de la petite morte' (*Le Séjour*, 71–4), who, after her death, wanders in the world of the living, a ghost who is unable to communicate with those whom she once loved.

Acute awareness of solitude is yet another trait that Chessex believes to be typical of the Vaudois, a race of solitary individuals who rarely break out of their loneliness. In 'Le Miroir de Dylan Thomas,' he puts in the mouth of the Welsh poet, who is a foreigner among the Vaudois, words that describe their difficulty in escaping their solitude. Thomas says that they are 'enfermés derrière les barreaux de leur prison' (*Le Séjour*, 239). Naturally, solitude is a major theme of Swiss Protestant writers, and, says Chessex, may be found in the works of Yves Velan, Georges Haldas, Alice Rivaz, and Alexandre Voisard (*Saintes*, 130, 169, 187, 203). He suggests in *Portrait des Vaudois* that the proliferation of societies and clubs in the Vaud is the result of a fear of solitude and is an attempt to find companionship with other Vaudois. 'Une vieille peur doit nous pousser les uns vers les autres,' he speculates, 'un effroi rêveur, une angoisse d'être oublié, de mourir seul à l'Hôpital derrière un paravent' (174). Such fears are the direct result of a Calvinist tradition that stresses the sins of the individual, his damnation, and his situation as a specific and isolated individual before God. Chessex lists among the effects of Calvinism 'culte de la solitude ennoblissante, particularisante, mais souffrance aussi de la solitude qui pèse comme une tare sur cette race biblique privée de prophètes' (*Saintes*, 10).

Faced by solitude, the awareness of passing time, and the sense of the precariousness of human existence, Chessex expresses in his writing the feeling that life is empty and has nothing to offer. Writing of this feeling in the works of Jaccottet, he describes it as 'l'effrayante disparition, le sentiment brutal du vide, du dépouillement horrible comme une mutilation' (*Saintes*, 143). The same feeling is expressed in these lines: 'Nous n'allons vers aucun autre rivage / Que la brume et le givre entre les eaux' (*Une Voix*, 31). The poet questions this emptiness, but receives no response; he appeals for answers, and is greeted by silence: 'Nulle réponse. Un monde vide accueille / mon appel. Une nuit lasse et vide / où je m'épuise à penser à ma vie qui s'épuise / comme ce soleil blanc, squelette de l'ombre' (*Le Jour*, 23).

Man is shown as powerless to find any solution to his sense of emptiness; he is a victim in a hostile world that takes no account of him. This is a world in which men are 'bagnards, sans appel, à perpétuité ... comdamnés de droit divin pour être un jour sortis de leur mère' (*Les Dessins*, 24). Addressing the dead poet Gustave Roud, Chessex wonders why this is so, and who decided it should be so: 'Qui décide, Roud, qui juge? / Quelle immatérielle fileuse tient l'écheveau des vies?'[12] There are, of course, no answers to such questions, but one may see in them a trace of the harsh Calvinist belief that all is preordained in man's existence, and it is useless to raise questions or to protest.

Chessex's texts do not paint a cheerful picture of the human lot. None of his characters succeeds in achieving lasting happiness, and all of them have to face the reality of death. Jean Calmet fails in his quest for freedom and commits suicide; Alexandre loses the two beings he loves most, and also kills himself; Mange loses Monna, and his daughter ends her own life; Jonas does not find the freedom and happiness that he seeks in Fribourg; Jean Burg finds only temporary happiness with Geneviève, before she dies and he is reclaimed by a jealous God; Raphaël Turner plays out a role that he is powerless to reject and that leads him to suicide. Such characters are typical of mankind in general: victims of a blind and cruel fate. Alexandre compares our lot to that of a pheasant lying mangled after a combine harvester has passed over it, or to that of a fox dying of rabies. Both animals, like human beings, are victims of a cruel force that blindly eliminates them.

The vision of existence proposed by Chessex's texts is familiar to many readers because it resembles in some ways what other writers have termed the absurd. Like Malraux, he depicts the individual as a helpless and humiliated victim of an impersonal fate, a being destined to suffer and to die for no apparent reason. Like Camus, he represents the universe and whatever forces govern it as irrational and inexplicable in terms of human logic. Like Beckett, he often sees life as a pointless journey from oblivion to oblivion, a journey in which we achieve nothing of lasting value. Like all the writers of the absurd, his consciousness is dominated by death: an ever-present, unjustifiable, and feared presence that is the final and irrefutable proof of the absurd.

What distinguishes Chessex's vision from that of these other writers is, of course, its foundation in Calvinism. Here is a religious background that might have afforded protection against the fears inspired by death and the idea that man is a sinner. But that belief has been rejected, leaving, however, in the consciousness of the writer, a continued awareness of death. His texts demonstrate an inability to escape the deleterious aspects of Calvinism – the insistence on man as a fallen being, a sinner condemned to suffer and die – while showing no belief in the more positive side of religion: the possibility it might offer of salvation. His is also a vision of death that insists on the horror of its physical manifestations: decay, decomposition and the rotting of the flesh. This is no abstract concept of death, but a fear of it as it affects the living organism. Coupled with that is the fear of old age and of the passage towards decay. His vision is best summed up in the words of Jonas, as he contemplates his son's grave: 'Vanité! Il n'y a pas de mémoire, pas d'esprit, pas d'amour de Dieu. Il y a un cerveau, un coeur, un corps promis à la pourriture depuis leur naissance, et la mort étend son règne sur le monde comme la neige enferme ta tombe dans l'aube trompeuse' (*Jonas*, 149).

6
Les Justes

Like the Romantics, Chessex produces texts that constitute both metaphysical and social revolt. In fact, he claims that all his works have a social dimension in that each one is a condemnation of attitudes that he considers prevalent in his country (Garcin, 39). As one might expect, it is a particular kind of Calvinism that he sees as the force behind these attitudes.

Chessex levels his attack mainly against the leaders of society in the Vaud, against those respectable bourgeois who are the very pillars of that society, and whom he calls 'les justes.' He uses this term to refer to them because they are sure of their own righteousness, of the justness of their beliefs, and of their duty to impose their own standards. They think in abstract categories of right and wrong, and they apply these ideal criteria indiscriminately to others. 'Tous sont abstraits,' he says, 'tous se sont inventé un monde théorique qu'ils prétendent appliquer à tout prix sur le nôtre' (*Carabas*, 84). His attitude to these people is unequivocal: 'Une de mes haines: je déteste les justes' (*Carabas*, 83).

'Les justes' seek to impose a restrictive morality that would prevent any open enjoyment of life. Such enjoyment is seen as sinful, especially if it is sexual in nature. However, in order to make these restrictions seem reasonable, 'les justes' often disguise them as 'moderation' or the avoidance of extremes. Chessex pours scorn on their pusillanimous mouthing of respect for moderation: 'Je les déteste, ils n'ont jamais compris que l'excès est une bête puissante et qu'il faut sentir une bonne fois craquer toutes ses digues, toutes ses barrières, pour être libre et pour être heureux' (*Carabas*, 25). He imagines a representative of 'les justes' whom he dubs 'L'Ecclésiaste'

– a name chosen to suggest this person's propensity for preaching, since it refers to the author of the Book of Ecclesiastes, who is also known as 'the Preacher.' This person summons Chessex to answer for his pleasures and excesses, and he is particularly severe towards Chessex's flaunting of the unsavoury side of his character. Such things should not be openly displayed, for they are unseemly. In their place is proposed: 'Equilibre! Humanisme! Classicisme, enfin!' (*Carabas*, 77).

'Les justes' are those who oppose laughter and merriment, and Chessex mocks their feeble amusements and 'ce rire nerveux des justes qui croient se salir en riant' (*Carabas*, 47). They would confine life within careful, safe limits, which leads Chessex to tell them: 'Mais vous vivez d'une morale de fonctionnaires, d'un ragoût de chiens chouchoutés incapables d'imaginer l'ivresse du loup' (*Carabas*, 85). In their presence, the narrator of *La Tête ouverte* feels suffocated, and exclaims: 'Il n'y a pas d'air ici' (19).

The main occupation of such people appears to be, like that of the God of Calvinism, to observe, judge, and condemn. Chessex himself, after returning from a period spent in Catholic Fribourg, was immediately aware of being watched. He could sense 'le regard des autres vrillé en moi' (*Carabas*, 197). Typical of 'les justes' is the woman who acted as judge during Chessex's divorce, and who made clear to him her disapproval of his 'immorality.' As he thinks of her and of her absolute certainty in her disapproval, he wonders: 'D'ailleurs, je me demande comment on peut juger. Avocat, oui. Juge, non' (*Carabas*, 83). Daumier's work springs to his mind, and he thinks of all the petty criminals sentenced with a light heart by those who are sure that they are right.

In *La Tête ouverte*, he transposes 'les justes' to a French pension, where they become Madame Lequatre, who owns the establishment, and such boarders as Monsieur Jean and Monsieur Antoine. These people spy on the narrator, judge him behind his back, decide that he is immoral. It is also 'les justes' who find Mange guilty of immoral conduct, who become 'le tribunal des justes' (*Ardent*, 216), and who destroy his happiness with Monna. Such people are represented by the prophet who says, in one of Chessex's poems: 'Je ne me courbe pas / Je ne me casse pas / Je ne demande rien pour moi / Je dénonce' (*Le Calviniste*, 113). In *Carabas*, he gives a long list of other typical members of this group, ranging from 'vieux libéraux bouffis de vanité garantis par l'armée' to 'notaires libristes promenant de comité en comité leur nostalgie des braillards de l'Eglise du Réveil,' from 'énergumènes calvinistes dressés sur leurs principes' to 'philanthropes radiophoniques grimaçant entre Tartuffe et l'Amour médecin,' from 'cuistres penchés sur le tiers-monde' to 'superbes analystes de la situation politique' (84). What they all have in common is their unhesitating belief in their own rightness and righteousness.

There is something of the artist's traditional dislike of the bourgeois in Chessex's attack. This is particularly true of his accusation that 'les justes' are too sure of themselves and too unquestioning in their attitudes. Like such writers as Sartre, Camus, and Ionesco, he is distressed by their lack of reflection and their inability to see that there can be no certainties in life. They are like the narrator of 'La Mamelle des morts' and his friends, who prefer to ignore or to treat as madmen those who talk of death and the grimmer side of life. They dismiss the character called Stéphane as a lunatic when he talks of death, and they finally have him locked away.

Maître Mange's wife displays a similar refusal to be shaken from her comfortable assumptions. A respectable, unemotional woman, she is untouched by Mange's passions and his ability to feel strongly. He is helpless in her presence, unable to communicate with her, and dismayed by her inability to be moved by the many things in life that touch him deeply. One of the reasons why he falls in love with Monna is that she *is* touched by such things.

Unquestioning acceptance of a particular morality springs in large measure from a deep and typically Calvinist respect for authority, and this is seen particularly in the attitude towards political and religious power. For many Vaudois, authority is represented by Berne, the seat of political power and the force that imposed Calvinism on the Vaud. Jean Calmet, despite his ironic attitude towards this city, is intimidated by 'l'autorité de Berne, son histoire de père et de ciment de la Confédération' (*L'Ogre*, 168). He cannot help but be impressed by its 'banques énormes et solennelles, une santé de vieillard vigoureux et prospérant sur son tas d'or' (171). People who can say 'On est de Berne' immediately create a sense of strength and invulnerability. This phrase means: 'On est du côté des costauds, on est défendu, soutenu!' (*Portrait*, 125).

In the eyes of Jean Calmet, the figure on Swiss coins is an excellent representation of the authority of Berne, of institutionalized Calvinism, and of the mystique of Swiss confederation. He sees in this figure, with its muscular body and its air of calm assurance, 'l'homme incarnant la Suisse [qui] avait une force calme et une sûreté qui blessèrent immédiatement' (*L'Ogre*, 204). An even better representative is the statue of the ogre that he sees in Berne. He equates this ogre with his father, of course, and he sees both of them as emanations of the Calvinist God. But they also represent the social manifestation of that God. They are symbolic of a society based on authority and the continual scrutiny of others' behaviour. Consequently, when Jean's dead father reappears at times when Jean is asserting his freedom, we may see in this not just the intervention of the God of Calvinism, but also of Calvinist society in its role as punisher of those who disobey its rules.

The principal of the school in which Jean teaches is also a representative of an authoritarian society. A pillar of the establishment, he is a deputy and a colonel in the reserve as well as principal of the school. He is a powerfully built person whose physical size reflects his power over others. When the students contest his authority with a sit-in, he appears with a whip in his hand, and drives them from the school.[1] Like God and Jean's father, he seems to see everything and to sense wrongdoing. He sits as a kind of judge in staff meetings, and he is compared implicitly to Jean's father when we are told that, when summoned into his presence, Jean feels 'la même peur qu'il subissait en se rendant au cabinet de son père' (121). He is directly assimilated to God when he is described as 'Dieu-Directeur-des-hommes' (122), and he is depicted as God's representative in the social order when called 'le lieutenant du Créateur, le Roi-Dieu, le père de l'Etat' (141). He too is an ogre, for when he smiles at Jean, the latter 's'apprêta à être assommé et dévoré' (123).

The school over which this man reigns, with its rigid hierarchy and its imposition of strict discipline, is a microcosm of society. 'Ici, tous étaient au service de l'ordre, qui ne tolérait aucun écart,' we are told (151). Even Latin, the language that Jean teaches, is connected with authority. This is conveyed by the fact that the coin on which the symbolic figure of Switzerland appears bears the Latin inscription *Confederatio Helvetica*. Latin is thus seen as the language associated with the state and with central power. It is 'la langue paternelle ... la langue sacrée, la langue de la puissance et de l'indestructible' (*L'Ogre*, 205).[2]

Jean's suicide may be seen, not just as a rejection of a religion, but as the rejection of a society formed by that religion. His final refusal to give in to this society takes the form of removing himself definitively from its power. But he is also a victim of that society, an individual who can find no escape from it except in death. It is interesting in this context to notice that he is often represented in the posture of a sacrificial victim. When he makes love to Thérèse, he lies on the bed with his arms spread, as though being crucified, and when he is seized by a fit of outrage and madness in a café, he falls across the table, with his arms outspread. It is also significant that he commits suicide with a razor like his father's. The very symbol of an authoritarian society and an ogrelike father is the instrument of his death.

Chessex's fiction contains many other characters who may be seen as incarnations and representatives of this society. Prominent among them is, of course, a variety of judges. The divorce judge before whom Mange appears seems like God Himself, and makes Mange think of the Day of Judgment. He is 'émanation du Juge suprême' and the courtroom is 'théâtre de la punition' (*Ardent*, 176). The judge who strips Mange of his right to practise law is also described as 'l'émanation de Dieu' (216). Various other people who are part of the judicial system likewise serve as reminders of the power of 'les justes.' The *Procureur*, for example, because his role is to prosecute offenders, is one such person. Inspector Renard (whose name, as well as linking him to the fox and to evil in the world, also suggests the traditional policeman's cunning) is a tool of 'les justes' in revealing Mange's connection with a woman implicated in drug trafficking. Mange's father-in-law, who is instrumental in his rise in the profession, is another representative of Calvinist society, one whom Mange imagines judging him long after the older man is dead.

The most obnoxious of 'les justes' in *L'Ardent Royaume* is undoubtedly the 'vénérable' Gerstein. This man, who is the head of Mange's Masonic lodge, represents religion and society. A large man, he breathes power and authority, and he symbolizes for Mange 'autant de mythes à la fois classiques, familiers et insupportables' (165). He is shown as an avatar of God who, during the lodge's ceremonies, appears 'solennel, ancestral ... glorifiant la sagesse du Grand Architecte de l'Univers' (166). When he expels Mange from the lodge, he seems like God expelling Adam from Paradise – for sins that, like Adam's, are caused by a woman.

The two institutions that stand for the power of 'les justes' in this novel are the prison and the home for the mentally retarded. Mange is disturbed by his visits to the prison because he can sense its oppressive nature. It reminds him of his own guilt, and he feels as though some superior power is watching him when he enters it. The institution for the retarded holds those judged unfit to live within society. Significantly, it is housed in a grim old castle that dominates the town at its feet, as though set up as a warning that those whose conduct does not fall within the accepted norms will be separated from the rest of society.

People and institutions like these were once an accepted part of Mange's life. At the beginning of the novel, he is a respectable lawyer, a deputy, a Mason and the owner of a major legal practice. As a lawyer, he is seen to uphold the morality of 'les justes' as it is expressed in the legal system. But Monna frees him from this and makes him change sides, as it were. He sympathizes more and more with those of his clients who are in prison, and especially with one who is accused of fomenting disorder within the army (which is, of course, another symbol of authority). He has the feeling that 'il passait de l'autre côté de la barrière' (151), and, when ejected from his Masonic lodge, he tells Gerstein: 'Je n'ai jamais été des vôtres' (188). The change is complete when he finds himself accused in a court of law.

Mange falls foul of 'les justes' because, under Monna's influence, he embraces scandal and disorder. He brings Monna into his professional life, has her work in his office, takes her on trips to see clients. He mixes two worlds, refuses hypocritical pretence, and he does not hide his 'sin.' By openly flaunting his liaison with Monna, he shows scorn for the values of 'les justes' and he becomes a threat to them. They have no choice but to condemn and reject him. In the end, he is 'Maudit! Rejeté! Blessé à mort!' (219).

The respectable bourgeois who condemn and reject Mange and others like him are not the only representatives of 'les justes.' An equally repugnant product of this society are those whom Chessex calls 'les nouveaux justes' (*Carabas*, 97). By this he means those left-wingers and radicals who oppose bourgeois society and its values, but who themselves are bound by an authoritarian and unbending orthodoxy. He says that they are 'confortablement installés dans leur conformisme de gauche et ils se donnent des airs audacieux, des airs avertis, des airs de martyrs de leurs idées' (*Carabas*, 98). They condemn and execrate with a Calvinist fervour all that is not in conformity with their beliefs, and they are really just 'aristocrates accrochés à la tribune populaire par une vieille nostalgie calviniste de la punition et de la harangue' (*Carabas*, 99).

Chessex dislikes all conformists, all those who are so sure of themselves that they never question their beliefs. He says in an interview: 'Je n'ai pas ici à attaquer la gauche ou la droite, j'attaquerais les deux, c'est plutôt mon tempérament' (Garcin, 144). He is above all a *révolté* who rejects any attempts to impose belief or order. He professes particular admiration for those writers and artists who refuse labels and membership of literary movements, and who are usually described in manuals as 'attardés et isolés' (*Carabas*, 133). He believes himself to be one of these, and he affirms: 'Je me considère de droit comme l'un de ces parias, comme l'un de ces proscrits que les mages de la critique rejettent avec une moue de dédain' (133). He refuses all such attempts to classify, arguing that 'il est doux d'être inclassable, d'être réfractaire à toute organisation policée, vertueuse ou appliquée' (*Carabas*, 133). However, he realizes that he has not escaped this kind of labelling, and that because of his refusal of left-wing dogma and his insistence on his individual freedom, he has been called an 'anarchiste de droite' (Garcin, 41). This label, like all such tags, he believes to be a stupid oversimplification.

Of the writers who, like himself, refuse assimilation by 'les justes,' Chessex singles out Cingria for praise because 'il refusait de faire partie de la société parce qu'il avait refusé très tôt le monde contemporain, ses structures, ses polices' (*Cingria*, 13). Even a writer like Jean Ziegler, whose left-wing views are not shared by Chessex, is praised by him because he is a *révolté*, and Chessex appreciates in his writing 'une façon de se lancer à l'eau, de crier, de dénoncer, de se faire attaquer, de se faire menacer de mort' (Garcin, 143). But of all his contemporaries, Chessex particularly appreciates Chappaz, because he shares with him the same instinctive dislike of 'les justes.' He says with pride: 'On nous a reproché, à Chappaz et à moi, de sortir de la bienséance, de la décence, du salon, et de partir à la bataille' (Bevan, 56).

Chessex's characters also share his attitude of revolt, and they are outsiders whom society despises. Jean Calmet, as a child, attempts to rebel against his father's authority by committing petty thefts. Of all the Latin writers whose work he teaches, he prefers those of the Decadence, who reacted against the authority of the High Classical period. He admires the young for their sense of freedom, their disrespect for authority, and their revolts and sit-ins. Alexandre Dumur too is an *exilé*, and his sympathies go instinctively to the poor, the rejected, and the despised: the cripple whom the other customers in a café mock and brutalize; an old woman eating a crust and a piece of mouldy cheese in a country café; the aged, sick animals on display in a menagerie; the rabid fox shot by a gendarme. Raphaël Turner is a Judas figure, rejected and reviled as a traitor, but who gladly embraces his resemblance to 'l'homme le plus méprisé, le plus haï de tous les hommes' (*Judas*, 68). Mange revolts openly against society and is condemned by it. These are all victims of society whose lives are ruined by what one critic has called 'leur échec à vivre selon leur désir ... leur impuissance à briser la barrière que la société oppose à leur naturel épanouissement.'[3]

Chessex claims that he has always stood firm against 'les justes.' As a teacher of literature, he has taught what he chose and in the way he chose, even though he works within a system constructed by 'les justes.' He says with some pride: 'Je ne leur ai jamais obéi. Jamais cédé' (*Carabas*, 87). But it is particularly as a writer that he has stood firm, because it is as a writer that he has suffered the most pressure. Swiss writers who decide to speak their mind and to resist both a stifling religion and an oppressive society are immediately condemned as 'un ramassis d'obsédés sexuels, de violents malins, de porcs habiles à faire monter leurs tirages en corsant leurs torchons d'érotisme faisandé et de bassesse' (*Carabas*, 72). There are several writers in Switzerland who are treated this way, but Chessex mentions particularly Maurice Chappaz, whose works are dismissed by the critics with the comment: 'Chappaz salit son nid!' (*Saintes*, 209); Crisinel, of whom Chessex says 'les justes avaient compati à sa mort, ils s'étaient sentis encore plus forts, encore plus justes' (*Carabas*, 88–9); and Cingria, who died in a work camp where he was sent by 'un fonctionnaire personnellement ennemi des esthètes décadents et parasites ' (*Reste*, 90).

It is tempting to see something of a persecution mania in Chessex's insistence on the dislike shown to writers and to those who disagree with official values. There can be little doubt that there is a goodly measure of such mania in the hero he creates in *La Tête ouverte* – a young man whose whole existence is dominated by the belief that he is being spied on, judged, and condemned. There is an almost pathological fear of 'les justes,' of whom he says: 'Ils rampent, ils marchent à pas de loups vers mon repaire' (15). At times, his protests are hysterically shrill, as when he says: 'J'ai senti le regard aigu des guetteurs dans les taillis, j'ai perçu la respiration contenue des chasseurs' (18). But one should not confuse a writer with his or her characters, however much the writer's attitudes may customarily be put into them. In *La Tête ouverte*, Chessex is attempting to depict a psychology that is not his own: that of a victim of persecution mania. He is aware, of course, that this attitude may be attributed to himself, and he has said ironically: 'Accusez-moi de délire de persécution et vous ferez ma réjouissance. Voilà ce que c'est de se gaver des *Confessions*' (*Carabas*, 49).

The fact is that Chessex has some right to dislike 'les justes.' Several of his works have provoked scandal in his own country, and particularly in the Vaud. He belongs, as Jérôme Garcin says, to 'cette race d'écrivains combatifs et sévères qui pourfendent avec entrain les juges et les moralisateurs excessifs,'[4] and, consequently, he has sparked many hostile reactions: attacks in the press, threatening telephone calls, anonymous letters.[5] *La Confession du pasteur Burg* provoked a hostile reaction in Protestant circles with its portrait of an excessively severe cleric and hypocritical parishioners.[6] *Portrait des Vaudois* and *Carabas*, which portray the Vaud in all its beauty, but which do not hide the sordid aspects of its society, produced, in addition to the usual letters and telephone calls, a number of death threats (Garcin, 39).

Chessex feels that he shares dislike of 'les justes' with many francophone Swiss writers, and he believes that the best of them are subject, as a result, to this kind of attack. It is for this reason that he rejects the accusation that he is marginal, and that he does not represent Swiss literature. Indeed, he says: 'Je crois pouvoir dire en toute modestie humoristique que je suis, en fait, l'un des témoins les plus justes, les plus au centre de la vie helvétique francophone contemporaine' (Bevan, 56).[7] As has been pointed out, Crisinel, Chappaz, Cingria, and many others have been the object of the hatred of 'les justes,' and Chessex argues that he is writing in the same vein as they are.

Chessex's works are clearly a reaction against a particular society. He reveals a side of Switzerland that many of its inhabitants would prefer to keep hidden. Behind the tourists' image of picturesque scenery and a calm, mild people, he shows a society obsessed with a strict code, and the imposition of authority. In his own words, he has shown 'la vie dans ce pays, non seulement dans ce qu'elle montre de riant et de solaire, mais dans ce qu'elle a profondément à mes yeux de suicidaire, de dramatique, d'isolé, d'enfermé de neutre' (Garcin, 35). In the words of François Nourissier, a novel like *L'Ogre* shows 'la terrible société des Justes, vertueuse et taraudée par les tentations, calviniste jusqu'à la haine de vivre, puritaine mais secouée de frissons de violence et de désir.'[8]

The Swiss try to hide the other face of their country. They try particularly to deny the importance of death in their national consciousness, since this contrasts with the supposed pleasantness of the land and the happy disposition of its people. Yet, says Chessex: 'En Suisse, jusque sur les billets de banque, la mort à la faux ricane parmi des femmes de trois âges' (Reste, 43). One manifestation of this obsession is the inordinate number of suicides in Switzerland, yet this is a taboo topic. Chessex attacks 'cette façon que nous avons d'être aseptisés: tout est mis chez nous sous cellophane, dans les boîtes de conserve, dans la propreté, dans l'immunisation perpétuelle' (Garcin, 74). He even welcomes the spread of rabies into Switzerland because this is death in an epidemic form that even the Swiss cannot ignore.

The prevalence of suicide is part of a more general disposition towards violence that the Swiss prefer to hide. The taste for violence can produce outbreaks of murderous racism like the one that once took place in Payerne, and that is described in *Reste avec nous*: a group of Nazi sympathizers murdered a Jew named Bloch. It can result in such aberrations as the neo-Naziism of Mollendruz – a character in *L'Ogre* who lives in a world of racial hatred and dreams of political violence, surrounded by a collection of Nazi memorabilia that is presided over by a portrait of Hitler (yet another ogre). It can provoke the kind of daily violence practised against immigrant workers, who are badly paid, made to work like horses, fed on scraps, and lodged in a barn. The Italian immigrant is dismissed as 'un sauvage', is physically abused, and has his religion mocked (Portrait, 34). This attitude can breed scorn and violence towards outcasts, the crippled, and the deformed, like that described in 'Loin du bal' (Portrait, 39–44), directed against a toothless, simple-minded dwarf who is taunted, made to dance, and generally degraded. It can bring about neglect and cruelty towards the old, who are shut up in institutions, where they are punished for being incontinent, mocked by other inmates, and where their only way out is often suicide. And all this violence in the Swiss character is hidden behind a bland and virtuous exterior.

Because of its emphasis on strict morality and its repression of certain instincts, Calvinism can actually exacerbate those instincts. Repressed desires and emotions can burst forth in often violent and unpleasant ways. The sect described in *Judas le transparent* is an excellent example of how this can happen, for the violent punishments that it practises scarcely conceal a suppressed sexuality. The society that Chessex depicts is fundamentally violent because the strict morality of Calvinism really encourages the violent streak in human nature. Alexandre Dumur echoes this belief when he talks of 'tant de pièges, de baves, de poisons, de violences cachées' (*Les Yeux*, 16). He recites a list of suicides, murders, and assorted acts of violence that he attributes to repressed desire, which he is careful to distinguish from 'le bon désir heureux qui se montre et s'assouvit en pleine lumière' (17). Raphaël Turner looks at his village, like Christ looking down on Jerusalem, and he talks of its hidden crimes, describing it as 'un cloaque inspiré' and 'plus gluant que Sodome' (*Judas*, 114).

What makes the restrictive morality of 'les justes' even more difficult to bear is the hypocrisy that often lies behind it. The important thing for these people is the pretence of morality, a façade of respectability. But, hidden by this, there is usually a willingness to compromise and to live lives that are not in strict accord with Calvinist values. Pastor Burg, who is a 'true' Calvinist, is amazed by the 'pouvoir de dissimulation' that he discovers in his parishioners (*La Confession*, 27). Typical of them is the local notable known as H., who is Geneviève's father. He is a wealthy man who buys off criticism by contributing large sums to the Church. His private life, however, is one of many excesses, and Burg describes him as 'alcoolique, glouton, débauché' (44). Because of his wealth and influence, the Church tolerates his behaviour, and Burg's predecessor as pastor turns a blind eye to H.'s sins. A similar case is that of the Bâtonnier in *L'Ardent Royaume*: a respectable figure in the judicial system who has Mange dismissed from his profession for sexual misconduct, but who is, in Mange's words, 'un chaud lapin' (80). However, unlike Mange, this man maintains a show of respectability, never divorces his wife, and never flaunts his liaisons.

As well as hiding sexual immorality, this pretence of strict adherence to Calvinism may also conceal a rampant materialism. Whatever spiritual values 'les justes' may profess, their motive is often profit and the amassing of a fortune. This, Burg discovers, is the main preoccupation of his flock, and when he attacks their materialism, they react at once by attempting to silence him. It is this spirit of materialism that has led 'les justes' to take a city like Lausanne, which was once an attractive place with well-kept parks and fine buildings, and turn it into an ugly, concrete desert. 'Béton, laideurs, profit, modernités, architectures aberrantes: aucun plan d'ensemble, aucun art,' is how Chessex describes modern Lausanne (Garcin, 139). But even worse is Montreux, which caters entirely to rich tourists with its hideous hotels and its peddling of 'typical' Swiss knick-knacks. It is now 'honte d'une côte qui descendait, chênaies et vignoble, jusqu'au mare nostrum lémanique' (Portrait, 161). Montreux is no longer part of the Vaud or Switzerland as Chessex knows them, but has become 'une boutique de suisseries, de petits coucous, de petites pendules, de petits ours et de petits chalets' (Garcin, 141). He contemplates the handiwork of 'les justes' and asks them: 'Est-ce que vous ne voyez pas que ces laideurs nous tuent?' (Portrait, 166).

Linked to the degradation of cities is the systematic destruction of the countryside for profit. It is being torn up in order to build hotels, ski resorts, highways, and other profit-making ventures. 'On nous salope nos paysages,' he complains (Carabas, 117). In tones reminiscent of an Old Testament prophet predicting doom, he warns: 'Le pays meurt, messieurs les propriétaires,' and he points to 'les bulldozers, les bunkers, les motels, les hangars, les usines ... et les nuages de supershell' (Portrait, 17). The quiet village squares, the rustic fairs, and the small farms are being replaced by 'des machines hurlantes aux micros stéréophoniques' (Portrait, 261). In a cry of hatred for those who carry out this destruction, he says: 'A l'ancienne terre romane et savoyarde, à l'ancienne terre de Calvin, se substituent des moeurs de parvenus, de texans, de voyageurs de commerce et d'entrepreneurs pressés de graisser leur patte crochue' (Portrait, 261).

The mentality of many such profiteers is summed up by the 'maître du domaine' depicted in Reste avec nous (54–5), whose life is spent calculating the profit to be gained from his land, his livestock, and state subsidies, which he then balances against the cost of running his farm, marrying his daughter, and providing for his own funeral. This is the mentality that has made Switzerland synonymous with money and with banking. The national obsession with money is, Chessex says, 'comme une maladie qui peut surgir n'importe quand' (Garcin, 143). 'Les justes' have created Switzerland and the Vaud in their own image, and they exploit their country for whatever they can get out of it. 'Mais je n'exagère pas,' Chessex exclaims. 'Ils ont fait ce pays. Ils l'ont nourri et s'en sont repus' (Carabas, 86).

Chessex does not paint a pretty picture of Swiss society, and particularly of the society of the Vaud. But he sees it as his duty as a

Vaudois and as a writer to reveal the horrors and crimes that a certain kind of Calvinism can produce, and the sort of society over which 'les justes' preside. What he reveals is 'un pays dur. Vindicatif. La rogne éclate en bagarres, en vengeances cruelles, en obscurs coups liés à l'escarpement abrupt, à l'angoisse qui brouille les cerveaux, à la forcénerie de ce vin puissant qui énerve les plus détachés' (*Portrait*, 189). We are far from the tourists' view of postcard scenes and smiling country folk.

7

The Affirmation of Life

Although Chessex's texts are often dominated by the presence of a stifling religion, the shadow of death, and the fear of evil, it would be wrong to represent them as reflecting nothing but these influences. As well as conveying the importance of such forces, his work is also a reaction against them. His essays and his poetry openly reject the oppressive weight of Calvinism and its vision of life, even as they reflect upon it. The characters of his fiction also make a conscious effort to live free of this religion. Jean Calmet attempts to escape the memory of a father who incarnates the God of Calvinism for him; Alexandre Dumur fights against the power of the devil in his life; Jonas Carex deliberately flees the home that represents his Calvinist upbringing, and he looks for freedom with Anne-Marie in Fribourg; Mange seeks to free himself from 'les justes' in his love for Monna. Benoît, Benjamin, and Sarah live a triangular sexual relationship that is an effort to escape both conventional morality and the shadow of death that threatens Benjamin. And these efforts do meet with some success. There are moments of freedom and happiness in Chessex's work, times when an oppressive religion and its sad message are pushed aside, and when the sheer joy of living breaks through the clouds of remorse. Chessex's texts are not all gloom and obsession with death. Although they delineate the forces that oppress the Calvinist mind, they do so in order to make the enemy clear. Then they react against these forces. His writings are an affirmation of life and freedom as much as they are an examination of the forces of Calvinism and death.

There are periods of respite when the possibility of a benign God, the giver of good things, is glimpsed. The section of *Le Calviniste* entitled 'La Gloire de tes dons' expresses the belief that there are things in life that make living worthwhile. In 'Pâques 1976,' we experience the simple joy of approaching summer, of caressing a pet dog, of 'cette lumière où la grâce d'exister / De nommer, de louer / En cet instant s'est entièrement sevrée du malheur' (58).

Such moments may be brief, but the realization of their brevity becomes an incentive to enjoy them as fully as possible. In certain texts, the fear of approaching death can inspire fierce attachment to life: 'Oui nos jours sont de l'ombre sur la terre / Il n'y a pas d'espérance ici-bas / Mais nous nous attachons du crâne et des nerfs / Nous nous attachons' (*Le Calviniste*, 84). Chessex depicts a crow perched on a tombstone, like a messenger of death. But he turns to this messenger, acknowledges the message, and adds that he has many things to do yet, and that he intends to cling to life (*Feux*, 20). The fear and anguish that are never far from the surface, by contrast with the joys that life offers, make life seem more desirable. Addressing this fear directly, as though it were a familiar friend, he says: 'Car par toi le monde acquérait plus de profondeur / Le matin était plus aigu, le soir plus tendre' (*Le Jeûne*, 22).

Fear of death and love of life become two sides of the same coin. They are inextricably mingled in Chessex's work, as they are in Gustave Roud's and Schubert's. Speaking of his emotion when attending a memorial service to Roud, during which Schubert's music was played, Chessex points to the sadness and suffering expressed in the work of both these men. But this sadness is joined with love of life and attachment to it. As he listened to this music, he decided that he, too, expresses and would continue to express the same mixture of emotions in his own writings, 'parce que la méditation de la mort était là, et parce qu'aussi ma passion de la vie était là' (Garcin, 49).

Often this appreciation of life in the face of death becomes eager and even furious affirmation of life. At such times, Chessex is one of those writers 'qui écrivent comme on fait l'amour, comme on partage le vin et les viandes rouges avec des amis.'[1] In *Portrait des Vaudois*, he describes how, shortly after the cremation of his father, he was walking in Lausanne, oppressed by the burden of gloom provoked by his father's death, when he suddenly realized that a fresh wind was blowing, there were trees growing in the gardens of houses, and life still had pleasures for him. At that moment he felt part of the life flowing in the world around him, and he affirmed his love of that life. The same will to live now and as intensely as possible is expressed in many poems. 'Avant la mort nous pouvons croire au monde / Aimer ce sable dont tu parles, ces plantes, ces nuages' (*Une Voix*, 30), we read in one such poem, and in another: 'Mais je m'accroche à la journée / je me souviens de la lumière / je désapprends la langue morte / et l'habitude de céder' (*Chant*, 32).

These moments of joy provide temporary escape from death, periods when death recedes from the consciousness and has no more hold over it. 'Tu marches vers ta vie / Tu marches, la mort ne pourra pas te ravir' the poet assures himself (*Chant*, 28). He abandons himself to the forces of life that are stirring all around him as spring pushes winter and thoughts of death away, and he exults: 'Ce matin je suis riche et pesant de tendresse / j'ai les poumons pleins de soleil infatigable / j'ai poids, j'ai place, j'ai voix, j'ai la journée' (*Chant*, 30).

Chessex's comments on a novel by Pierre Gascar may well be applied to such passages in his own work: 'La vie n'est pas méchante, disent ces pages.'[2] And it is as well that he can feel and express this love of life, for without it his texts would be very depressing indeed. He himself knows this, and he points out that life would be unbearable for him were it not for the pleasures it provides and for the sense of attachment to life provoked by such pleasures. He has said: 'Si je n'étais pas attaché charnellement à ce monde, je me serais suicidé depuis longtemps' (Garcin, 66).

Many times, Chessex's texts go beyond even this fierce attachment to life, and they become a celebration of excess, of outrageous and gluttonous pleasure. Critics have not been slow to seize on this aspect of his work. *Portrait des Vaudois* has been called a book of 'tous les excès qui le tentent'; *Carabas* has been described as full of 'coups de gueule ... impatiences ... saboulages'; his work as a whole is said to be 'vivement adonné à l'excès'; and Chessex himself is 'le sensuel et carnassier Chessex.'[3] Another critic points out that this goes beyond the will to live life fully and becomes an attempt to push the limits of human experience as far as possible, to live life at the extreme.[4]

Of all of Chessex's literary production, it is *Carabas* that is most striking in its evident taste for excess. With its pitiless and sometimes complacent catalogue of the author's sexual exploits, its revelation of acts that still provoke his shame, its bitter attacks on 'les justes' and on several other pet hates, and its violent affirmation of attachment to life and its pleasures, it is an obvious celebration of excess in all its forms. The following partial list of intemperate 'achievements' gives some idea of the tone of much of this book: 'J'ai absorbé des hectolitres de vin blanc, j'ai divorcé deux fois ... j'ai fait un enfant à une jeune fille, j'ai sauté à motocyclette dans le bleu Léman, je suis devenu alcoolique et je me suis remis, j'ai donné un coup de couteau à un soldat, j'ai chouté Monseigneur l'évêque de Lausanne et Fribourg dans un modeste escalier matinal, j'ai siroté de l'urine d'institutrice, j'ai vomi un souper de pochard dans le Malraux de la Pléiade, j'ai jeté l'anneau de mariage de mon père dans une bouche d'égout' (*Carabas*, 12). In the same book, Chessex claims: 'J'appartiens à la race des buveurs et des cogneurs' (15). *Carabas* demonstrates, on page after page, the will to live life at its very limits and to explore everything it has to offer.

Other works also reflect this desire, of course. It can be seen in the lives of such characters as Raymond Mange, who abandons everything to pursue his passion for Monna, and who 'avait besoin de chaleur, de lumière rouge, de viande et de vins chaleureux dans son ventre et son sang' (*Ardent*, 52). It is true of Alexandre, who luxuriates in his excessive drinking, his sexual appetites and even his acute sense of guilt (*Les Yeux*, 151). It is the case of Raphaël Turner, who pushes his taste for betrayal to the point of becoming Judas; and of Aschenbach, who whips up his followers to acts of appalling cruelty and self-immolation. It can be seen in Burg's severe Calvinism. It is even true of such minor characters as le père Cormier, one of Jonas' teachers who is tantalized by Calvin because 'les excès le fascinaient, comme l'attiraient les rigueurs de l'Inquisition' (*Jonas*, 145).

Characters like these demonstrate that emotion, passion, intense experience are essential parts of the refusal of death. Chessex sees art as the expression of such emotions, and he has said: 'J'ai toujours été lié ... à la représentation des sensations' (*Garcin*, 48). His own writing, he says, is not cerebral in nature, but has its origins in the emotions that he feels in the face of death, the natural world, life, women, and Calvinism – all those things that form the woof and warp of his texts. Explaining why, despite his interest in philosophy, he chose to be a writer and a teacher of literature, he says, in typically excessive fashion: 'Je ne crois pas tellement que le talent passe par le crâne: il vient d'abord du ventre. Les idées, je m'en fous.'[5]

Passionate experience of life is also a response to 'les justes,' who would prefer moderation at all times. It is equally a response to death and its central position in Calvinism. It is, in fact, the omnipresence of death that provokes excess:

Ma gourmandise s'explique: je vis dans un immense ossuaire, à tout instant j'ai besoin de retrouver la chair chaude, la chair saine pour faire fuir les défroques claquetantes et les haillons terreux qui me sautent dessus. Je veux les seins palpitants, je veux le ventre lisse et chaud, je veux la salive et le souffle contre les charognes qui me poursuivent, contre la cloche des morts, contre les urnes, les faire-part, les oraisons, les A-Toi-La-Gloire, les cancers, l'autoroute, la cirrhose, l'hôpital, le tablier de caoutchouc, l'éther, les vers, la pluie dans la fosse, la dalle grotesque, et les nécrologies papelardes. (*Carabas*, 215–16).

This may be taken as Chessex's credo, an expression of his belief in excess, which he also conveys in these words: 'Je choisis l'abondance et la surcharge contre la mort. L'empoigne avant la fosse' (*Carabas*, 204).

There are several symbols of life and attachment to it in Chessex's texts. Wine, for example, is frequently shown as one of the finer things that life provides, as 'ce sucre et ce mica et ce silex ... contre l'hiver, contre l'eau noire qui lavera nos crânes ... contre la boue froide où nous nous enfoncerons ... dans la dégueulasse pluie des morts' (*Carabas*, 96). The wine of the Vaud is seen particularly as something associated with the land that he loves, and as a kind of antidote to the grip of Calvinism and of 'les justes' on that land. He even writes an ode to wine, addressing it as 'porteur de terre' and 'vin de la lumière noire' (*Comme*, 59). Food in general, but particularly heavy food and red meats, are another symbol of life, and such characters as Mange, Alexandre, and Jonas are eaters of hearty meals. In burlesque praise of the pig, Chessex celebrates that animal as symbolic of attachment to the earth and as a provider of succulent meat (*Portrait*, 103–11).

The young are one of the major representatives of freedom and life. *L'Ogre* in particular praises their rejection of the morality of 'les justes' and their enjoyment of life. Jean Calmet approves strongly when his pupils, carried by the tide of revolt that swept Europe in 1968, rebel against the authority of the principal and occupy the school. Just to look at them frees him from memories of his father, and the carnival atmosphere of their demonstrations fills him with joy. Mange, too, years after the events of May 1968, events in which he did not participate, looks back to them as an outburst of vitality that he regrets having missed. He hopes that Monna at least was able to know 'le joli mois de mai 68, l'amour, le gai bordel dans la rue' (*Ardent*, 56).

Mange associates Monna in his mind with May 1968 because she is for him the most perfect incarnation of all that opposes death, Calvinism, and 'les justes.' This may seem strange at first, since Calvinism represents woman as sin incarnate, as temptation and the cause of man's damnation. She is directly linked to death in the Calvinist mind because she is the cause of mankind's fall. Chessex reacts against this view of her by showing her as the opposite of all these things. She thus becomes, in his work, a privileged entity in which these opposites meet, the incarnation of both life and death, the paradoxical representative of all that Chessex fears and all that he seeks and celebrates.

The female characters in Chessex's fiction are often shown as a positive, life-enhancing force because they serve as consolation and protection. Because of Monna, Mange finds that 'la terre était habitable' (*Ardent*, 172). In the short story entitled 'Un Petit Vent frais' (*Où*, 99–107), the character called Paul, a rather simple-minded young man who is bullied by his employer, finds the miseries of life become bearable because a woman consoles and protects him. Jean Calmet is fortified by Thérèse, and he gives in to the forces of death only when she abandons him. The narrator of *Morgane Madrigal* celebrates Morgane as a kind of all-embracing presence. He frequently refers to her sex organs as a warm, protective passage to the shelter of her womb, as 'labyrinthe rose où me perdre' (37). Because of her 'odeur marine' (*Jonas*, 155), Anne-Marie reminds Jonas of the sea creature in whose womblike warmth he, too, would like to seek protection.

Women are also seen as opposing death in a more active way, as a kind of life-force that makes it retreat. When terror of death closes around him, Chessex depicts himself crying to the woman he loves: 'Et toi, mon ange, ma douce diablesse au fruste sexe, fais reculer la nuit!' (*Carabas*, 164). Mange turns to Monna when his daughter's suicide oppresses him, and Jean Calmet uses Thérèse to fight memories of his father. Benoît and Sarah find in their lovemaking a means of escaping the oppressive presence of Benjamin's approaching death, and Benjamin himself seems to find in their pleasure the strength to face his own unpleasant end. Woman's effect on the oppressive weight of death and despair is clearly seen in *Les Yeux jaunes* when Alexandre first meets Paula. In a mood of suicidal despair, he is contemplating the sad and hopeless animals in a travelling fair, seeing in them mirror images of man's own dismal lot. Then Paula appears, and he suddenly feels restored to life.

Woman becomes identified in many texts with life. She is the very centre of existence, 'femme au milieu de toute vie' (*Carabas*, 142). More than respite, protection, and consolation, she is life itself, the very forces that oppose death. The young girls whom Jean teaches, for example, are a source of strength to him when he is oppressed by morbid thoughts. Anne-Marie is depicted as a force that consistently intervenes in Jonas' morbid cogitations to remind him of the importance of life. 'C'est vers la vie qu'il faut tendre, que chacune de nos forces doit se mobiliser, se durcir, jaillir,' she encourages him (*Jonas*, 131). It is under her influence that, at least for a time, he turns again towards life. The daughters of Aschenbach represent attachment to life and pleasure in the midst of a sect given to remorse and the celebration of death. Monna is so linked in Mange's mind to life, that, when he is overcome by guilt at his daughter's suicide, Monna alone gives him the courage to live. Hence, finding himself one day in an old church, surrounded by reminders of death and of a cruel God, he turns from 'cette odeur de péché répandue sur toute chose,' and he embraces Monna, who is life, love, and 'l'ardent royaume' (*Ardent*, 185).

The joys of life naturally become associated with woman. During the first days of his liaison with Monna, Mange is 'comme drogué par l'extraordinaire joie qui coulait dans ses veines comme du feu' (*Ardent*, 80). He finds a new appetite for life under her influence, begins to enjoy such pleasures as eating and drinking good wine in her company. In the New Year celebration described in *Portrait des Vaudois*, it takes the arrival of one woman amid the group of sombre, timid, and subdued men for the prospect of pleasure and enjoyment suddenly to appear. She has only to raise her glass, declare 'Santé! Moi, c'est Martha!' and the whole atmosphere changes (220).

Woman is also represented as a principle of liberation, as freedom from the restraints of Calvinism and the society of Calvinists. Cécile in *La Tête ouverte* is seen by the narrator as a means of freeing himself from 'les justes,' represented by his landlady and her boarders. He parades Cécile in front of them, and when he wants to escape their stifling society, he seeks out 'Cécile qui rit' (39). In the same way, Mange flaunts Monna before the respectable society of Lausanne and uses her to liberate himself from that society.

The power to free from remorse is also one of the attributes of the women whom Chessex depicts. So, Jean Calmet lays to rest for some time the ghost of his father (i.e., of remorse) through his liaison with Thérèse. In her arms he discovers 'une volupté enfantine, protégée, où toute crainte avait cédé' (*L'Ogre*, 109). Jonas is able to respond to the devil by saying that Anne-Marie has cleansed him and that he no longer considers himself guilty. All the usual Calvinist obsessions are thrown off as he declares himself free of the old laws and restrictions, of what he calls: '*Mon* Deutéronome' (*Jonas*, 169; italics in original). He sees this as a return to an original purity, like that which mankind might have known before the Fall, a purity that he attributes to 'le corps et l'âme d'Anne-Marie, seuls capables de me rendre l'origine perdue et l'eau printanière du fond de la terre' (169). In similar fashion, Mange sees Monna as transporting him to a kind of Eden in which sin has no meaning, and he describes her as 'Sainte Monna. Non plus terra incognita, mais terre promise, terre atteinte' (*Ardent*, 185)

It is in *La Trinité* that the most sustained attempt is made to escape guilt and the fear of retribution. The dying Benjamin encourages Benoît to become his wife's lover because he wants all three of them to be free of these oppressive forces, and he hopes to find his own happiness in theirs. 'Nous savons que nous devons être parfaitement libres, vous et moi, pour faire ce que nous avons à faire. Et le faire sans aucun regret,' he informs Benoît (53). The latter, despite the qualms of his Calvinist conscience, does find moments of freedom with Sarah, and he comes to admire in her 'cette liberté presque transparente à force d'être naturellement ressentie et visible' (71). For him, the other two are the supreme example of freedom from all the Calvinist obsessions that still grip him at times. 'Pas plus de remords que de bagages,' he says of them (73).

For Chessex the writer, woman also plays the role of literary inspiration, of the life behind the text. She is freedom from the Calvinist sense of guilt that presents writing as a sin and an offence to God. It is Anne who provides Alexandre with the inspiration to break away from this view of writing and to create his books. Various women have also inspired many of Chessex's poems, and he describes the one whose presence may be felt behind many of the pages of *Carabas* as 'cette merveille, et par elle l'écriture, dressée comme un chant dru contre la mort' (149).

In Alexandre's case, woman is inspiration because, in the form of

Anne-Marie, she provides the stability that enables him to write. He refers to her as 'ma joie, ma sécurité' (*Les Yeux*, 37). But women are also stability in the life of the community, an element of order that stands against the death and disappearance of the group. It was the women who held out the longest against the imposition of Calvinism on the Vaud, who clung to the old religion and protected the priests. Now that they have accepted Calvinism, they hold just as firmly to that, and are 'le ciment des paroisses et la garde prétorienne des ministres' (*Portrait*, 87). It is women who preserve the traditions and resist the destruction of the old way of life. 'Elles sont plus rapides que nous, plus tenaces, plus acharnées,' writes Chessex. And, for those who want to save the best in that way of life, 'mieux vaut se tourner vers les mères et les grands-mères à psautiers et à robes noires, régentes des traditions et des nourritures' (90).

Woman is, in short, everything that opposes death, restraint, Calvinism, and 'les justes.' She is often idealized and treated with almost religious awe. Chessex is inspired in many pages by what he calls 'la révérence éblouie des femmes' (*Carabas*, 62). Morgane Wagner is even told by her lover and admirer: 'Je suis un mystique sans Dieu, moi, Madame, vous êtes ma lampe sainte et mon icône parce qu'en vous je révère tout le sacré possible en ce monde' (*Morgane*, 51). On one occasion, he refers to her as 'le Graal' (151).

Of Chessex's female characters, it is Morgane who best sums up the view of woman as a life-force who also inspires religious adoration. After she and the narrator make love for the first time, she says as she leaves the room, 'Mandala' (25). Subsequently, there are many similar references. Morgane's apartment, for example, is lined with photographs that the narrator interprets as mandalas; women's sexual organs are referred to as a 'rose' or 'mandala' (63, 77, 130); Morgane shows a marked interest in books and works of art that contain mandalas. In eastern religions, the mandala is a design used in worship, and it consists of a series of concentric geometric figures. The purpose of these figures is to draw the mind of the worshipper towards the centre from which they all emanate, and which represents the divinity from whom life originates. By associating Morgane with the mandala, the narrator of *Morgane Madrigal* suggests that she, too, is a centre from which life forces radiate, and that she is to be treated with the same religious wonder as one would show a deity.

But as well as inspiring religious awe, woman also provokes love, and in the bleak world of Calvinism, in a universe ruled by a jealous

God, love is seen as another force that affirms life. Chessex's characters, when they fall in love, find their existence suddenly bearable. When Burg realizes that he loves Geneviève, he declares, 'On pouvait habiter le monde' (*La Confession*, 102), and he ceases to see life as a vale of tears and an antechamber to another world. One might compare *La Confession du pasteur Burg* to Jaccottet's *Leçons*, which, according to Chessex, teach that 'l'amour lumineux fait que la vie peut reprendre' (*Saintes*, 144). More than making life bearable, love actively opposes death and serves as a way of exorcising it. Jean Calmet, Mange, Benoît, and Alexandre all make love as a response to the presence of death, and seek in love for various women a means of rendering the thought of death less fearful. Jonas speaks for all of them when, oppressed by his son's death, he tells Anne-Marie, 'En fait, tu es la seule à pouvoir me tirer de là' (*Jonas*, 154).

Like woman herself, love and sexuality are sometimes linked to religion. Jonas, forced by a prostitute to wash himself before having sex with her, compares this act to the purification that a priest must undertake before celebrating religious rites, and to Jesus' washing of his disciples' feet. The atmosphere surrounding the sex acts described in *Morgane Madrigal* is referred to as 'recueillement' (200), and Morgane herself is compared to 'le Souverain Bien de saint Thomas' (204). She even becomes the Mother of God in a blasphemous parody of the Hail Mary: 'Je vous salue Morgane, mer de sel, eau nocturne, le délire est avec vous, vous êtes magie entre toutes les femmes et le suc de vos entrailles est béni' (205). Benjamin claims that it is in the sex act that he has known his only 'intuitions vraiment aiguës' (*La Trinité*, 157) and that 'quand je respirais l'odeur des femmes, j'étais comme immergé dans l'absolu' (158).

Love is also an antidote to the power of death because it is a form of attachment to life. Although death had once seemed preferable to life, Burg decides 'pourquoi ne pas aimer cette vie, ses habitants, et même ses maux?' (*La Confession*, 90). He comes to see the body, not as a vile thing linked to sin and corruption, but as the temple of the Holy Ghost, as Saint Paul puts it. Love is seen as a lasting force that will endure even beyond death: 'Seul l'amour ne passera pas' (91). When thoughts of death come to him in the night, he has only to look at Geneviève, and they disappear. Under the influence of his love for her, he sees the celebration of Christmas in a new light, as evidence of God's love for man. 'J'avais vécu dans la nuit et la mort,' he says (108), but like Paul on the road to Damascus, he has become 'l'objet d'une conversion' (109). All this is accomplished by his love for Geneviève.

Burg finds the strength to reject the Calvinist vision of life and to discover that love *is* life. He begins to see the world around him with a new keenness. 'L'oeil est plus vite ému, plus attentif à la beauté des sites et des êtres,' he declares (89). One of his favourite games with Geneviève is to close his eyes and to let her describe what she sees around them. The lesson is obvious: through the eyes of love, he sees the world in a different light. Jonas, too, realizes that woman is life, because she gives life and because love of her attaches man to it. He lays his head on Anne-Marie's stomach and says, 'Là est la vie' (*Jonas*, 191).

Love replaces the Calvinist fear of punishment with respect for others. Hence, Burg's plan to punish H. by seducing his daughter is forgotten when he falls in love with her. His love for Geneviève is now extended to humanity, and he no longer despises his parishioners. It saves him from all his Calvinist obsessions, replacing them with peace and contentment. Even his view of Scripture changes, and he now sees in it, not the vengeful God of war and destruction, but a loving deity who cares for man. Gone now is the feeling of guilt associated with the flesh. Jean Calmet forgets his avenging father, Burg sees only a God of love, and Mange 'retrouvait l'innocence' (*Ardent*, 82).

The world created by this God of love, and particularly the natural world, also become reminders of life and of the forces that preserve life. Instead of seeing signs of death in nature, Chessex and his characters often see the presence of life. For example, the recurrence and rebirth of life are suggested by the seasons and by the arrival of spring. Even in the depth of winter, the poet looks forward to spring and the advent of new life: 'Du plus profond des fosses / Prisonnier de la terre fétide et des mousses / Je t'appelle printemps millénaire de la joie' (*Une Voix*, 63). There is always the promise of life and of the inevitable return of spring, suggested by the title of the poem 'Le Printemps gagne' (*Une Voix*, 69). When it does arrive, spring is celebrated as though it were a return to the very beginning of life: 'L'aubépine me parle / Sur la colline de miel / Ce matin la mort elle-même / Cède au vent de mai' (*Elégie*, 36).

Easter in particular is seen as a celebration of rebirth, not just because it comes at spring, but because of its religious connotations of resurrection. In the chapter of *Portrait des Vaudois* entitled 'Le Printemps du fond de la terre,' Chessex depicts an Easter Sunday in the Vaud, when 'du fond de la terre jaillit le printemps avec le vin de la communion, les feuilles, le pain, les tiges et les bulles de bonheur dans le cou des merles' (9). He shows us the faithful arriving at church to celebrate Christ's resurrection, the signs of new life all around them in nature, the sense that winter has now gone. He concludes: 'Vaincus l'hiver et l'affreuse mort où le corps et le coeur s'étaient engourdis comme des serpents sous la pierre froide' (13).

Day, in contrast to night, is another such symbol of life and hope in nature. The whole of the volume *Le Jour proche* raises the hope of approaching day that will dispel night and the presence of death. In the poem 'Eveil,' for example, the poet, in the midst of night, says, 'Déjà j'explore le jour docile et blanc' (13). The feeling that life is reborn as day approaches is conveyed in the lines 'La montée de l'aube / Ce jour de juin / M'a comblé' (*Le Calviniste*, 47), and the poet's description of the cock crowing from behind the barn as the sun rises carries the same feeling of relief that day has come.

Certain poems suggest that the individual would do well to abandon himself to the rhythm of birth, death, and rebirth in nature represented by the passing seasons and the passage from day to night and back to day. The poet argues that man should exist as part of nature, undergoing the cycles of death and rebirth like all other living organisms. 'Ainsi devrions-nous peut-être passer nos journées / Pareils aux branches, aux fruits dans les haies / (Peut-être serions-nous moins surpris par la mort / A vivre près des arbres doux et forts ...)' suggests one poem (*Une Voix*, 55). Another one expresses the desire to live as naturally a part of the world as the grass of the fields. If he could live this way, says the poet: 'J'échappe à la mort, je suis l'herbe / L'herbe, la verdeur devant l'hiver ... / Je suis l'herbe acharnée à durer' (*Elégie*, 44).

The desire to abandon oneself to the cycles of death and rebirth that are part of nature is symbolized by the sea monster that is often evoked in *Jonas*. The biblical monster represents death when it swallows Jonah, but as the quotation from the Book of Jonah set at the beginning of the novel reminds us, the monster also regurgitated Jonah. It conveys, therefore, the hope of resurrection and escape from death. In many myths, a hero is swallowed by a monster or descends to Hell, and appears again. The story of Jonah is just one of these, and Jonas explicitly points this out by referring to Uve Steffan's interpretation of the story as a parable of life after death. It should also be noted that in the Bible we are told that it was a 'fish' that swallowed Jonah (Jonah 1: 17). Jonas points out that the early Christian symbol for Christ was a fish. By linking the sea monster to Christ, he emphasizes further its role as an image of resurrection. Jonas' interest in these symbolic allusions to rebirth indicates that he, too, looks for life in death, the reappearance of life as part of an alternating and natural pattern.

These allusions to the presence of life in death are less common, however, than direct celebration of nature as a source of life. As well as being the dwelling place of the devil, and associated with death, nature is often portrayed as a source of the life forces. It is, consequently, a major element of much that Chessex has written, almost a character in his fiction.

Most of Chessex's texts express a deep love of nature, and particularly of the natural beauty of the Vaud. Ones that deal directly with the Vaud and its people, like *Portrait des Vaudois*, *Carabas*, and *Bréviaire*, contain many descriptions of the beauty of the Vaudois countryside. The poems often celebrate nature and the poet's joy in it. The fiction, too, contains descriptions of nature, for characters such as Jean Calmet, Alexandre Dumur, Jonas, and Mange enjoy walking in the countryside and savouring its calm. One is often reminded, when reading these passages, of Chessex's famous predecessor and poet of nature, Jean-Jacques Rousseau. Comments such as 'je crois profondément à la nature' tend to reinforce such comparisons in the reader's mind.[6]

Chessex displays a direct, earthy appreciation of nature. He evokes the smells, the sounds, and the 'motte, fumier ... liqueur éclairante' that he finds in it (*Portrait*, 20). He praises the countryman's down-to-earth love of the land, the attitude that says 'la terre est simple. Lourde, légère, grasse, caillouteuse' (*Portrait*, 22). Yet, like Rousseau, he also shows the breathtaking beauty of his land. He describes the hot sun on the stony ground and ruined buildings, the insects in the grass, and the sound of a snake slithering under a stone (*Bréviaire*, 38–9); fields of wheat, with the dark forest in the background and a deep blue sky above (*Bréviaire*, 44–5); herbs and grasses, the smell of wild flowers and hay (*Feux*, 21–3); streams of sparkling water (*Feux*, 27–30); birds of all sizes and species nesting in hedges, trees, and roofs (*Feux*, 1–3).

'Au centre du livre, personnage principal dont les pouvoirs extraordinaires fascinent ... voici la nature,' writes Chessex, commenting on Pierre Gascar's *Le Meilleur de la vie*.[7] He could as easily be commenting on any of his own books, and one critic sums up this side of Chessex's writing by saying, 'Chessex est l'ami des forêts, des lacs, des jeunes filles et des petits animaux.'[8] Chessex himself would consider this love of nature as typical of the Vaudois and of the French-Swiss, for he claims that 'l'écrivain romand est marié à son paysage.'[9]

The connection between Chessex and his characters on one hand, and nature on the other, is so close that it is as though nature speaks to them. In the case of Jean Calmet, it quite literally does that. On his way home one evening, he encounters a hedgehog, and he has the sudden feeling that here is a messenger who has something of significance to say. He is sure that the animal is 'le symbole d'une liberté gaie et sauvage, la preuve qu'aucune domination ne soumet jamais les grandes forces telluriques qui sourdent, qui jaillissent' (*L'Ogre*, 41). Fortified by this message, he overcomes memories of his father. Later, at another critical moment in his life, he meets a cat that actually does speak to him. It tells him to forget his gloom, to put his father's image from his mind, to enjoy life and the spirit of Dionysus.

Jean's dialogue with the cat is a representation on a fantastic level of the sense of communion that he feels with nature. He feels it particularly strongly as he lies in the grass on a sunny day, listening to the sound of a nearby river. At that moment 'Jean Calmet se savait frère de cette eau: elle coulait en lui, elle le traversait, elle l'emportait à travers la plaine' (78). What characters like Jean sense in their moments of pantheistic communion is a life-force within nature, something that Robert Kanters describes as 'la vie des choses, ce grain de la pierre ou de la chair qui nous assure d'une palpitation cachée.'[10]

One may discern in Chessex's texts what he points to in René Char's: 'La ... nature effervescente toute soulevée par les forces qui l'habitent.'[11] He says elsewhere that nature contains a life-force that the sensitive observer may often feel and see around him or her. 'Toute la nature est portée par un courant de passion: de l'arbre au cerf, de la racine au sanglier se tendent violemment les vigueurs naïves,' he writes (*Reste*, 53). Because he loves the countryside and is an attentive observer of it, he has, since his childhood years, been aware of these forces: 'Ainsi j'apprenais à considérer l'arbre, le buisson, la colline comme des êtres vivants, habités de présences puissantes, riches de multiples dangers, magies et significations' (*Reste*,

62). It is these forces that speak to Jean Calmet through the cat and the hedgehog. They manifest themselves to Alexandre Dumur through the foxes with whom he has an instinctive sympathy. Chessex, too, feels a kind of harmony with such animals, and he has said that 'depuis toujours il m'a semblé que la part sauvage de ma nature était incarnée dans l'animal' (Garcin, 133). He goes on to point out that man, too, is an animal, but that he has lost the ability to sense and to express the life in nature as animals do. We must try, he argues elsewhere, to rediscover in the animal 'sa force panique, sa beauté immémoriale, sa fraîcheur de force parfaitement pure' (*Portrait*, 243).

In ancient religions, the life-forces were often personified by various nature gods, and Chessex seems at times to look back to these beliefs. Even Jean Burg, the strict Calvinist, suggests something of the kind when, walking in the forest, he feels the stirring of life all around him, and he comments, 'Je comprends les hommes qui ont divinisé la forêt. Un dieu veille dans cette ombre. Sa présence est là, palpable, certaine' (*La Confession*, 68–9). One name that was given to the god of nature was Dionysus, and it is precisely to this god that Chessex alludes when he describes Jean Calmet as being filled with the spirit of Dionysus. 'L'Esprit de Dionysos' is the title of that section of *L'Ogre* in which Jean is shown turning away from memories of his father and seeking life. It is also at this time that he meets Thérèse, who incarnates freedom for him, and who brings the spirit of Dionysus into his life. Another name given to the god was Pan, and Chessex describes himself, in a moment of intense joy in nature that seems almost to be a kind of possession, as being 'une bête dans les pattes de Pan' (*Carabas*, 37). Traditionally, when humans were possessed by these spirits, they entered into a sort of madness or dionysiac frenzy. It is, in fact, just such a frenzy that takes hold of Jean Calmet when he is sitting beside Thérèse in a café. He starts to shout that he is pure, that he is not evil, and he falls across the table 'comme frappé par la foudre sacrée' (*L'Ogre*, 105).

This attitude to nature is tantamount to a rejection of the Calvinist view of it as full of sin and a reminder of death. It presents life rather than death in nature, joy rather than guilt. It shows the life-forces as pure, beyond any idea of sin, and it sees love of nature as a glimpse of Paradise here on earth. Nature becomes something akin to Novalis' conception of it as being 'le Paradis ... épars dans la nature autour de nous' (*Saintes*, 70).

Nature is also set up in opposition to Calvinism because it is a principle of freedom. It has been said that 'seule la nature, lorsque Jean Calmet et Raymond Mange s'y abandonnent, lorsqu'Alexandre Dumur s'y plonge, semble apporter un élément libérateur.'[12] These characters escape memories of their childhood, which was steeped in Calvinist restraint, by losing themselves in the contemplation of nature and in experiencing the life-forces in it. In *La Tête ouverte*, liberty is represented by the sun that the narrator looks at through the windows of the train bearing him away from Madame Lequatre's pension. It is also symbolized by the sea that he looks at when feeling particularly restricted. The sea, which has frequently been visualized in literature as standing for freedom, and which provoked Baudelaire's 'Homme libre, toujours tu chériras la mer,' suggests boundless liberty to the young man oppressed by provincial small-mindedness. Animals, too, can be seen as representatives of freedom, for they live outside the civilized restraints that man imposes on himself, outside all ideas of sin and evil. Foxes, cats, birds, and the hedgehog all play this role. It is the cat, however, in the children's story *Marie et le chat sauvage* that conveys this belief in its simplest and most charming form. In this tale, a young girl becomes the friend of a wild cat, but the cat cannot give up its independence and be tamed by her. Because she loves the cat, Marie accepts that it must live wild, and she restores it to freedom. The fox plays a similar role, for it refuses man's restraints and is consequently a persecuted victim. It is 'détesté, piégé, traqué' (*Reste*, 75), but persists in living free, and becomes in Chessex's eyes a heroic figure, 'l'animal traqué qui doit apprendre, au milieu de nos polices, à conserver la part sauvage' (Garcin, 133).

Nature and animals in nature are images of freedom from guilt, of a primordial innocence. They exist apart from the categories of good and evil that man invents and that are codified by religions like Calvinism. Chessex writes of experiencing nature as a state of innocence that existed at the beginning of time, before man introduced religions and codes of conduct. He looks at the natural world, and he sees 'perfection céleste dans le vert et la solitude / C'était l'innocence, c'était l'origine' (*Elégie*, 69). It is a cat that tells Jean Calmet to forget his father, to abandon remorse. 'Regarde-moi,' it says. 'Est-ce que je me fais du souci? Est-ce que je macère dans le remords ou la tristesse?' (*L'Ogre*, 117).

Much of Chessex's work is built around this celebration of nature, which, together with woman, becomes the force that inspires in him the will to live and to create. As one might expect, the two forces are often linked, and Chessex's work, like Voisard's, 'assemble en un même corps diffus l'amour de la femme et l'amour de la terre' (*Saintes*, 204). When the poet wishes to express his love of a woman, he frequently chooses to compare her to his other love, nature. She becomes a beautiful day, a tree, a torrent, a bird's song, the forest, and countless other aspects of the natural world (*Chant*, 19). The narrator of *Morgane Madrigal* calls Yolda, one of the women in the novel, 'lupa mater, renarde des neiges, fouine haletante ... souple fennec' (202).

Women are shown as having a deep affinity with nature, as though they are incarnations of it. Jean Calmet calls Thérèse 'la fille au chat' because of her feline associations in his mind. When he looks at her, his emotions are described in terms of the natural world. He feels 'des cascades jaillir au fond de lui, des précipices ... où tombaient des pierres millénaires ... Le vent montagnard ... dans les pins' (*L'Ogre*, 93). Her very name, Dubois, suggests a relationship to nature. Morgane appears to the narrator in a dream in which he associates her with a waterfall and a clearing in the woods. Even Jean Burg sees Geneviève as part of the natural world, for when he thinks of her, it is usually against the background of the countryside where he loves to go walking with her. He sees in her a 'parenté de la lumière qui poudroyait sur les prairies' (*La Confession*, 64). Alexandre Dumur links Anne to nature, and, when he watches her walk towards him 'avec elle s'avançait tout un paysage de pentes herbeuses, de lacs immobiles sous les sapins ... de sources fourmillant dans l'herbe' (*Les Yeux*, 118).

As the source of life, woman is associated, as one might expect, with Mother Nature. When he evokes his own mother, Chessex thinks of 'une prairie, des pâquerettes, et le vent léger de mars' (*Portrait*, 255). Like nature, his mother was an element of strength, a barrier against suffering and pain. He writes with deep emotion of 'cette vertu de résistance, de concentration, de foncée terrienne et gaie' that was part of her (255). She too, like nature, provided joy in his life, and he still links her in his mind with the wind, the snow, and the sun that he remembers from childhood.

Woman may also be seen as the very incarnation of the life-forces in nature, of the mysterious and frightening power hidden in the world. One reason why she is referred to as a witch is that witches traditionally communicate with and are channels for these forces. The old woman in 'Le Mal retourne au mal,' who lives alone in the forest, communing with nature and unlocking its powers in the herbal remedies that she concocts, is one such force. She is explicitly linked to witches when she is told, 'Vous auriez été brûlée pour moins que ça, il n'y a pas si longtemps' (Où, 214). As well as linking Thérèse to Dionysus, Jean Calmet also calls her Circe and Morgane – the names of famous sorceresses of the past (103) – and he compares her to the fairies and witches of folklore when he refers to her as 'l'esprit des fées' (196). At one point, he even calls her one of the 'génies des montagnes et de l'eau' (95). In *Morgane Madrigal*, Morgane, too, bears the name of a witch, is frequently compared to Medusa, and is associated in the narrator's mind with 'scènes et pratiques de sorcellerie' (127). Virginia Aschenbach readily admits that she may be 'une sorcière oubliée là, dans ce hameau' (*Judas*, 72).

Woman is seen, then, almost as an integral part of nature. And women and nature are, in their turn, linked to the erotic, which is also represented as a manifestation of the life-force. These three elements of the forces come together in the many stories in which characters make love in the countryside. Mange and Monna, Jonas and Anne-Marie, the characters in 'La Clairière' (Où, 201–4) make love in surroundings that are themselves charged with erotic feeling. A similar phenomenon is observable in 'Secrets de la colline' (*Le Séjour*, 111–14), in which a man hides himself to spy daily on a young woman who comes to sunbathe naked on a secluded hillside. For many such characters, nature itself seems spontaneously to suggest sexual images and to contain erotic allusions. Hence, Gilles Roux sees some pinks that suggest 'des orifices sacrés' and notices 'la bave des escargots' and 'le poil des pavots de rocaille' (*Le Séjour*, 116). Describing wild poppies in *Bréviaire*, Chessex refers to 'indécente fleur qui ravives ma faim de bouches, de plis, de trous en sang' (45). In 'Matin de Don Juan,' he sees in nature 'souvenir des seins hantés / Et du sexe de petit-lait des jeunes filles' (*Le Calviniste*, 53). The narrator of *Morgane Madrigal*, looking at an alpine lake and the mountains around it, sees 'le col doucement nu, les mamelons dressés ... la chute des reins ... la cascade entre les deux valves neigeuses' (59).

Only Pieyre de Mandiargues among contemporary writers in French so consistently links nature and sexual desire. Chessex – again like Mandiargues – sees nature as bursting with life-forces that are associated with the erotic impulses in man, and he has written: 'Justement, l'air n'est jamais si vif, le bois si dru, les truites du ruisseau si rapides et si chargées de magie panique, les parois de terre rose si spirituelles et si terriblement pareilles à de la chair que lorsqu'Eros les aiguise' (*Carabas*, 158). So closely are women and the erotic linked to the life-forces in nature that he claims, in the same text, that these forces are hardly apparent unless there is a woman to serve as an intermediary between him and them.

Women, sex, nature all combine to express Chessex's attachment to life and his desire to live free of the restraints of Calvinism. Life is exalted in the face of death, freedom in the teeth of constraint. He refuses in many passages the sense of guilt that Calvinism would impose on his appreciation of life, and he affirms the importance of the life-forces in their various forms. His texts are not a simple expression of Calvinist fears and of the importance of death. They also attempt to erect barriers to such fears.

8

The Flight from Calvinism

Chessex's texts are the chronicle of an attempt to escape a certain experience of Calvinism. They depict characters who spend most of their lives fighting against its influence, and they frequently affirm all the values that are the direct opposite of those preached by this religion: freedom, love, sexual enjoyment, pleasure, and, above all, love of life. They represent, at times when these anti-Calvinist values triumph, a defeat of Calvinism and the fear of death that it inspires. However, this triumph is only temporary, and the shadow of Calvinism always falls over these texts at some time.

The difficulty of escaping the hold of Calvinism is due largely to the fact that this religion is an integral part of a land that Chessex loves. He reacts against some aspects of the Vaud, its society, and its religion, but he is a product of that region. His origins in the Vaud are evident in almost every work that he has written, and François Nourissier's description of *Carabas* fits any of Chessex's texts: 'Livre d'un Suisse, et qui ne pouvait être conçu, écrit, crié nulle part ailleurs qu'aux rivages lémaniques.'[1] The setting of most of Chessex's fiction is Switzerland, and particularly the Vaud.[2] His characters are mainly from the Vaud, while his essays depict the people and the way of life of that region. He has described himself as 'le Vaudois du lac et du Synode' and as having within himself 'la folie calviniste et les vertiges de la transgression' that are typical of Vaudois (*Carabas*, 223). He has passed these traits on to many of the characters in his fiction, and he himself says, 'Je fais le Portrait des Vaudois' (*Portrait*, 253) – a comment that applies not just to the book of that title.

He realizes that much of his inspiration comes from the Vaud, its people, its history, and its religion. He has looked elsewhere, but he has always had to come back to his roots here in order to find what he wants: 'Chaque fois pourtant j'ai retrouvé terre, j'ai repris pied terriennement, et Vaudois, sans plus douter, j'ai été forcé de l'être – de le devenir! – par la vigueur de l'évidence' (*Portrait*, 254). He has now reached the point, he explains, where, although he loves Paris and willingly travels to France, he must always return to the Vaud because he cannot live and write without it. 'J'ai besoin de ce pays comme Baudelaire avait besoin de Paris. Je déteste en sortir parce que je perds ma foule et mes paysages,' he writes (*Carabas*, 116).

The Vaud is the source of Chessex's being, of his inspiration, and of his texts. But it is not the only such source. The other major one is his father, and it is instructive to compare his attitude towards his father to his love of the Vaud and to his attempts to get away from certain things associated with the Vaud. One may easily discern in Chessex's attitude to his land the same apparently contradictory feelings that he and such characters as Jean Calmet show towards their father. Both father and country are stifling, restrictive forces that must be rejected in order to reaffirm freedom and identity; yet both are essential formative influences that are loved and respected. Jean Calmet and Chessex himself feel relief at the death of their fathers. We have noticed this sense of relief on the part of Jean; Chessex, too, admits to having felt 'ce sentiment scandaleux de liberté' when his father died (*Portrait*, 256). But Chessex and Jean loved their fathers, and Chessex in particular felt a deep attachment to a man whom he also admired.

Chessex is well aware of the similarity between his attitude to his father and his feeling for the Vaud. His father was strongly attached to this part of Switzerland, and he was mainly responsible for revealing the natural beauty of the region to his son. He also fostered in his son an abiding interest in the people of the area. Consequently, there was an early link formed in Chessex's mind between his father and the Vaud. 'Mon père est devenu le pays,' he says (*Portrait*, 254). Both these forces helped form him, so, when his father died, it was as though he had lost one of the sources of his being. Therefore, he looked to his roots in the region to find again and to reinforce the remaining source. Speaking of his father's death, he says, 'J'ai déjà dit qu'elle m'avait lié au pays, que le pays m'avait saisi depuis cette mort, que je m'étais reconnu un lieu, une origine depuis cette horreur décisive'.[3] A tragedy such as this in writers' lives may often turn their attention to the country or the region associated in their minds with that event. He writes: 'Enfants, adolescents, leur vie a connu un drame (une mort, une douleur, ou l'attente, l'impatience passionnée et immobile) qui pour toujours leur apparaîtra lié à *leur* pays.'[4]

Chessex's inability fully to escape the influence of Calvinism is very easily understood if one takes into account this sense of belonging to a particular region and of being linked to it forever by memories of his father. The Vaudois characters in his fiction experience the same difficulty, and for the same reasons. Like Chessex, they are attached to a land by their love of it, and to the religion of that land by their upbringing.

The example of Jonas is the most instructive. He leaves his Calvinist area of Switzerland for the more liberal atmosphere of Catholic Fribourg. This is a flight from Calvinism and the region that formed him and an attempt to find again a time when, in his youth, he lived freely in this city and loved Anne-Marie. His flight is an effort to rediscover freedom, love, and life. When he meets Anne-Marie again and resumes his liaison with her, it seems that he has succeeded. However, the death of the son whom he never knew often comes between them, and he is never able to forget the presence of death. He also finds that he cannot really escape his Calvinist upbringing. He feels like Jonah regurgitated by the monster, finding himself again unprotected by the values and the sense of freedom he had tried to rediscover, victim again of the harsh beliefs of Calvinism. Even his love for Anne-Marie is not unwavering, for, having claimed that he loves her, he begins to doubt. He goes as far as to wonder if he is capable of love. Calvinism, with its terrible doctrine of punishment by a vengeful God, has rendered him unable to love freely. 'Calvin avait raison,' he is forced to admit (*Jonas*, 235).

Although he seems, towards the end of the novel, to reaffirm his love of Anne-Marie, this hesitation is indicative of the continuing influence of a religion he never really abandons. He is obliged to admit to himself that he is 'ce Poisson qui va de la vérité à l'erreur sans se décider' (236). He wavers between love and denial of it, between belief in the goodness of God and His grace, and inability to believe. The God of Calvin never fully relinquishes His grasp on him, and the last sentences of the novel are a despairing admission that this dark, vengeful God will always have some hold on him: 'Malgré mon amour de Dieu, malgré le Fils, malgré notre fils, Anne-Marie, la grâce est morte et j'ai l'âme desséchée. Et je sais aussi de *source* sûre: il n'y aura pas de Résurrection' (236; italics in original).

Jean Calmet, Maître Mange, and Alexandre Dumur are likewise pursued by the God of Calvinism, and they are never able to release themselves completely from the influences and memories of childhood. Jean Calmet's father, an incarnation of all these influences, pursues him to the end of his life, and finally triumphs when Jean commits suicide with the very razor that he associates with his father. Both Mange and Alexandre are visited by memories of their Calvinist upbringing and by the presence of death at critical moments in their lives, and they, too, may be seen as victims of that upbringing.

Escape from Calvinism in its social manifestation is also impossible, for 'les justes' always seem to win. Dr Calmet represents society as much as he represents an image of God, and Jean's death may be seen as the triumph of 'les justes' over him. Maître Mange is hounded and condemned by a society that refuses to accept his wish to live freely his love for Monna. Jean Burg discovers a new face of God, a loving image, but he, too, falls victim to the old God of Calvinism when Geneviève is taken from him, and 'les justes,' in the form of his parishioners and Geneviève's father, easily defeat him. Alexandre Dumur, too, becomes an outcast, misunderstood by the respectable bourgeois who cannot tolerate his marginal way of life, and who are partly responsible for driving him to suicide.

Even woman, although she is a shining image in Chessex's work, a principle of life and love, is finally powerless against the weight of a Calvinist past. Anne-Marie is unable to make Jonas abandon his past life and to put an end to his hesitations. Monna cannot protect Mange against a society that is bent on his destruction. Thérèse cannot overcome the pursuing presence of Jean's father. At the most, these women provide such characters with moments of joy, with protection that is temporary, and with an incentive to live that does not last. An old man represented in one of Chessex's poems, after a lifetime of seeking freedom through women, has to admit that the God of Calvin has finally won: 'Maintenant je suis vieux et je suis aveugle, Dieu vainqueuer / Je n'ai plus ma force d'arbre et mes mains tremblent / Que me reste-t-il de tes filles innombrables? / Que me reste-t-il de leur rire sous mes doigts morts?' (*Le Calviniste*, 114).

The ultimate victory of Calvinism, however, lies in the fact that the attempt to live freely and fully may itself be seen as a product of this religion. It is a reaction *against* a particular influence and therefore dependent upon it. Rather than spontaneous movements of joy and affirmation of life, they are the product of a religion that denies such things. They are, as it were, the negative image of something that must always be present in order to produce the image. This is particularly evident in Chessex's praise of excess and excessive appetite for enjoyment. He shows Calvinism as a religion of excess, one that preaches an extreme kind of purity and that threatens the direst punishment for sinners. It is surely the extreme nature of this religion that provokes an equally extreme reaction and praise of a different kind of excess.

But the most unfortunate result of the reaction against Calvinism is in the attitude to women that many texts betray. To represent woman as a temptress, an excuse for sin, the cause of man's death and damnation, has long been part of a type of Christianity. This traducing of women denigrates them as human beings and relegates them to the rank of unregenerate instruments of the devil. It is a view that Chessex struggles to reject, yet it clearly maintains a hold over his imagination. Worse still, when he reacts against it, he constructs a view of women that is, in its way, just as unfair and unflattering. By negating the old Calvinist view of women with one that is its exact opposite, he produces a new vision that is also unworthy of them. To treat women as idealized beings surrounded by an aura of religiosity is no more worthy of them than to see them as Satan's handmaidens. To represent them as conduits for the forces of life rather than as instruments of the devil is still to see them as instruments and to deny them a will and an individuality of their own. As inspirers of the writer (always a male writer, in Chessex's work), they are likewise depicted primarily as a medium for other forces and as subordinates whose main function is to support and to nurture the writer.

The very attempt to produce a picture of 'woman' is itself an unfortunate result of a Calvinist attitude. Calvinism talks of 'woman' as a class, imposing on a group of individuals an identity that is invariable for all of them. Chessex's attempt to respond to this produces another view of individuals as a class. Although he may have a conception of them as a group that he considers more flattering than the Calvinist one, this is still an abstract and general view that takes no account of women as individuals. And it is interesting to note that he projects in his text no view of the male sex as a class.

The best that one can say of Chessex's view of women is that, in some of his texts, the women characters still manage to project a certain individuality. Monna is a spirited, living character who has the courage to assume her unsavoury past. Thérèse is also a free spirit who refuses to be tied to Jean Calmet and who supports the students' revolt of 1968. Anne-Marie has lived independently and brought up Jonas' child on her own. Anne leaves Alexandre when she can stand his behaviour no longer. These are acts of independent women that often require courage, but they are usually reported fairly briefly, and their implications are not developed. The text rarely points out explicitly how remarkable some of these women must be. The problem is that these female characters are seen through the eyes of male characters and narrators, who tend to treat them as elements in their struggle to escape Calvinism. The women may assert themselves as free individuals in their acts and in their lives, but all this is seen by men who recuperate such acts for their own needs. And, of course, many of those needs are sexual. While the women do not become just sex objects, they are often remarkably willing to 'comfort' the male characters in their hours of need.

The one apparent exception to the general rule is Sarah, who makes no bones about using men for her own needs. She explains to Benoît, lest he misunderstand the situation, that she always takes the lead in her relationships with men: 'C'est moi qui commande et qui varie. A la première minute, je leur fais comprendre qu'ils *servent*' (*La Trinité*, 98; italics in original). But even Sarah is seen through the eyes of Benoît, and it is mainly his needs and emotions that are presented. One might also argue that, even when she uses men like Benoît, she is being manipulated by her husband and is serving his needs as much as her own.

Nor does Chessex's praise of women, or his insistence that they are incarnations of life and the life-forces, dispel the fear of death in many cases. In fact, this fear is at best driven into the background. Death usually triumphs and comes to the fore again at the end of his fictional pieces: Jean Calmet, Alexandre Dumur, Raphaël Turner all die. What is more, they die at their own hands, indicating that death has won in their minds and in their lives, and that they can no longer fight against its influence. In the course of his novels, other characters also die: the pastor's wife in *Les Yeux jaunes*, Jean Calmet's pupil and his father, Jonas' son, Mange's daughter, Benjamin, and Geneviève. This list does not even include the many deaths in his short fiction.

As for the attempt to see and appreciate life in nature, it too frequently fails. Love of nature provides only temporary respite from the fear of death, which inevitably returns. Life and rebirth may be presented as part of nature and the recurring seasons, but so is death. For the individual who must die, it is of little consolation to know that life goes on in nature after his or her death. Often, Chessex finds it impossible to imagine living as part of nature, accepting its cycles and seeing death as part of them. He writes, 'Je voudrais vivre comme un arbre / Croître de tout mon bois vers la lumière / ... / Mais je perds ma réalité. Chaque jour m'approche / Du dernier seuil' (*Une Voix*, 30).

Chessex's texts oscillate between life and death, Calvinism and escape from it, freedom and restraint, remorse and innocence. He affirms life, but death remains an ever-present reality; he rejects Calvinism but never fully escapes it. In his work each of these elements exists as the mirror image of its opposite; each contains the other. Jonas, with his hesitations between two realities, his inability to commit himself finally to one of them, his tormented soul divided against itself, is the best representative of this aspect of Chessex's work. In Jonas' case, as in that of Chessex and many of his characters, the origin of these conflicting impulses, the very measure of all his experience of life, the impetus that sets all his acts in motion, is the Calvinism that lies at the source of his being.

9
Division and Unity

Chessex's texts are far from being straightforward statements of unequivocal attitudes. They are, in fact, full of complex and apparently contradictory beliefs. His is a work that is based on paradox and on what may often seem to be irreconcilable opposites. It has been said that 'Chessex's work is ... marked by contradictions,' and that various conflicting beliefs 'dialoguent, s'alternent, se disputent l'âme qui en est leur centre.'[1] These are clearly texts that strike the reader as divided against themselves, and there is no point in looking for clear-cut and unambiguous stances in them.

This does not mean, however, that they are a mass of many conflicting contradictions or that they should be dismissed as chaotic. A closer look at them reveals that the attitudes expressed fall into pairs of opposites. As the foregoing analysis has attempted to show, every belief put forward is accompanied by its opposite; every hope by its concomitant fear. Rather than containing many contradictions, therefore, the texts are built around two poles, two main lines of thought, just like Calvinism itself, which sees the world as divided between good and evil, God and the devil. Despite all Chessex's attempts to escape the influence of Calvinism, its mark remains in the very structure of nearly everything that he writes. This division is best summed up in the quotation from Hemingway used as an epigraph to *Où vont mourir les oiseaux*: 'Nous avons servi un maître la nuit, et un autre le jour.'

The division into pairs of opposites is perceptible in many aspects of Chessex's writing. His texts are marked, for example, by an ever-present fear of death, accompanied by a longing to live fully. In the words of one critic: 'D'un côté les plaisirs des sens et l'attrait de la chair, inassouvis; de l'autre, la conscience du mal et la hantise de la mort.'[2] Another critic says, 'La violence du goût de vivre exacerbe, chez Chessex, la terreur de la mort.'[3] His texts show a never-ending will to escape the cruel God of Calvinism and a longing for the protection afforded by belief in Him. They reveal the attraction of that God, but also the traps and snares of the flesh set by the devil. Chessex has admitted this particular division in his work between God and the devil, the spirit and the flesh, for he has said that writing is for him 'faire l'ange et c'est faire la bête, puisque boue et rosée céleste sont mêlées dans le même amour' (Jotterand, 38). Maître Mange finds in his love for Monna the same division between 'solitude et désir, horreur et attente, nuit et lumière, ravine et éblouissement' (*Ardent*, 162).

Even the conception of God found in these texts is not unmixed. Beside the vengeful God of Calvinism stands the more loving and understanding one that Pastor Burg glimpses. Sometimes Catholicism seems to offer a more appealing image of God and of religion, and the attraction of the Catholic faith struggles in Jonas Carex's soul against his Calvinist heritage. Although the possibility of Catholicism as a more acceptable religion is never fully explored in his texts, it is clear that Chessex has been attracted by it. He writes in *Carabas* of a period spent in Fribourg, studying (like Jonas) in a Catholic institution. 'A Fribourg,' he writes, 'on pardonnait et on chantait, on célébrait la Gloire, on aimait tendrement et doucement. Chez moi, on s'accablait de remords, on mentait, on se tordait de désir derrière sa façade, on dénonçait, on se suicidait' (*Carabas*, 197). And yet he returned to the Vaud with its Calvinism because its influence over his mind remained so strong, and because it was the source of his inspiration.

A measure of the importance of the division within Chessex's work is his instinctive realization of the same characteristics in the writings of others. Cingria and Chappaz, for example, both present a view of life that is, in Chessex's opinion, split between two poles. He talks of Cingria as a man who deliberately cultivated paradox, and who was divided between his Swiss heritage and his appreciation of the Catholic Middle Ages, between his love of solitude and his need of others (*Cingria*, 12, 21). He looks on Chappaz as a writer whose literary production is split between his Swiss background and his cosmopolitanism, and he appears 'partagé entre la rage et la tristesse, entre le besoin de célébrer et le besoin de massacrer, entre la louange et la protestation puissante' (*Saintes*, 209).

Chessex is equally aware of his own divided self. He readily admits that he is both a secretive and an open person, that he keeps his inner divisions hidden, yet often reveals them, that he loves solitude, but flees it (Garcin, 171-2). He has a spiritual and mystic vision, while also being attached to this world, and he quotes with approval Galland's description of him: 'Chessex est un mystique qui aime le miel et le lard' (Jotterand, 37). Looking back on his own hesitations, on his nostalgia for an upright life, on his many 'sins' of excess, and on his division against himself, Chessex admits to a feeling of disorder and of having failed in some way. He writes: 'J'avais besoin d'être fidèle et je trompais. J'avais besoin de sûreté et je multipliais les démissions' (*Carabas*, 33). His attitude to the world in which he lives, and to his activity as a writer, is equally divided, and he describes his life as 'ecrire dans un monde effrayant que j'aime violemment et que je déteste violemment' (Jotterand, 38).

Not surprisingly, many of the characters that he has created share these dichotomies. They fear death, yet are attracted to it, and they often commit suicide; they adore women but are unable to rid themselves of the idea that women are the devil's instruments; they see both life and death in nature; they try to escape from Calvinism, yet they know it attracts them. Because they are divided, they are able to see the division within others. Jean Calmet realizes that his colleague Verret 'demeurait ce curieux mélange d'orgueil et d'humiliation' (*L'Ogre*, 80); Mange sees that Inspector Renard is a dangerous and relentless enemy, yet, in his way, a pleasant companion; Benoît discovers in Sarah a free spirit who loves life, but who is attached to her husband and who commits suicide after his death.

The protagonist who sums up all these characters best in their hesitations and divisions is Jonas Carex. Jonas feels the force of both Catholicism and Calvinism, of his austere background and of 'la magie profonde et ramifiée de Fribourg' (*Jonas*, 185). He longs to recapture his youth, his old sense of freedom, his love for Anne-Marie, yet he fears them and finds himself 'tournant autour de l'obstacle, tenté, repoussé, à nouveau séduit et inquiet' (188). The split within himself between good and evil is symbolized by his dialogue with the devil – a kind of exteriorization of a duel inside him in which the two halves of his being argue. He sees in his more lucid moments that it is as though 'la transparence et la saleté fatalement se fussent rejointes en moi, dans mon pauvre esprit écartelé' (215). The novel culminates in a frenzy of indecision as he hesitates between Anne-Marie and a return to his old life, between love for her and a sense of remorse, between hope of salvation and fear of damnation, between Fribourg and his home.

The reason sometimes presented for this division within both Chessex and his characters is that they belong to a land that is divided. Switzerland is divided by religions, language, and traditions. Jonas describes his country thus: 'Au sud, la France, le Léman, les vignes dans l'austère soleil protestant. Au nord, le pays de Fribourg, la Nuithonie catholique et romaine, la cohabitation des langues germaniques et du français, la révérence du latin d'Eglise et des pompes cérémoniales de la célébration baroque' (25). This division, Jonas says, was felt instinctively by the writer Lucien Bodard, who, crossing in a train from one of these regions to the other, roused himself from a drunken sleep and exclaimed: 'Ici, on change de pays' (26).

Within this country, the Vaud itself is a region of contrasts. *Portrait des Vaudois*, with its insistence on the Catholic past of this area and its Calvinist present, its depiction of the appetites and excesses of its people behind their austere beliefs, captures this division. It has been said that this book shows the Vaud as 'mélange de latinité et de calvinisme, de joie de vivre et de rigueur réformatrice, de lumière et d'ombres.'[4] As for the Vaudois as Chessex reveals them, they are equally divided. The typical Vaudois is shown, according to another critic of *Portrait des Vaudois*, as 'un être double, à deux penchants, l'un solaire, l'autre secret.'[5]

There is, then, within Chessex's vision and within his texts, an obvious division between two poles. However, just as the apparent welter of contradictions in his work proves to be, on closer inspection, a somewhat simpler division into pairs of opposites, so the pairs of opposites may be seen as concealing a fundamental unity. There is often in his writing a deliberate effort to look behind seeming distinctions towards a more unified concept of life, an attempt to reconcile the apparently irreconcilable. What may appear to be a rift between two opposites is sometimes represented as two sides of a single reality.

The major division evident in his writing – the one between life and death – is presented in some instances as a false dichotomy. Life and death may be seen as linked rather than as mutually hostile forces. Death and decay are shown, for example, as the necessary precondition for life, which is pictured as growing out of them. The hedgehog that speaks to Jean Calmet of life and affirmation of the life-forces, and that is the very representative of life within nature, lives in an undergrowth of dead and rotting vegetation. From this vegetation comes an odour that is 'chargée d'émanations putrescentes et à la fois toutes neuves comme la saveur laiteuse des racines' (*L'Ogre*, 41). The alternating of seasons in nature, of winter and spring, of life and death, may also be seen as symbolic of the fact that life and death are inseparable. Although he does not ultimately see spring and rebirth as consolation for the death of the individual, Chessex's insistence on the alternating rhythms does show a realization that these are two faces of the same reality.

Here and there in Chessex's writing are symbols of the indivisibility of life and death, people or things that draw together these two forces. Jean Calmet's mother, for example, is seen by him as a source of life, the giver of his very being, but also as an old and rapidly declining force that stands on the brink of death. He associates her with those fabulous and magic beings who represent life, and he calls her 'Ophélie,' 'Mélusine,' and 'Morgane,' but he also says, 'Tu étais toutes les fées des contes et maintenant tes os saillent et les rides lacèrent ton visage' (*L'Ogre*, 165). The young girls whom he teaches and whose vitality he admires are also connected with death. The pupil who dies is one such symbol uniting life and death, especially in the scene in which, almost at death's door, she makes love on a plot of ground reserved for her in the cemetery. Another such symbolic presence is the girl whom Jean observes placing a flower in the open mouth of a skeleton exhumed from the ruins of a cloister. The flower that represents life and the grinning skull that is death are here brought together, as are the live and vibrant girl and the skeleton. As he watches her place the flower in the grave, 'les tresses blondes de la petite Burgonde ont frôlé les os du saint surgi de l'éternité' (76).

In *Reste avec nous*, Chessex describes a procession celebrating Corpus Christi. He shows us what is really a funeral procession, in which one man represents Christ with his crown of thorns. Earlier that day, the man's mother has been to the cemetery to remember her dead, and has put flowers on the tomb. But, despite the funeral connotations, this is a procession that takes place in the spring, the participants are decorated with flowers, and they are possessed by 'l'ardente tendresse de vivre' (106). Since this particular festival is held in honour of the Eucharist, which is itself a celebration of life in death, of the risen Christ, and of salvation through his flesh and blood, the links between life and death are further reinforced. This whole celebration brings together for Chessex two realities that are really one.

According to Georges Anex, 'L'art de Jacques Chessex, ou pour mieux dire, sa vision et sa visée d'artiste, ne séparent pas la face lumineuse de la vie de sa face obscure.'[6] Anex points out that, in such works as *Où vont mourir les oiseaux*, Chessex always observes light in the midst of darkness and life in death. Yves Velan agrees that, despite the two poles of Chessex's writing, he produces texts in which 'le résultat n'est pas l'ambiguïté, c'est au contraire le va-et-vient.'[7] Chessex, for his part, strives consciously towards a vision in which opposites are united. He rejects the Calvinist view of a world in which God and the devil, good and evil, and a host of other mutually opposing forces strive for mastery. He argues that there is a unity beneath the surface of life and that a dualistic view of the world misrepresents the truth. 'Je crois qu'il faut bannir tout dualisme, profondément et une fois pour toutes,' he says (Garcin, 172). He rejects in particular the familiar distinction between spirit and flesh, the soul and the body: 'La chair est dans l'esprit, l'esprit est dans la chair ... Je ne crois plus qu'il y ait antinomie entre l'âme et le corps mortel' (172).

The view of the deity that Chessex finds the most reasonable, and that he sometimes strives to observe in creation, is that of a God who is Himself double, in whom good and evil, right and wrong, light and dark are joined. This deity would combine the traditional roles of God and the devil, and would be these two forces in one. He would show what one poem calls a 'visage du dieu double' (*Comme*, 67). It is this double deity that Raphaël Turner serves in his role as Judas. Turner sees himself as an instrument of the devil and of evil, but he also serves God since it is God's will that he betray Aschenbach. (Just as it was part of God's plan that Judas betray Jesus.) He believes himself to be the chosen one of God *and* of the devil, and he says: 'De tout le royaume, je suis le seul élu des deux armées ... Au milieu, Judas. Ni chaud ni froid' (*Judas*, 17). He is, in fact, serving some superior power or logic that combines good and evil, God and Satan. Because of this, although he is the very embodiment of evil, he is also innocent, since he is carrying out a superior will. This combination of evil and innocence is conveyed by the very title of *Judas le transparent*.

The idea of Creation as Chessex tries to capture it in some of his texts is in the image of this double-faceted God who unites all opposites. Raphaël Turner says of the world that 'c'est beau et ... ça sent le rot. C'est vrai que c'est pur et que ça pue comme une diarrhée d'alcoolique' (120). Philippe Nadal says that, in his poetry, Chessex shows the world as, 'pas de fleur sans la flétrissure, pas de mémoire de Dieu sans l'image du règne de Satan, oui, pas de pomme sans la morsure dedans, pas de fruit sans le ver qui ronge, pas de chair sans la putrescence.'[8] In other words, this is a world in which everything always contains its opposite and is defined by it.

Bearing in mind this attempt by Chessex to view life as the *combination* of opposites, certain elements of his texts may be seen as representing the blending of opposite forces. Those parts of his vision that are the battleground of opposing forces may also be seen, in another light, as privileged areas in which opposites meet. They represent the combination of opposites as well as being divided by warring forces. Woman, for example, becomes the being who brings together life and death, good and evil, rather than a being split by them. She is the instrument of the devil, but, *at the same time*, the means of salvation. As well as representing temptations of the flesh for a man like Burg, she is *also*, in the form of Geneviève, a means of discovering a loving God who works for man's salvation. She is the threat of death through sin, but, as Mange comes to realize, she is *simultaneously* life and intense enjoyment. Because of her association with the erotic, she is a being in whom the life forces *and* the threat of death coexist.

The comparison of Morgane Wagner to the centre of a mandala conveys particularly well the idea that woman is an essential unity in whom apparent opposites are reconciled. The centre of the mandala is the point from which the forces of both life and death radiate, the ground occupied by the deity from whom everything in existence comes. For the narrator of *Morgane Madrigal*, Morgane can be identified with this centre because she is life and freedom to him, while also suggesting death. She is the sum of all things, and he tells her, 'En vous seule est l'Un, Morgane, le centre à retrouver, la Rose où je bois le battement du monde' (206).

Nature, too, may be seen as a combination of the poles that represent the two extremes of Chessex's vision. The devil lurks in every tree, valley, and river, yet nature is God's creation and an emanation of Him. Death lies in nature, but so do the panic forces that produce life. Like woman, nature is linked to the erotic and to life, while containing within itself winter, death, and decay. Of the elements of nature, it is the moon that man has frequently regarded as representing the opposing rhythms of nature. Because of its periodic changes, its waxing and waning, birth and death, it has often been seen as symbolic of the double face of nature. Chessex, too, has seen it in this light, and has called it 'la lune, exactement associée aux maléfices et à la beauté de la nuit' and 'monde liquide ... plein de la mort vivante' (*Reste*, 43). Among the animals, it is the fox that best sums up this double nature for Chessex, since it carries rabies and death, but it also clings to life, endures, and represents the wildness of nature.

The unity of life as Jonas sometimes glimpses it is conveyed by the biblical sea monster. As we have noted, the monster represents death that swallows man, but, since it regurgitates Jonah, it is also the hope of rebirth. It stands for the Calvinism that pursues Jonas and that would engulf him, but also for safety, protection, and return to the maternal womb. It is described in the Bible as a fish, and is therefore linked in Jonas' mind to the fish of astrology (the sign under which he and Anne-Marie were born). The two-headed fish of the zodiac symbolizes the double nature of life and of man, especially the combination of their physical and material side with their spiritual and mystic one. It is 'le poisson double de l'astrologie ... les deux têtes, les deux corps inversés – une tête dans l'élément physique, dans l'humide, dans le corps charnel, l'autre tête fascinée, captée par la vie de l'esprit, par les mystères et les pouvoirs de la transcendance' (*Jonas*, 121–2). The fish is also a symbol of Christ, who likewise has a double nature since he is life in death and rebirth after death.

The Vaud itself, although the origin of many of the apparent contradictions within Chessex's view of life, may be seen in another light as the ground on which the two sides of his vision find a fundamental unity. As one critic points out, the Vaud is, in many of Chessex's texts, 'un tout ... un ensemble.'[9] In *Portrait des Vaudois*, Chessex describes a minister greeting his congregation at Easter, while behind him is the church where once priests and monks also stood in the Easter sun greeting the faithful. Before Calvinism was imposed on it, the Vaud was Catholic, and the same festival, celebrating resurrection and life in death, was held. These are just two faces of the same religion, and the Vaud has embraced both religions. Behind the two forms of Christianity, the Vaudois celebrate the same belief in rebirth and life. Even the pastor who now conducts the services has the same gestures, the same air, and performs basically the same ritual as his Catholic predecessor.

Today the Vaud and its people are still not invariably partisan upholders of just one faith, and sometimes these two religions coexist and accept each other, as at Echallens, where Catholics and Protestants live peaceably together and use the same building to worship (*Portrait*, 27). Symbolic of this reconciliation is Maître Manuel. Born a Calvinist, Manuel resembles 'un prêtre bourguignon du quinzième siècle' (200). He is fascinated by Catholicism and by the Latin heritage of the Vaud, and he lives a life devoted to reminiscence of the Latin, Catholic, and Burgundian past of his region. He sums up in himself the double nature of the Vaudois: Calvinist with a Catholic past, Swiss with a Burgundian history, influenced by both Germanic and Latin cultures.

There is also at times a glimpse of the realization that, behind the diverse forms of Christianity, there is another more basic religion with which they share something. As the pastor described in *Portrait des Vaudois* celebrates Easter, signs of spring and of nature coming alive are all around him. The Christian rite of Easter is linked to the rebirth of nature, and through it, to pagan beliefs that saw life *in* nature and personified that life in the form of certain nature gods. Dionysus and Pan are the two gods whom Chessex evokes in *L'Ogre*, while Burg, in *La Confession du pasteur Burg*, senses some god like them in the forest. Both Christianity and these pagan beliefs, despite their apparent hostility to each other, express the fundamental truth that there are life-forces in the natural world.

Chessex also believes that the Vaud and its people combine love of order with love of revolt, a desire for security with a turbulent will to be free. Their pleasure in the army and in performing their military service conveys this double love. The army stands for order but it also represents periodic military service and escape from an ordered and comfortable bourgeois life, a chance to live and camp in the open, and to avoid routine. 'Les Vaudois aiment aussi ce défi-là,' he adds, 'cette rébellion, cette manière de dire non en filant par la bande et en cognant s'il le faut, cette manière de relever la tête et de secouer ce qui comprime, parce qu'on nous a trop ceinturés' (*Portrait*, 75). Behind their staid exterior and their love of order, the Vaudois can be a violent and often cruel people, Chessex says, and he recounts, as we know, many tales of violent deeds in the Vaud. He sums up his compatriots: 'Les Vaudois sont patients, habiles, soudain le torrent s'enfle et bondit, la lumière devient noire, le sang cogne' (77).

For Chessex it is the region of the Vaud called La Côte that conveys best all the diverse aspects of this part of Switzerland. He sees this place as the product of a certain spirit that is associated historically with the romanesque, and that unites many strands of the Vaudois past. It is 'l'endroit où je sens le mieux que l'esprit vaudois est le produit de cette culture romane, c'est-à-dire à la fois lémanique et paysanne, rhodanienne et terrienne, qui lui assure l'équilibre' (*Portrait*, 179). But La Côte is just typical of a wider area around it that combines many elements of history, culture, and religion in a unity that is typically Vaudois: 'Composite, divers, le pays? Non, un pays complet comme on dit qu'un pain est complet, un pays géographiquement juste parce qu'il surgit sur un espace plein et total comme la terre promise, et c'est ce qui donne à tous les Vaudois ce sentiment d'être d'un tout, d'une cohérence: le pays *tient*' (*Portrait*, 57; italics in original).

It was pointed out in chapter 2 that Chessex's texts may be described as mythical, because in them he tries to deal with the problems that preoccupy myth and religion, and because he tends to employ mythical images in order to do this. His way of looking at the Vaud, and at life in general, may also be termed mythical because he tries to look beyond surface appearances, beyond the apparently tranquil life of people (especially those of the Vaud) to the deeply disturbing metaphysical preoccupations of their lives: death, salvation, human suffering. He often depicts these concerns in stories of universal application involving characters who are individuals, but also representatives of mankind. Hence certain characters, animals, and elements of nature are transformed into representations of man and his destiny. The sea monster in *Jonas* becomes a symbol of life and death, of hell and salvation; the fox symbolizes the presence of evil in nature, the revolt against society, the inevitability of death; Jonas, Jean Calmet, Mange, and Alexandre Dumur become all men struggling to live free and to face death. One might say of Chessex, as he has said of certain other writers, that he is aware all the time of 'les dieux, les métamorphoses ou les débris de la part mythique dans la simplicité quotidienne, dans l'air de la chambre ou du pré' (*Saintes*, 12).

Ancient myth dealt precisely with these concerns in stories that were of general application. It tended to see the apparent contradictions of life as being two sides of the same reality; to see life and death, light and dark, good and evil as two aspects of the same thing. The deity who created this one reality was 'the totality of the universe, the harmonization of all the pairs of opposites.'[10] In this sense too, there is an attempt in Chessex's writing to project a mythic view of life. The symbolic presences in his work are often combining symbols: the sea monster, the fox, the panic deities combine within themselves the opposites of creation. Woman especially is one such symbol. Chessex depicts, in characters like Anne-Marie, Geneviève, Monna, and Thérèse, women who are not just individuals, but womankind. On this level, they are the meeting place of the apparent opposites of life and death, good and evil, freedom and servitude.

On the 'mythical' plane, then, Chessex's writing may be seen as an attempt to view life as a unity behind its contradictions. As Henri-Dominique Paratte says, Chessex's vision has 'cette unité existentielle, quasi organique, qui rapelle aisément Ramuz.'[11] But it is Chessex's friend and publisher, Bertil Galland, who best sums up his attempt to view life as a mythic harmony when he writes: 'Réfractaire à l'abstraction, Jacques Chessex n'a pas retrouvé son unité dans une doctrine ou une idéologie. Il a rassemblé tous les pans de son être en visionnaire, dans le mouvement enveloppant de mythes privilégiés et charnels.'[12]

There is no doubt that Chessex does try to adopt this vision in much of what he writes, and he is immediately aware of the same search for unity in the writings of others. He is struck, for example, by Judrin's technique in *Le Balancier* of taking one popular saying or proverb and quoting beside it another that conveys the opposite meaning. Chessex sees in this an awareness that there are two sides to any truth and that opposite 'truths' do not necessarily cancel each other out. He praises Judrin's conclusion that 'pour retrouver la vérité, il fallait réunir l'ange et la bête, Dieu et Mammon, le bouquet de fleurs et le prix du boeuf.'[13] He admires Cingria for his writings and his life, which display 'le mariage prodigieusement fertile en lui de l'Orient byzantin, de Rome et de La Lotharingie' (*Cingria*, 44). The attempt by Cingria to combine many parts of his life and of his experience leads Chessex to describe him as 'pèlerin et poète de l'unité' (*Saintes*, 37).

Yet this view of life is not always the one that is uppermost, and Chessex's texts are not always expressions of the unity within the opposites of existence. Despite the attempt to go beyond a dualistic and purely Manichean conception, the old Calvinist view of a divided existence is never fully evicted from the text. Indeed, the overall vision often remains one of division and dualities, and his texts are frequently unable to escape the Calvinism that experiences life in terms of clear-cut distinctions between good and evil, God and the devil. In the poem 'A Calvin,' the poet says, 'Je suis l'amant de Dieu,' and he goes on to depict God as a jealous God who tolerates no vision but His own, a vision of a world split between opposing forces. The poem concludes: 'Je suis l'amant de Quelqu'un qui ne partage pas / Choisis, idiot, rêve imbécile / Il n'y a pas de couture sur mon territoire / En moi la vérité est happée ou noire' (*Le Calviniste*, 108).

In this, as in so many other things, the characters of Chessex's fiction mirror his plight. The tragedy for them is that, even if they glimpse the unity of life, they cannot live it. They are unable to maintain in their own lives the precarious equilibrium between the conflicting aspects of life as they live it. Jean Calmet finally gives in to guilt and remorse, and turns to death; Mange erects Monna as a kind of deity, abandons everything for her, and inevitably feels this is all a failure when she is forced to leave him; Jean Burg forgets his spiritual role by living exclusively for Geneviève, and he believes that he is punished as a sinner when she dies; Alexandre gives in to the sexual excess that Louis incites in him. These characters all become victims of an excessive view of life that drives them to one extreme. They are overcome by precisely the excess that Chessex so often praises, and by so doing, they are no better than the Calvinist, whose view is also an excessive one because it places exclusive emphasis on one pole of existence and attempts to deny or combat the other.

10

The Text as Unity

Chessex's writings are full of paradox. They are divided by apparently hostile forces that confront one another, turning the text into what sometimes seems to be a battleground. On the textual level too, however, these forces actually fall into pairs of opposites. Chessex's work is based on a whole series of apparent dichotomies, of opposing pairs of forces or influences. These forces are brought together in the text, which becomes the place in which they meet and in which they are finally reconciled. The text is used as a principle of unity, a means of joining two conflicting visions.

The most basic division into opposites, the one that is there, as it were, at the birth of the text, is the one of 'influences' or intertextual presences. Chessex's writing belongs to two literary traditions: one based in French Switzerland, and the other in France. This double influence is itself due to the fact that he writes in a language that belongs not just to the region of his birth, but also to France. At the same time, this language is spoken and written differently in the two countries, and has produced two distinct literary traditions, each with its own power over the francophone Swiss writer. A common language thus produces two different forces, both of which are at work in Chessex's writing.

Chessex's first loyalty (and that of his texts) is obviously to the region where he was born. He is proud of his Vaudois heritage, and he sees his roots in the Vaud as the very origin of his texts. To abandon these roots for some other tradition would be to cut himself off from the source of his inspiration. The presence of the Vaud is, consequently, very noticeable in his fiction. Almost all his novels and short stories are set in the Vaud, and the major characters are Vaudois. Even in *Jonas*, which is set in Fribourg, the reader is still constantly aware of the presence of the Vaud, for it and its religion determine most of Jonas' acts and are his usual point of reference. Only *La Tête ouverte* is not set in Switzerland and does not have a Swiss protagonist. Even in this story, however, there are echoes of the Vaud, for some of the characters have traits that are typical of 'les justes' and the respectable Calvinists of Chessex's own land.

Just as important as the physical presence of the Vaud, with its own particular scenery, its people, and their Calvinist mentality, is a literary tradition. The Vaud, and other parts of French Switzerland, have produced writers who have created a distinctly French-Swiss literature, and Chessex has his part in that tradition. In fact, he deliberately embraces a literary tradition of which he is very conscious, and to which he wishes to make his own contribution. 'Je ne me sens pas du tout écrasé ou dominé par mes aînés,' he says. 'J'ai tenté d'assimiler la qualité d'une tradition, le génie d'une pensée, pour les féconder à mon tour et leur apporter une part de ma nature' (Bevan, 58).

Several writers may be counted among those 'aînés' to whom Chessex makes reference. Among them, Jean-Jacques Rousseau is a major figure whose presence may be felt not just in Chessex's writing, but in the literary production of a good many French-Swiss writers.[1] Although Chessex does occasionally mention Rousseau, little has been written about the intertextual presence of this major predecessor in his writing. It is not our intent here to give an exhaustive account of that presence, but merely to mention its more obvious manifestations since it does constitute a link between Chessex and a national tradition.

The most obvious similarity between the two writers is their love of nature and the many descriptions of the natural beauty of Switzerland to be found in their texts. They share what might be termed a typically 'romantic' attitude to natural beauty, which produces lyrical descriptions of it as a living thing that seems to reflect or even inspire the emotions of the beholder. In all such descriptions there is a feeling that this is a living presence, a source of some dark energy with which the individual may commune. Chessex is aware that he, like Rousseau, sees this side of nature, and he has said, 'Je crois très profondément à la nature. Ce que j'apporte, moi, est une certaine sauvagerie, comme Rousseau était sauvage.'[2] Commenting on his love of nature as being 'romantic,' he says, 'J'ai tripoté le clavier de Rousseau et de Schubert' (*Carabas*, 202).

The element of confession in these writings also reminds one strongly of Rousseau. Indeed, the very title of *La Confession du pasteur Burg* invites comparison to Rousseau's *Confessions*. *La Tête ouverte, Les Yeux jaunes, Jonas, La Confession du pasteur Burg, La Trinité*, and several short stories are narratives in the first person singular in which the speaker openly reveals and confesses his fears, emotions, and turpitudes. In *Carabas*, Chessex launches into a whole series of confessions in his own name, no longer bothering to place a narrator between himself and the text. In many volumes of poetry, but especially in *Comme l'os* and *Le Calviniste*, the poet's persona confesses his darker side. *Comme l'os*, which dwells mainly on his love for two women, is described by Patricia Serex as 'dix confessions sublimes et sobres,' while Gérard Valbert says of *Le Calviniste* that 'Jacques Chessex écrit ses poèmes comme d'autres tiennent un journal.' Other critics have said of his work as a whole that 'Chessex ... se dénude, s'offre, s'explique,' and that 'Chessex ... dévoré de culpabilité, ne cesse de se confesser.'[3] One poem in *Comme l'os* says, 'Je scrute une âme tachée de regret' (50), and in *Carabas* Chessex admits quite simply, 'Je parle de moi' (21). The act of writing becomes a kind of dialogue with himself, a means of freeing himself of his obsessions, an 'inventaire de quelques hantises' (*Carabas*, 110). The reader of Chessex's texts becomes, to use Chessex's description of his own experience when reading Alice Rivaz, 'lecteur d'un journal intime' (*Saintes*, 189).

Both Chessex and Rousseau may be seen as products of a Calvinist tradition that lays emphasis on recognition of one's darker side. This produces a desire to delve into one's innermost secrets and evil desires, and what David Bevan calls a 'littérature de sublimation et d'intériorisation, une littérature à la première personne du singulier' (Bevan, 8). Chessex recognizes this aspect of the literature of French Switzerland, and he has said, 'Ne pas se raconter est rare dans ce pays de confessions et de journaux intimes' (*Saintes*, 181). Calvinism encourages writers such as Chessex and Rousseau to emphasize in their confessions the 'sinful' aspect of their lives, the more shameful of their deeds and their desires. Chessex, like Rousseau, is remarkable for 'l'espèce de franchise qu'il met à se peindre sous les traits les plus noirs.'[4] This is particularly evident in *Carabas*, which becomes at times a catalogue of the most unpleasant traits that Chessex can find in his own life and character. But he is clearly aware that, like Rousseau, he is open to the accusation of taking pleasure in an excessive display of self-abasement, and his response to this criticism is the same as Rousseau's: 'J'ai choisi de me montrer sous mes vraies couleurs' (195). Alexandre Dumur produces a similar reply to the criticism that he overemphasizes his turpitudes in describing his life: 'Mais j'ai juré de tout dire!' (*Les Yeux*, 50).

Yet another trait that some of Chessex's texts share with Rousseau's is a sense of persecution. While this does not become the mania that we find in Rousseau's *Confessions* or the *Rêveries*, it does loom large in such works as *La Tête ouverte*, in which the narrator feels that everyone around him is his enemy. Like Rousseau, Chessex feels that he has been unjustly attacked for some of his writing. The scandal provoked in his own country by texts like *La Confession du pasteur Burg* and *Carabas* is the cause of this feeling, and one must admit that, in this case, his sense of persecution is not entirely unjustified.

One more obvious link between Chessex and Rousseau is their nostalgia for childhood, which both see as a kind of paradise. Maître Mange often feels regret at having lost his childhood, and he is 'repris ... par l'émotion de son enfance' (*Ardent*, 83). Much of his love for his daughter is expressed by evoking her early years, and by imagining the world of happiness and love that this time in her life must have meant for her. Alexandre, Burg, and Jonas also remember themselves as children, and, even when thinking of the harsh Calvinist upbringing that they received, they feel a certain nostalgia for the security of those years. Chessex, too, in *Portrait des Vaudois*, talks of his years in Payerne and of the sense of happiness and security provoked by these memories.

After Rousseau, the most influential writer in Swiss-French literature is probably Ramuz, and it has been said, 'Il ne serait pas excessivement présomptueux d'affirmer qu'il n'existe point d'écrivain romand contemporain qui n'ait sa dette envers Ramuz' (Bevan, 7). Whatever the truth of this statement as far as it concerns Swiss-French writers in general, it certainly applies to Chessex. He has frequently written about Ramuz and has praised his work and its role in creating a distinctive literature in the Suisse Romande. He says, 'Pour moi, Ramuz a la taille de Tolstoï. Je crois que j'ai ressenti Ramuz, non pas comme un père dévoreur, mais comme quelqu'un qui me tendait la main' (Bevan, 58). The resemblance between Chessex's *L'Ardent Royaume* and Ramuz' *Les Circonstances de la vie* is particularly striking. Both Maître Mange and Ramuz' Emile Magnenat are lawyers who are ruined by their love for a woman, but who are happy to sacrifice themselves for her.

Besides recognizing the importance of these two predecessors, Chessex affirms his kinship with several contemporaries from the Suisse Romande. He admits that Cingria has always fascinated him, and that his fascination led him to write a book on this poet (Garcin, 92). He says that he admires Philippe Jaccottet, and describes him as 'un poète important d'une très grande sensibilité' (Bevan, 60). He has always felt a great friendship for Maurice Chappaz, has frequently praised his work, and sees his own *Portrait des Vaudois* as being a kind of companion volume to Chappaz' *Portrait des Valaisans* (Bevan, 56). His respect for Chappaz is such that he dedicated *Portrait des Vaudois* and a chapter of *Carabas* to him. He likewise expresses admiration for Jacques Marcanton (whom he compares to Malraux, Joyce, and Mann) and for Georges Borgeaud (Bevan, 60).

Finally, one should mention Chessex's frequently expressed admiration for Gustave Roud. This poet's influence has been felt by many francophone Swiss writers, and Chessex acknowledges himself to be one of them. He says that Roud first inspired him during his adolescence to write poetry, and to realize that, despite all the difficulties experienced by Vaudois poets, it was possible to write poetry in the Vaud. He describes the texts written by Roud between 1920 and 1950 as 'quelques-unes des oeuvres les plus indispensables que j'aie lues' (Garcin, 85). It was this admiration that led him to seek out Roud, who was known as a rather reclusive figure, and to begin a friendship that ended only when the older man died.

These writers are all part of the literary tradition of the Suisse Romande, and Chessex's love of their texts links him to that tradition. Of all of these affinities, it is his love of Ramuz' work that is the most instructive. Although the archetypal Swiss writer in many ways, Ramuz was read and published in France, and he saw himself as also belonging to a French literary tradition. One reason why Chessex appreciates his writing so much is that it pointed the way beyond a purely regional literature towards France. He says: 'Vaudois, j'ai ressenti Ramuz, au contraire, comme un formidable ouvreur de routes vers la France et vers l'univers. Quelqu'un qui, au lieu d'opprimer et d'assassiner ses cadets, nous faisait sortir du provincialisme, de la bêtise, de la mesquinerie' (Bevan, 58).

Chessex is very much aware that being a francophone writer in Switzerland has its problems and dangers. Like many writers of the

Suisse Romande, he is conscious of belonging to a linguistic minority that often feels threatened by the German-speaking majority.[5] At the same time, francophone groups outside France may be regarded by the French themselves as marginal, provincial, and of little importance, and their writers may be dismissed as being apart from the mainstream. There is even a danger that Francophones outside France may themselves accept this verdict and adopt a kind of self-defeating provincialism. Chessex sums up the problems of writers like himself: 'Il est très difficile d'être un écrivain suisse français. Longtemps nous avons été les parents pauvres de la francophonie.'[6] He speaks with envy of the ease with which German-Swiss writers seem to be accepted and read in Germany, and he says that 'il suffit d'être écrivain de Genève pour se trouver séparé de la culture française.'[7]

It is because of the threat of marginality that Chessex is particularly proud of the Goncourt Prize that he received for *L'Ogre*. This constitutes recognition of his work in France – a recognition that eluded even Ramuz. He says that his prize was a source of great personal pride, that it restored much of his confidence in himself, and that 'le fait d'avoir été reconnu, et à plus forte raison, écrivain vaudois, écrivain d'origine suisse, reconnu et couronné d'un prix français d'une telle importance, a fortifié ma confiance en moi' (Garcin, 98–9). But acceptance by French literary circles is also recognition that there exists a francophone literature outside France that is worth noticing. He says: 'Dans ces conditions, ce prix est sans doute ma chance, mais peut-être aussi celle d'une littérature francophone déjà existante à l'intérieur d'une grande communauté de langues et de livres.'[8]

He is also particularly grateful for the friendship and support that French critics have often shown him when those in his own country have been scandalized by his publications. He speaks with gratitude of the support of French critics when *Carabas* was published and almost universally condemned in Switzerland, and he especially appreciated the encouragement of the critic André Stil for such works as *L'Ardent Royaume*, *La Confession du pasteur Burg*, and *L'Ogre* (Garcin, 40–1). Parisian publishers and critics are seen by Chessex as invaluable allies who have frequently recognized, by their support of his writing, the contribution that Switzerland has made and is making to literature in French.

As for Paris itself, it is seen as the centre of a culture that he admires and shares. It is a city that he loves and that he feels the need to visit regularly. While admitting that he could never live there, he says: 'Paris, c'est une langue ... Paris, c'est un certain nombre d'édifices et de centres sacrés où le génie du lieu parle très haut' (Garcin, 96). He is conscious that Paris offers something that is his and part of his culture, something that, as a Francophone, he shares with the French. 'Quand je vais rôder à Paris,' he says, 'c'est un véritable besoin, ce n'est pas du tout une mondanité, c'est une façon de retourner à la source pour boire l'air qui est le mien. J'ai besoin de Paris comme j'ai besoin du Pays de Vaud' (Bevan, 55).

Chessex's love of Paris is extended to France in general. This affection is conveyed particularly well in the section of *Carabas* called 'Une Tranche de melon.' He here describes himself, having crossed the lake from Switzerland to France, sitting in a café at Evian, watching the people around him. Everything seems to have its own distinctive traits; everything seems different from his own part of the francophone community; everything seems very French. He is struck by 'la jetée où les pêcheurs à béret basque sur des mines décidées d'anciens combattants installent une couleur locale qu'il est définitivement impossible de confondre avec celle d'un port voisin valaisan ou vaudois' (93). He feels a deep and abiding affection for this country as he savours a glass of Beaujolais, sticks a French stamp on a letter, and watches some soldiers drinking at the bar. He tells himself: 'C'est la France. J'habite à une heure de l'autre côté de l'eau. Je parle cette langue, de mes fenêtres je vois cette côte, ces montagnes vertes, la nuit je regarde le serpent de lampes d'Evian juste en face de Lausanne comme un reflet. La France!' (93).

Chessex clearly needs the French presence to nurture his work, and he is very conscious of belonging to a French literary tradition as much as to a Swiss one. He has said: 'Je me sens très profondément lié à la France par l'écriture, la langue, l'héritage, etc.' (Bevan, 55). He feels a deep affinity with many French writers, an affinity that is as important to him as the one he has with Swiss writers. His literary tastes and his own themes and style have been influenced by several French writers. 'Giono, Bernanos, Malraux, Arland, Morand auront été ces initiateurs du goût et des choix,' he writes.[9] He also says that Michel Tournier, in such works as *Vendredi ou les limbes du Pacifique*, and *Le Roi des Aulnes*, has had a decisive effect on him (Garcin, 156). Gide is likewise a writer whom he has always respected, and an obvious parallel may be drawn between *La Confession du pasteur Burg* and *La Symphonie pastorale*, with their austere Swiss ministers who do not understand their own emotions and whose inability to do so leads to deceit and the destruction of the girl with whom they fall in love.

But the major contemporary French presences felt in Chessex's work are those of Paulhan and Ponge. He says that, in the early 1960s, he fell under the spell of Paulhan and 'le génie de la litote, la distance ironique, l'oeil perçant de cette chouette surprise en plein jour' (*Carabas*, 38). The rigour and precision of such early works as *La Tête ouverte* and *La Confession du pasteur Burg* may be attributed to Paulhan's influence, an influence that Chessex finally found somewhat stifling. While recognizing the absolute necessity, at that stage in his life, of listening to and taking advice from Paulhan, he says that finally 'je me suis cru, par lui ... arasé, coupé, tué' (Garcin, 24). But Paulhan's opinion always remained important in Chessex's mind, and whenever he writes, the question that he still asks himself is 'qu'est-ce que Paulhan aurait pensé?' (Garcin, 26).

Ponge, too, taught Chessex the importance of brevity and accuracy. While writing, as a student, a dissertation on Ponge, Chessex learned from him the need for concision and the avoidance of excessive emotion. He says that Ponge taught him to 'dénier l'instant premier, le cri, l'extase appolinienne, la folie dyonisiaque [sic] qui étaient en moi' (Garcin, 21). This influence too became stifling, and Chessex admits that 'après m'avoir fécondé, m'attirant vers le réel, m'attirant vers la pulpe des fruits, vers la chair des femmes, Ponge m'a littéralement coupé la parole' (Garcin, 128). For some years, Chessex turned away from poetry, and it was not until he escaped the negative side of Ponge's influence that he began writing it again and produced *Elégie soleil du regret* in 1976.[10] Nevertheless, Chessex still concedes that Ponge also inspired him, and that 'Francis Ponge est le fondateur, le premier critique et le maintenant de la poésie contemporanie.'[11]

In addition to individual writers, there is one French literary movement that has a particularly strong intertextual presence in Chessex's writing, and that is naturalism. *Maupassant et les autres* is Chessex's homage to the naturalists, and in his preface to this work he says: 'Je me suis reconnu, dans cette famille d'esprits très diverse et cohérente, une parenté de tempérament, d'idées, d'attitudes à l'endroit de la littérature et du siècle' (9). Elsewhere, he has said that his pleasure at receiving the Goncourt Prize was all the keener because 'comme [les Goncourt], j'appartiens à la tradition naturaliste.'[12] Critics have, of course, noted the affinity too, and have said that the naturalists are 'tous cousins de l'écrivain suisse,' that *Maupassant et les autres* is a 'salut adressé à ses pairs,' and that Chessex himself is 'inégalable dans le néo-naturalisme.'[13]

More specifically, Chessex believes that he is in a direct line of descent from Flaubert. He sees *Carabas* as particularly Flaubertian in its attack on 'la bêtise' and in its exuberant style. Like Flaubert writing *Madame Bovary*, Chessex read the pages of *Carabas* aloud as he wrote them, testing their style and the force of the attacks that he mounts in it against various forms of stupidity and a host of *idées reçues* (Garcin, 43-4). One might also draw a comparison between *L'Ardent Royaume* and *Madame Bovary* in their depiction of a certain type of hypocritical provincial society, and in their description of one individual's attempts to escape this in an adulterous liaison. The leader of the Masonic lodge in *L'Ardent Royaume*, with his self-sufficient, bland assumption that he represents morality, progress, and all the 'right' values is a latter-day Homais. Looking beyond their texts to the two writers themselves, one might even see the rather long moustache that is evident in many photographs of Chessex (and his burlesque praise of moustaches in *Carabas*) as a homage to Flaubert.

There is also an obvious affinity with Maupassant. Both use short fiction to express their vision, although Chessex's *oeuvre* is not as dominated by short works as Maupassant's. Both writers, in the words of one critic, use the short story to express 'des obsessions de violence, de suicide, de pourrissement et de folie.'[14] They have a similar view of life, with the same emphasis on the futility of human acts. Although this view is not quite such a constant in Chessex's writing as it is in Maupassant's, it is very clear in such works as *Carabas*. As François Nourissier points out, certain situations in Chessex's fiction – when Dr Calmet steals his son's first love; the fiasco that Jean Calmet experiences when trying to make love to Thérèse; the many visits to cemeteries – would not be out of place in a Maupassant story.[15] Bertil Galland says that the resemblance to Maupassant is due mainly to Chessex's 'plongée dans les existences médiocres qu'il transfigure puissamment, feignant le cynisme, élevant le quotidien à l'ampleur du fantastique.'[16] One might even see the famous moustache as being as much a homage to Maupassant as to Flaubert.

This extensive French intertextual background and the admiration for French writers are ample proof that Chessex looks as much to France as to the Vaud. It does not mean, however, that he abandons in any way his sense of being first and foremost Vaudois. Although he is part of a specifically French literary tradition, although he writes in French, and although he is read and published in France, he is not French. Like many Belgians, Québécois, and other Francophones outside France, he has his own land, literature, and history. He makes this very clear: 'Or, je suis vaudois: j'ai une certaine façon de sentir qui est celle de ma race. La langue nous est commune aux Français et à moi, mais pas ce fond, ce brassage, ce malaxage par l'histoire, par la famille et la fibre' (*Carabas*, 136). Despite his love of France and its culture, he says: 'Je ne veux pas jouer au Français de France' (*Carabas*, 137), and he rejects the accusation that this attitude is 'ridicule affectation provinciale de gaucherie et de pudeur fruste' (*Carabas*, 137).

What Chessex is doing when he reflects the intertextual presence of French literature in his writing is to affirm his place in a literary and linguistic community while maintaining that he is a distinct part of that community. He sees himself and his texts as belonging to a French literary tradition, to which they bring their own perspective – a perspective that springs from his roots in the Vaud. Both these elements and national traditions nurture his work, which is not so much divided by them as a place in which they meet. It is a blend of influences and forces that come together and meld. His Calvinist obsessions, the typically Vaudois setting, the particular society of the Vaud are combined with a naturalist's view of life and with metaphysical concerns that are also part of a French tradition. As a Vaudois and a teacher of French literature, as a writer who has a place in two cultures and literatures, he is in a unique position to combine in his texts two different but equally important sources of inspiration.

This attempt to overcome boundaries and to combine traditions is aided by the fact that one of the major influences on Chessex's work, the French influence, is seen traditionally as a 'universal' one. The whole tenor of French literature since at least the seventeenth century has been to deal with matters of universal concern. What constitutes the French tradition is, as it were, its attempt to go beyond specifically national or local questions to deal with ones that affect mankind. This is particularly true of the modern writers who deal with 'metaphysical' questions. As we have seen, Chessex too is a writer of 'metaphysical' texts who raises questions of universal import.

Chessex is naturally aware of this aspect of French literature and culture, and he says that it is important to him that his texts be read in France, because he, too, aspires to the universality that is part of the French tradition. In one interview, he says: 'Je sens la nécessité d'avoir des lecteurs français, justement pour tenter d'approcher cette dimension universelle' (Garcin, 100). For him, contemporary French literature is represented principally by those 'metaphysical' writers whose concerns are universal and supranational. He says that another reason why he was so pleased to receive the Goncourt Prize was that, at that time in France, these writers were closely identified throughout the world with French literature: 'Il y avait Malraux, il y avait Aragon, il y avait un certain nombre de poètes, Jean Grosjean, Guillevic, Jean Tardieu, André du Bouchet, Jacques Réda' (Garcin, 100). Being acknowledged and read in France meant that he could measure himself against these names, hone his own talents in their company, and take his place among writers of universal significance. When he writes now, he can think of these others, and say to himself, 'Je vis avec eux' (Garcin, 101).

In his own texts, Chessex attempts to do what these writers do. The stories of Jean Calmet, Jean Burg, and Maître Mange are those of individuals of no particular importance, of ordinary and, in many ways, mediocre individuals. Yet they are stories that raise questions of concern to all men and women. Jean Calmet struggles against life-threatening forces, the despair of death, and the failure of love; Mange's life of routine and monotonous conformism becomes a life illuminated by love and threatened by death; Jean Burg, whose experience and life are certainly very different from that of most readers, and who is almost inconceivable outside a Swiss Calvinist milieu, struggles with problems of good and evil that all men and women must face at some time. Robert Kanters' comment on *L'Ogre* applies to most of what Chessex has written: 'Le talent de M. Chessex est de nous obliger à faire le saut de sa simple histoire vaudoise à la plus vieille – à la plus constante – histoire de l'hunamité.'[17] Another critic, writing about the stories in *Le Séjour des morts*, makes the same point: 'Ce n'est pas seulement la Suisse protestante que Jacques Chessex nous dépeint dans ces instantanés. On dirait que son regard embrasse cette fois une humanité plus vaste.'[18]

One of the reasons why Chessex feels a particular debt towards Ramuz is that the latter also attempts to open his works to this universal dimension. Ramuz showed the way for subsequent Swiss writers, and he is described by Chessex as 'quelqu'un ... qui nous ouvrait la voie à la littérature universelle' (Bevan, 58). Ramuz représents a strain of Swiss literature that breaks out of provincialism and seeks to deal with wider issues, and it is precisely to this strain that Chessex also belongs. It is not just the French part of his inspiration that leads him to look beyond national boundaries, but his Swiss heritage too. Even that peculiarly Swiss and Vaudois element of his background that is represented by a particular type of Calvinism is an incentive to break out from a purely local mould. Chessex makes it clear that the Calvinism described in his writing is typical of a certain part of Switzerland, yet the very questions it obliges him to ask are ones of universal concern. By forcing him to consider issues of life and death, good and evil, servitude and freedom, questions of man's destiny and the presence or absence of God in human affairs, it helps him to join a French metaphysical tradition that approaches the same questions from a different (usually atheist) perspective. These two traditions join to raise Chessex's texts above national boundaries into the realm of the universal.

Chessex himself knows that it is precisely these questions of universal significance in his Vaudois background that are the inspiration for his texts. 'Je suis Vaudois, c'est une fibre naturellement profonde et métaphysicienne,' he says. Then, listing the elements of that 'fibre' that are of particular importance to him, he talks of 'un sentiment profond de la mort ... la pente vers la destruction de soi ... une façon de réfléchir sur l'extraordinaire ampleur de l'autre vie' (Garcin, 15). By being Vaudois and seeking inspiration in that fact, Chessex is affirming his texts as supranational in their scope.

The text as Chessex creates it combines two different literary traditions and consists of narratives or poems concerned with matters of import to all mankind. The text thus becomes a principle of unity that blends two distinct national forces in order to create a third one that goes beyond national boundaries. But the text is a unifying principle for another reason, too: by its very nature it imposes order. This is particularly true of the poem, and in 'Jeûne du livre' the poem is described as a means of fixing the disorder of existence, its fugitive impressions and disparate experiences. It stands against emptiness and destruction, and: 'Ainsi la détresse même ne peut rien / Quand le Livre vénéré parle / Contre l'incohérent' (*Le Jeûne*, 82). The text is seen as a principle of stability in an existence threatened by contradictions and apparent opposites. Hence, says Chessex, the poetry of Voisard is an expression of 'son horreur du précaire, sa certitude de surveiller ce qui se détruit à notre insu et d'incarner nos propres vies dans des poèmes.'[19]

In the writer's own life, the act of writing brings order, and the best illustration of this point may be found in the life of Alexandre Dumur. This writer's existence is one of order, devoted to literary creation, until Louis enters it. Louis is represented as the devil, a principle of disorder who disrupts Alexandre's attempts to write and makes his life degenerate into chaos. When he does try to restore order, it is by devoting himself again to his writing, and by fixing for himself a set routine of literary creation. The book he is writing now begins to take shape, and he says: 'Mon livre se corsait d'autant mieux que je demeurais isolé de mes coupables va-et-vient' (*Les Yeux*, 135). As his attention to his text increases, so does the calm in his life, but when his attention flags, the disorder takes over again. The book that he finally produces is rejected by his publisher as an inferior product – one that has not imposed the necessary order on chaos. It is interesting to note that Anne, too, is a principle of order in his life, but only as long as she encourages his literary activity. 'En quinze ans elle m'a aidé à écrire mes livres en organisant cette paix un peu particulière,' he says (31). But, once she joins Louis against Alexandre and abandons her support of his writing, Anne becomes a principle of disorder, too.

Chessex's own experience as he describes it would seem to support this view of literature as order. He claims that at a time when his own life was becoming more and more disorderly, he clung to literature and literary creation as a principle of stability. This was the time when, under the influence of Paulhan and Ponge, he was producing texts of extreme concision in which he sought to impose a rigorous and precise style. He comments: 'Plus ma vie était désordonnée et plus j'étais tenté d'écrire un récit neigeux, tendu, ivre de correction et de rigueur' (*Carabas*, 38).

The reader, too, may experience literature as stability. The language of a literary text, the language that confronts the reader on the page, sets down the disorder and dichotomies of experience in a more orderly form. This is particularly the case of poetry, in which the form imposed by language is somewhat more tightly governed. This is why, according to Chessex, the best novels and prose writing are almost a form of poetry, since their style is practically as rigorous as that of poetry. Cingria, in his prose works, is still a poet because of the importance he attaches to style and the careful use of language.

The same is true, Chessex argues, of Ramuz, Proust, and Rabelais. The works of such writers restructure the chaos and diversity of human experience and achieve what Chessex calls 'l'apothéose connaissance = conquête = poésie = prose, une assumation et une récupération totale du monde' (*Cingria*, 74). Such writers use language as a principle of unity. They show, like Louis Matthey, 'cette obsession du language, et sa seule foi irréductible: au commencement était le Verbe' (*Saintes*, 54).

The literary text is, then, seen as a form of unity because of its ability to seize and combine the disparate elements of life. It orders in a single form the apparent opposites that compose it. It is this unity that Chessex seeks to achieve in his texts, and speaking of some of his short stories, Jérôme Garcin says: 'Ce qui fait que les nouvelles du *Séjour des morts* sont des oeuvres d'art et non pas des théorèmes, c'est précisément qu'il y a une zone absolument indistincte où les choses se brouillent ... et ... vibrent au-dessus d'une tombe comme un chant qui n'est pas explicable' (Garcin, 61). The unity that Garcin senses in these tales is due to the way they show the presence of life in death, present characters in whom life and death coexist, and talk of the penetration of two aspects of existence that are generally considered irreconcilable – and it is all done in stylish, rigorous prose. This is not a *logical* vision, one that follows clear categories, and it is probably this irrational combination of logical opposites in the text to which Chessex refers when he rejects clear-cut distinctions and easy definitions in literature. 'J'appartiens essentiellement à une pensée illogique,' he says. 'Je ne peux pas souffrir la définition parce qu'elle est justement un arrêt, une privation' (Garcin, 64).

One of the reasons Chessex admires Cingria is that the latter ignored the usual distinctions between opposites, and revealed in his texts the unity that lies at the heart of experience, and that all great texts capture: 'Unité du monde, unité de la croyance, unité de la parole et de la voix' (*Cingria*, 77). Ponge, too, in his will to simplify and reduce, displays the same 'nostalgie de l'unité profonde du monde' (*Maupassant*, 167). Pierre Oster, by celebrating in his poetry the rhythm of the seasons, the identity of the past and the present, conveys 'l'unité dans l'instant coéternel et souverain.'[20] It is above all the poet among writers who seeks unity, and Chessex takes as a badge of glory the accusation made against the poet that he reports in *Portrait des Vaudois*: 'Cochon et ange! Les pieds dans l'auge et la tête dans les nuages, hé poète, méli-mélo, tu confonds tout, tu t'embrouilles' (15). Always a poet, even in his prose works, Chessex too builds a basic unity in his writing, and in the words of one admirer, 'il accumule de texte en texte, un large constat de réalités vues, sues, devinées et pour finir reliées les unes aux autres pan par pan.'[21]

This is, as I pointed out in chapter 1, a rather logocentric view of the text. It pictures the author as a unifying presence at the centre of the text, using language to spin a web that unites various strands into a more or less meaningful whole. The objections that may be made to this conception of the text have already been raised, and they need not be repeated. What is more important from our standpoint is the relationship of this view to Chessex's Calvinist background. It is easy to detect in his idea of the text as order and unity the same desire for rigour that we have observed in his attitude to religion. He is attempting to replace the strong central authority and organizing influence of Calvinism by the text, to substitute one logocentric view for another. For this reason, one may say that he often has a 'religious' attitude towards his writing. The remark quoted above, referring to the language of literature as 'le Verbe,' has obvious religious connotations, as does the title of such works as *Les Saintes Ecritures*, which is a collection of articles on literature, and *Bréviaire*. There is a kind of religious awe at times in Chessex's approach to literature, and one might say of him, as he has said of Cingria, 'il entre en littérature avec humilité et gravité, comme on entre dans les ordres' (*Cingria*, 36–7). Literature is seen by Chessex as a reflection of a lost Paradise, an attempt to recapture the original unity and undivided harmony of being when the primordial Word made all things. His description of Matthey's poetry shows his own longing for a unity that may be glimpsed in the text. He says that Matthey's writing is 'immédiatement assimilable au paradis perdu, au jardin bienheureux où tout accord, tout équilibre portent l'être. Le lieu de l'unité, de l'amour enfin sans partage' (*Saintes*, 51). The text, one might say, becomes a substitute for the rigorous unity imposed on life by Calvinism.

The unity of which Chessex speaks is also similar to religious experience in that it defies rational thought and logical boundaries, and it is sensed rather than intellectually presented. The text as he sees it attempts to provoke in the reader an experience that is not logical (and it is, therefore, in contrast to such 'intellectual' literature as the *nouveau roman*). It brings together apparent opposites and it encourages the reader to experience them simultaneously as two aspects of the same reality. His writing affirms, for example, attachment to life while describing the ever-present threat of death; it shows the struggle between good and evil, light and dark; it examines the attempt to achieve freedom while expressing nostalgia for protection and order. The text is the battleground of warring forces, but also the place in which they are brought together and meet. The reader sees and experiences, in the same text, the dual aspect of life. Each element of life as it is shown in the text depends on its opposite for existence, and it is defined by its opposite. We cannot, for example, understand the struggle to affirm life in these texts without experiencing through them the threat of death. The reader is thus obliged to take account of both sides of the equation while reading. The critic's words concerning *L'Ogre* are true of all of Chessex's texts: 'Dans cette perspective, il n'y aurait pas dans *L'Ogre* ... une relation d'opposition véritable entre le monde de la lumière et celui de la noirceur, mais plutôt une sorte d'interdépendance.'[22] What is being described here is an essentially religious experience, because it has to be lived as the text is read, and it cannot be explained logically, any more than one can explain the Christian idea of a God who is three-in-one, or a Saviour who dies yet lives. The reader, like the believer, has to experience these mysteries for himself or herself.

These paradoxical truths are sometimes conveyed in symbolic form. The unity of opposites is expressed in symbols that may be experienced on a nonrational, nonlogical level. There are certain symbolic presences in Chessex's work that unite in their one presence two apparently opposite and opposed sides of life. Nature, for example, is an ever-present background to the lives of Chessex's characters that conveys a wealth of disparate elements. It is sin and the devil, but also a possible source of salvation; it is death and cruelty, but also a place where the life-forces may be found; it is a source of danger and a threat to the individual, but also a cause of delight and intense pleasure. Woman is another such presence, combining sin and salvation, life and death. Even certain animals, like the fox and the mythical marine monster, are polyvalent symbols of similar opposites.

But it is most of all in the lives of the main characters in Chessex's fiction that the reader experiences the combination of opposites. He lives with Jean Calmet the exhilaration of freedom represented by Thérèse and the fear of death and repression represented by his father. The reader experiences Alexandre Dumur's lapse into chaos and death while sharing his search for stability and salvation. We know through Jean Burg the attractions of a jealous God, while also knowing how Burg lives religion as love and freedom when he meets Geneviève. We sense Mange's love of life and of Monna while also feeling his subservience to 'les justes' and an oppressive morality. These things are felt as divisions within a character, but they are also lived as essential and interdependent elements of that character's experience of life itself, and they are lived simultaneously and in the same text.

This experience depends, of course, on the reader's acceptance of literary characters as, in some way, representations or images of 'real' people. There is no point treating literary characters as the nexus of a series of linguistic signs if one is to appreciate the unity that they convey in Chessex's writing. The reader has to identify with Jean Calmet, Alexandre, Burg, and the others and to experience imaginatively the emotions and fears that Chessex describes as theirs. The reader has, as it were, to 'become' these 'people' for the duration of his reading. *Then* the reader will know how one can live and combine in one's existence a whole series of opposing forces.

Beyond the lives of characters, uniting symbols, and explicit expression of the unity in division, the text itself is the final meeting place and ground of unity. It is in the text that the reader encounters the characters and the symbols; it is the text that combines two national literary traditions; it is through the textual expression of characters, symbols, and intertextual presences that Chessex convinces the reader of the primordial unity of existence. But in order to experience this unity, the reader must accept and *live* the text on Chessex's terms. One has to be prepared to treat the text as language in the process of grasping a reality exterior to itself, and literary characters as 'real' people whose lives one may share. On these terms, the text is the most satisfying means of acceding to the unity that is so often absent from life as Chessex sees it.

11

The Text, the World, and Others

Jacques Chessex is a writer for whom the outside world exists in no uncertain manner. He is intensely aware of the physical presence of objects, details of everyday life, scenery and weather, and he tries to capture and convey this presence in his texts. He frequently displays for the reader the various features of the physical reality that surrounds his characters or that is the background of his poems and essays. His is what has been described as 'cette écriture au ras des choses, au niveau des phénomènes,' and this produces texts in which 'les choses jaillissent constamment sous ses yeux.'[1] He himself says 'j'écris ce que je vois,' and he argues that his goal is the same as Joyce's and Steinbeck's: to depict the universal by starting with the particular; to show specific individuals in their context in order to depict mankind (Jotterand, 38).

This goal is not easily achieved. Chessex is aware that language is not always able to grasp the world and convey it to others. But he does not treat language as a totally closed system that is entirely apart from any reality exterior to itself. He does attempt, therefore, to use language to come to grips with the world around him.

It is not our purpose here to analyse in detail how Chessex shows the outside world or how his 'realism' works. Mention must be made rather briefly, however, of some features of his depiction of the exterior reality. The most obvious aspect is, of course, his many descriptions of nature: the mountains, lakes, streams, meadows, and forests of the Vaud that appear in several novels and short stories, in certain poems, and in the descriptive passages of such works as *Portrait des Vaudois*, *Bréviaire* and *Reste avec nous*. Equally prominent are the descriptions of city streets and buildings in most of the novels. We see the school in which Jean Calmet works and the streets and cafés that surround it and the cathedral; the dark streets and garish lights of the prostitutes' quarter in *Jonas* and *Les Yeux jaunes*; the churches of Fribourg in *Jonas*; the background of Ouchy in *L'Ogre*. We are shown village streets and country cafés in *L'Ardent Royaume, Judas le transparent,* and in certain passages of *Carabas* and *Portrait des Vaudois*. The peace and serenity of country cemeteries is captured in *Le Séjour des morts, Jonas,* and *L'Ogre*. We see the inside of a successful lawyer's office (*L'Ardent Royaume*), a decaying mansion and estate (*Judas le transparent*), a quiet apartment (*Jonas*), a writer's study (*Les Yeux jaunes*). We can smell the sickly-sweet odour of rotting apples beneath the trees in 'Cueillir des pommes' (*Feux d'orée*) and the unpleasant smell of an old car interior in 'L'Après-midi' (*Feux d'orée*). We feel the heat of the sun in 'Foins' (*Feux d'orée*) and the bite of the cold in *Jonas*. Small details of external reality are sometimes picked out, creating a sense of the authentic and real: the grain in the wood from which a coffin is made and the hands of the man who lies in it (*Reste*, 117); the ring on a woman's finger (*Bréviaire*, 48); the lock of grey hair that falls over the forehead of Jean Calmet's mother (*L'Ogre*, 166). These places, sensations, and details of the external world exist with a force and a presence that constantly remind the reader of the importance of the physical world. Chessex's texts are, to quote the title of an article on him, 'la célébration du réel.'[2]

Chessex's preference among other writers is generally for those whose texts try to capture and convey physical reality, and his deep love of the naturalists is due in large measure to their attempt to do this. He praises them for being, 'les écrivains du réel. Un réel traité, trituré, un réel griffé, remâché, réinterprété viscéralement et humoralement' (*Maupassant*, 10). Many of those writers whom he singles out for praise, whether they are historically part of the naturalist movement or not, are precisely those who, in his view, have conveyed the presence of the outside world. Ramuz, for example, is compared to the Russian realists because he has their 'vigueur réaliste et rêveuse' (*Saintes*, 23); Pierre-Louis Matthey is said to create images that are 'toujours extraordinairement réalistes' (*Saintes*, 47); Bouvier's poetry has a simplicity that is reinforced by his 'pouvoirs réalistes' (*Saintes*, 184); Pierre Oster's work is praised for its 'attention passionnée au réel';[3] Georges-Emmanuel Clancier's texts are described as ones in which 'le "monde réel" surgit dans sa violence et sa beauté'.[4]

and Georges-Olivier Châteaureynaud is commended for his 'sentiment aigu du réel.'[5] Other writers are praised for the way in which they capture tiny details of the outside world and use them to create a sense of the real. Alice Rivaz displays this 'réalisme méticuleux' (*Saintes*, 189). André Malraux, too, in the midst of metaphysical speculations and considerations on great men and historically important events, seizes on small details, like the cat that jumps on De Gaulle's desk while the latter is discussing matters of state.[6] Writers such as these realize that attention to the world around them gives life to the text and that 'l'art suprême, c'est de montrer la beauté du vrai' (*Maupassant*, 65).

Chessex and the realists whom he admires all display a curiosity about the world surrounding them. That world is a constant source of interest that holds their attention and compels them to represent it in their texts. They are all like Charles-Albert Cingria, of whom Chessex says: 'Charles-Albert a la flânerie active, et rien ne lui échappe d'intéressant ou d'amusant' (*Cingria*, 35). In his own case, Chessex readily admits to a curiosity for all kinds of banal and unusual things, elements of the world outside that suddenly excite his interest. In *Carabas*, he gives an extremely long list of such items of interest to him. He includes in his catalogue, 'ce qui tourne et tournoie, le chahut, le tohu-bohu, la foire pleine d'éclats, l'agglutination, la surcharge, le foisonnement, l'irrégularité et la dissymétrie, l'ornement, le bizarre, les curiosités qui coupent le souffle' (53). The list then proceeds through (among many other things) street fights, crowds, religious processions, the Church of Saint Canisius, the hotels of Montreux, treatises on heraldry, casinos, and (of course) 'le sexe ouvert, le sexe secret ourlé bestialement dans ses boucles brillantes' (53).

Chessex's texts all show an avid, almost physical, desire for those things that excite his curiosity. It is a feeling somewhat akin to that 'sens gourmand' that he discerns in Paul Budry's descriptions of the countryside (*Saintes*, 27). Hence, when he describes himself in *Carabas*, he shows an individual who looks at and experiences the world in terms of appetite and desire to consume. He writes of 'le nez flaireur, les papilles exigeantes, la salive vite excitée. La curiosité forcenée' (62). He says that, when he writes about the world, he attempts to capture the fact that he experiences that world principally through the senses: 'Le museau hume, la langue tâte, la peau explore, la mémoire s'emplit, l'oeil n'oubliera plus ces figures, l'oreille la rumeur et le ton' (113).

By using the senses, Chessex tries to know reality and to put it in the text. His goal is 'connaître le poids des choses et des êtres.'[7] The text is used as a means of encompassing and appropriating reality, a way of fixing a world that is otherwise unstable, shifting, and threatened by death. It is this attempt to encompass and appropriate that he admires in Ponge's work, and he could be commenting on his own goals when he writes: 'Ponge veut désespérément, éperdument, connaître en exprimant' (*Maupassant*, 165).

Although all the senses are used in trying to grasp the world, it is mainly through the eyes that the process takes place. The visual quality of Chessex's texts strikes the reader forcefully, and it may be seen particularly in his descriptions of nature. 'Son regard prétend s'emparer de tout, plonger dans les profondeurs des êtres comme des choses,' writes Marianne Ghirelli.[8] Speaking of his methods of writing, Chessex emphasizes the importance that he attaches to observing and seizing on things with the eyes. He mentions his surprise on discovering that a writer of his acquaintance notes down everything that attracts his attention, and uses the notes when constructing his texts. His own method is different: 'Je note peu: je regarde.'[9] In this respect, Chessex is like Maître Mange, who looks at everything with intensely avid eyes, focusing on the details that particularly attract him: 'Il les buvait, les mangeait des yeux, les reprenait, les décrivait dans sa mémoire' (*Ardent*, 114). One of the many things that Chessex enjoys in Maupassant's work is this ability to see and to appreciate visually: 'Guy de Maupassant ... scrute, il retient, il écrit à chaud. La plume suit aussitôt le regard' (*Maupassant*, 20). The fact that Zola was a keen amateur photographer underlines, in Chessex's opinion, that his too was a visual imagination that used the eyes to capture the world for the text (*Maupassant*, 56–65).

Of course, the outside world is not composed just of things: it also contains other people. The curiosity that Chessex displays is naturally extended to the people who inhabit the world around him. In *Bréviaire*, he depicts himself walking at night in a darkened city, looking at lighted windows behind which shadowy figures move. He is possessed by a yearning to know who these figures are, what they are doing, and what kind of lives they live. Filled with a sense of what he calls the 'inépuisable secret des autres' (37), he decides that he must devote himself to discovering that secret. His goal will be 'adorer, célébrer leurs pentes, leurs cavernes, ne jamais perdre cette source, même si la boue menace, l'ordure' (37–8).

This same curiosity and desire to know others is projected into several characters. Jonas tries to read Anne-Marie's mind; Raphaël Turner wonders what drives Aschenbach to his extremes of religious fanaticism; Alexandre Dumur is tortured by the desire to know what dark thoughts lie behind Louis' yellow eyes. The narrator of *Morgane Madrigal* looks at Morgane, possessed by 'faim sans fin de son émanation, de sa couleur, de sa peau, de son souffle' (168). Most of all, Maître Mange is obsessed by an inexhaustible curiosity about others. When he sits in a restaurant, he speculates about the lives of the other customers; when he enters a hotel room, he immediately wonders who slept there before him; when he watches his wife, he tries to see behind her inexpressive features. Monna excites his most intense curiosity, and he tells her: 'Je voudrais te déchiffrer, Monna. Voir en toi comme en pleine lumière. Ton corps, ton coeur, tes hantises, tes peurs, tes désirs, tes rêves' (*Ardent*, 76–7). For Mange, others are a kind of unexplored land, and he is the explorer. 'Le secret des autres, quel voyage!' he exclaims (25).

Here, too, the eyes become a privileged way of knowing and appropriating. Like Roger Judrin in his novels, Chessex is 'un spectateur passionné, un indolent gourmand de l'esprit et du corps des autres.'[10] Many of his characters also watch others avidly and attempt to possess them in this way. The narrator of 'Secret des collines' comes daily to his hiding place in the hills to watch a woman sun bathing, saying: 'Je détaille, je caresse avec mes yeux, j'entre partout, je mange tout, j'explore, je reviens, je ressors' (*Où*, 113). The main character of 'La Femme cernée' (*Où*, 30–6) comes regularly to a particular restaurant in order to watch a woman customer and to speculate on the causes of her tired air and the black marks under her eyes. Dr Feld in 'Sur toutes les coutures' (*Où*, 159–63) makes all his women patients undress so that he can examine them. The narrator of *Morgane Madrigal* observes Morgane's body just as avidly, using it as a kind of starting point for his imagination and reveries about mandalas, mythical quests, and the source of art. When Morgane first offers to expose herself to him, it is because she knows he has need of this visual stimulus, that his need is 'de partir d'une image précise' (16).

As one might expect, it is Mange who provides the best example of this attempt to possess by looking. He first encounters Monna when he hires her to pose in the nude in a small apartment that he rents for this purpose. At first, he wants merely to look at her, to absorb her beauty, to itemize every aspect of her body, but also to see beyond that body. He tells her that his goal is 'vous observer, vous détailler, vous recomposer. Voir en vous, regarder vos pensées et votre désir, vous traverser, revenir, repartir, revenir encore, tout savoir de vous' (*Ardent*, 59). Even when he becomes her lover, he still uses his eyes as a means of knowing and possessing her. He observes her carefully, while a voice in him says: 'N'échappe pas, corps ... ne fuis pas, vision, éclaire, demeure, appartiens à mon regard' (101).

The desire to know others by watching them, to learn their darkest urges by watching these urges at work, degenerates easily into voyeurism. To watch others as they act out their fantasies is to know something of their fantasies and of parts of their psyche that are not usually accessible. Alexandre watches Louis eagerly for signs of the boy's growing desire for Anne, notices how he touches her and seems to prowl around her. His keenest pleasure, however, is to imagine them making love. He later takes a hotel room next to Anne's so that he can hear her making love to another man. Assuming Louis feels the same curiosity, he makes a hole in their bedroom wall so that Louis can spy on him and Anne. Anne, Louis, and her lover regularly engage in other games of voyeurism. Benjamin pushes his wife into the arms of Benoît so that he can lie in a nearby room imagining their lovemaking. Meanwhile, the pleasure felt by Benoît and Sarah is made more intense as they imagine him thinking of them. Maître Mange lies awake in his hotel room listening to the couple in the next room making love, and he pores avidly over a set of obscene photographs taken by one of his clients, watching at the same time how these images disturb his secretary as she looks at them. In *Judas le transparent*, Turner's two sons make Johanna undress and parade before them in their mother's clothes. As they attempt to possess her by watching her, their father spies on them through a hole in the wall that he refers to as 'un judas pour Judas' (36).

This complex play of looks, as characters spy on characters who watch other characters, is further complicated by the fact that the writer, too, is a voyeur who spies on the desires of the characters that he creates, and who tries to possess by watching. But the reader also has a role in this process. Since Robbe-Grillet's *Le Voyeur*, we have become accustomed to the idea of the reader as voyeur, as someone who looks over the writer's shoulder at the activities of his characters. At the same time, in so far as these characters are emanations of the writer, the reader spies on the latter's desires, too. In many cases, he may even be looking at exteriorizations of his own desires.

There is a whole series of attempts by reader, writer, and characters, in texts like *Judas le transparent* and *Les Yeux jaunes*, to seize on and possess one another by looking. The text becomes a means of knowing others and of possessing them.

The possession of others, whether they consent or not, is fundamentally an act of violence. There is frequently more than a hint of violence in Chessex's depiction of the attempt to take over others by looking at them. He readily admits to having a cruel streak in his nature, and he has said that '[la violence] est ma matière première, ma nature, l'esprit de cette matière et de cette nature' (*Carabas*, 151).[11] We have already noted this taste for cruelty and violence in his texts, and we have seen that it is linked to the element of cruelty in a certain type of Calvinism. But it is also connected with the desire to know others, which is pushed to the point of almost devouring them. Jean Calmet's father is an ogre because, like several other characters, he wants to know, possess, and control those around him. Chessex's novels show, as Robert Kanters points out, that 'la curiosité des autres êtres vivants peut nous conduire à les tyranniser, à les soumettre, à les dévorer.'[12]

This liking for texts that exemplify the desire to seize others, texts that are themselves attempts to assimilate reality, is part of Chessex's love of a literature of excess. He admires a literature that is violent and excessive because this is, in his view, a sign of its desire to seize on and possess reality. He sees it as a literature that expresses life and vitality, that affirms its power to dominate. He admires Flaubert and Maupassant because their works display 'ces grosses vigueurs troubles, précises, hargneuses, gourmandes, volontaires, tendues' (*Carabas*, 127). He claims that one can feel the physical presence of such writers, and of their taste for life, in the texts that they produced. The very violence of their writing makes the reality that they attempt to encompass seem more palpable, for 'le réel n'est jamais si dru que lorsqu'il est passé par les extases, les violences, les hallucinations des réalistes' (*Carabas*, 130). It is this excess that he would like to emulate: 'Et c'est bien cette sauvagerie que je voudrais faire passer dans mes livres' (*Carabas*, 131). As we have seen in an earlier chapter, Chessex does indeed convey some of the violence and lust for life that he admires in the naturalists.

And yet, despite the extraordinary strength of this desire to know the world and to know others, it is often a frustrated desire. The text is used as a means of knowing physical reality, and it demonstrates the desire to know and to possess others, but it does not produce entirely satisfactory results in either of these enterprises. Both the world of things and the individuals who inhabit it resist the will to assimilate them.

Although Chessex's texts show a continual desire to know others, to probe the human mind in all its unpleasant depths, to look at and assimilate other beings, they often do no more than illustrate the failure of this desire. Chessex is forced to conclude: 'Il y a une abominable distance entre les êtres' (Garcin, 55). This is also the conclusion that Mange reaches. He never fully knows Monna, and although he questions her minutely about her past, he is left feeling that this part of her, in which he played no role, forever escapes him. Her liaison with a drug seller, the latter's blackmail of her, her abandonment of Mange, are all things that cannot be understood or anticipated. He can never foresee 'l'insupportable secret des autres' (*Ardent*, 53), and even his wife, with whom he has lived for many years, remains an enigma to him, a bland and opaque exterior beyond which he cannot penetrate. The physical beauty of both his wife and Monna cannot be possessed, and it seems to reject his curious gaze. This beauty is 'splendeur éclatée, ou brouillée, ou détruite, ou simplement inatteignable à tout jamais comme les furieux mystères de chaque être' (47). Mange is forced to conclude: 'Sonder les coeurs et les reins, quelle duperie!' (25). Chessex draws the same conclusion in one of his poems, entitled, significantly, 'Impénétrable': 'Nous sommes des opacités les uns pour les autres' (*Elégie*, 41).

Other characters likewise fail to know the women who fascinate them. Jonas Carex does not anticipate that Anne-Marie is pregnant with his child, and he cannot understand, when he learns of this many years later, why she did not tell him. Turner's sons, obsessed by Aschenbach's daughters, never really understand what motivates them, and they do not anticipate Johanna's attempt to blind herself. Jean Calmet does not foresee Thérèse's abandonment of him for one of his pupils, and his jealousy blinds him to his own part in the process. Alexandre Dumur is totally incapable of communicating with Louis, of foreseeing his unpleasant tricks, or of warding off the disaster that they provoke. Benoît is startled to learn of Sarah's suicide, and concludes that 'l'âme se dérobe, change pour ne pas se livrer, ment et se ment, fuit dans ses repaires, pour finir meurt à ce monde sans que l'amant du monde ait jamais pu la connaître, ou même la voir' (*La Trinité*, 256).

It is not surprising that for most of these characters, who are males, it is women who excite the most curiosity. Woman is seen as the other, the most different and difficult to know of beings. Henri-Dominique Paratte points out that, for these characters, 'la femme, si belle soit elle, reste insondable de mystère.'[13] It is because she is so different that Mange cannot know Monna, that Alexandre misjudges Anne, that Burg is unable to see Geneviève will command his love and that Benoît cannot anticipate Sarah's suicide. The difficulty of knowing *any* other human is compounded by the fact that Chessex's characters try to know exactly the most unknowable of humans: those of the opposite sex. In this context, Monna's name is symbolic, recalling as it does Leonardo's Mona Lisa, the embodiment of the enigmatically feminine, the figure whose mysterious smile has always fascinated and baffled those who look at her.

The unknowability of others is expressed in terms of the psychological gulf between individuals, particularly those of opposite sexes. Other people are seen as being opaque because it is impossible to judge them from the outside, to see into their motives and inner drives. Chessex never expresses this gulf in terms of the inability of individuals to communicate because language itself fails as a medium of communication. The text is unable to seize others because others are by nature unknowable, not because language is unable to grasp them as something outside language. When he comes to describe the attempt to depict the objects of physical reality, however, he seems more aware that the problem lies at least partly in language itself.

Chessex is acutely aware that the physical world resists his attempts to assimilate it, and he writes of 'la résistance du réel aux ruses et aux pouvoirs de l'écrivain' (*Maupassant*, 131). Even Flaubert, Zola, and Maupassant had moments when they realized that their projects were not always successful, and that the complexity of the real world cannot invariably be grasped in words: 'Tous ces écrivains savent qu'ils sont perdants, que le monde aura raison de leur écriture et de leur mal' (*Maupassant*, 132). A modern writer like Le Clézio, who tries in somewhat different ways to exhaust reality by describing it, meets the same failure. His text *La Fièvre* shows starkly that words are frequently unable to come to grips with a reality that is alien to language: 'D'un côté des hommes s'acharnent à cerner des objets, à les comprendre, à les nommer, procès-verbal épuisant et forcené – de l'autre ce monde qui se refuse, qui relègue ces hagards dans leur irréductible étrangeté.'[14]

Chessex knows that the modern writer is more aware of the limits of words than the great nineteenth-century masters who set out confidently to capture 'reality' in their novels. One can no longer write as Zola did or show his confidence in words. The modern sensibility is represented by Ponge, who seeks to refine and reduce language to its barest essentials in order to find exactly the right words to grasp the world. Ponge carries on a twofold struggle: against the resistance of language to his manipulation of it, and against a reality that resists his attempts to possess it in words. The result is 'l'objet, ni le langage, ne se sont laissé prendre. L'objet est victorieux. Assassin du poème, parce qu'assassin du langage auquel il s'est constamment dérobé' (*Maupassant*, 166).[15]

In the face of this failure, Ponge turns away from the attempt to capture the world in words, and begins to write instead about that attempt itself. He describes his failures, and this very account becomes 'son dernier recours contre l'absurde et cette dérobade perpétuelle de l'objet et du langage' (*Maupassant*, 166). Strangely, the chronicle of failure becomes his only victory; the struggle becomes as important as any question of winning or losing. Chessex quotes approvingly Camus' words: 'La joie absurde par excellence, c'est la création' and he adds, 'conquérant, luttant, Ponge trouve sa dignité d'homme; sa méticulosité, son acharnement à rejeter les paroles abîmées par tant de lèvres, et la fureur qui le porte, lui assurent une victoire étrange, mais particulièrement précieuse' (*Maupassant*, 167).

Chessex is obviously aware that language does not always succeed in grasping a reality that is nonlinguistic. He sees that writers like Ponge cannot assimilate in their texts physical reality and the objects that are part of it because language is often unable to do this. But he does not believe that this is an invariable property of language, and that language must always fall short of the nonlinguistic world. He continues to write and to carry on the admittedly difficult task of describing the outside world, and he believes that he wins a kind of victory over language and the resistance of reality to it. His victory is somewhat different from Ponge's, which is achieved in an indirect manner by writing about the difficulties that he cannot otherwise overcome. Chessex is much less given to agonizing analyses and to writing about language. As we have noted, despite the influence of Ponge and of a particular sparse and unadorned style on Chessex, his natural exuberance and love of language come to the fore in the end. His is a much more spontaneous and vigorous attitude to the world and to language, one that naturally tries to come to grips with external reality and to assimilate it in words. He is aware that this attempt does not succeed fully; he is aware of the limits of language; he does to some extent write about these problems. However, his way is to continue to write, to carry on the struggle by direct contact with the world, whatever failures he may encounter. In many ways, Chessex is closer to Camus' Sisyphus than Ponge is. The quotation from Camus that he applies to Ponge is more appropriate to his own attitude of direct, tireless confrontation with the absurdity of the world and of language

Chessex feels unable to give up this struggle and to admit defeat, or even to seek an indirect Pongian victory, because his appetite for the world and for words dominates his awareness of possible defeat. He has a deep-seated urge to write, a need that has to be expressed. This is something as basic as a sexual urge, and he has described it as 'un besoin profond. Une nécéssité' (Garcin, 9). His lines about the meaning of poetry for him are true of all his texts: 'Tu es ma vraie fiancée / Mon églantier frais dans l'orage / Où je m'avance à ta recherche' (Chant, 38).

In any case, despite the failures inherent in most attempts to capture things in words, language, in Chessex's view, is not totally without some effect on reality. Although it may have difficulty encompassing the real, it can change it, and even create a new reality. By writing about the Vaud and his idea of it, he helps create that region. He and other Vaudois writers have contributed to the creation of an identity for an area that did not exist in quite the same way before. Chappaz has done the same for the Valais, and Voisard for the Jura (Saintes, 207–15; 197–202). Indeed, the writers of French Switzerland as a whole have brought into being, through their texts, a linguistic and cultural identity for that region: 'Ils ont transformé la Suisse Romande en inventant une écriture, une nouvelle manière de lire.'[16] The reader of their texts forms an idea of these areas from what he or she reads, and Chessex has been read widely enough in his own land for that land to have been changed by what he has written. He has, at the same time, influenced the outsider's perception of Switzerland and the Vaud.

In the same way, by writing about his father, Chessex has kept his father alive and has become, as it were, the creator of his father. Indeed, all the memories that the writer perpetuates in the text are to some extent created by him. Because these memories and images exist in the text, the reader perceives them and they become part of a new reality.

But the text's influence is not limited to the world of objects and of other individuals: it also has power over the writer. The text consists of words, and the writer is the one who creates the words. Language cannot exist without the individual who creates it. At the same time, the creator of words cannot exist without these words. He or she comes into being as a speaker and a writer when words are uttered and written down. As Philippe Sollers has written: 'En effet, il n'y a pas de sujet en soi ... puisque le sujet est la *conséquence* de son langage.'[17] Ironically (in view of his attacks on the Tel Quel group), Chessex would surely agree with this. In fact, he cites Flaubert as an excellent example of this process, pointing out that, when Flaubert tries to describe in words a world that he senses as chaotic and ephemeral, he is creating *himself* in those words: 'Flaubert n'existe que par le travail qu'il fait subir au magma voué au néant qu'on nomme le monde' (*Flaubert*, 122). The words that the writer creates, the words that express his inspiration, act on him as much as they do on the identity of his text. Chessex says of the poet: 'Le poète travaille sous l'empire du puissant souffle / Travaille? Est travaillé?' (*Le Jeûne*, 72).

The text has an especially lasting effect on a writer like Chessex because he has always used it as a means of explaining himself. He makes no secret of the fact that he is the subject of much of what he has written, and that his texts are very personal in nature. He uses the text as an instrument to reveal himself to himself, and *Carabas* in particular represents an effort to delve into himself. The text might be compared to wine, which Chessex also regards as a means of looking into himself and of releasing what is hidden there. Substitute the word *texte* for *vin* in the following quotation, and one has an excellent expression of what the text means to him: 'Le vin m'a rapproché de moi, je me suis admis, compris, pour une bonne part connu en lui' (22).

While examining himself, the writer creates himself in the text. Chessex's writing has evolved over the years from the simple, ascetic prose of *La Tête ouverte* and *La Confession du pasteur Burg* to the luxuriance of *Carabas*, and as he has sought himself in these works, so he has created different images of himself. He has changed as his texts have changed, has *been* changed by his texts: 'Vous voyez, les livres nous font, mes livres me changent, je n'ai jamais écrit une ligne qui n'ait eu sur moi la plus immédiate influence' (*Carabas*, 11). Each of Chessex's texts has created an image of him that is faithful to *that* text, and he is, in a sense, the product of each text. As he tells Jérôme Garcin: 'Je suis le fils de mes livres. A tout instant, dans cette expérience difficile, je change vers moi-même, je deviens ma plus vraie nature, mon plus vrai sens' (Garcin, 164).

By creating himself in his texts and then presenting the text to the public, the writer makes a gift of himself to the reader. Commenting on this process, Chessex addresses himself as a reader might speak to him: 'C'est qu'avec vous la plume va vite à son gré, vous allez, vous revenez, votre grâce est de nous donner ce qui parle, ce qui respire en vous exactement comme vous le trouvez.'[18] This is an unrestricted gift of all that a writer like Chessex chooses to reveal. 'Dans l'aventure on joue *toute* son existence,' he says (Garcin, 11; italics in original.) Chessex has never attempted to write *just* for his own satisfaction, or to create a literature for the restricted 'happy few.' He has always insisted that he likes success and wants to be read by the greatest number of people possible. He does not seek solitude, and he wonders: 'Comment être seul? J'écris pour des amis, pour une foule' (*Carabas*, 235). He makes a gift of himself to as many as are willing to accept the gift.

Maître Mange's failure to know Monna teaches us that it is impossible to grasp and to know fully another individual. Yet some form of communication is possible through the text. The writer offers himself or herself in a process that is a form of greeting. When he writes, he says: 'Bonjour. Je vous fais cadeau de ma journée. Ou je vous donne quelques rêveries. Un petit lot d'imaginations.'[19] It is the writer's way of holding out a hand to the reader in an effort to communicate through the gift of himself, his dreams and words. The text is offered as a means of bridging the gap between reader and writer, and, for Chessex, 'le poème ou le roman a besoin d'être en communication avec la comédie humaine, il a besoin de devenir regard, chair, sang ou larmes chez des milliers d'autres lecteurs' (Garcin, 103). It is up to the reader whether he accepts this gift. We are dealing here with a nonviolent offering that may be accepted or refused, and it is far from the violent effort to seize, assimilate, and impose that many of Chessex's characters make, and that he himself seems often to attempt. If the reader does accept, then, says Chessex, 'à ce moment-là, l'"hypocrite lecteur, mon semblable, mom frère" devient mon double.' (Garcin, 103).

The text does not succeed in completely assimilating the outside world and imposing stability on it. At the same time, it reveals the impossibility of ever possessing or fully knowing other individuals. Yet it achieves, in Chessex's view, a limited success in affecting reality and in enabling communication with the reader. In his attitude towards the text, with its emphasis on the need to accept partial success, Chessex seems finally to have escaped that Calvinist extremism that demands all or nothing.

12

Death, Memory, and the Text

A recurring theme in Chessex's fiction, poetry, and critical writing is the importance of the past and of memories of earlier times. The main characters in his fiction, for example, spend much of their time reliving their past. Jean Calmet remembers his childhood and the role of his father during that childhood. Indeed, his life as an adult is still governed by the influence of his father's actions at that time. Alexandre Dumur thinks constantly of his dead parents and of his childhood, and Jean Burg remembers those elements of his earlier years that led him to become a Calvinist minister. These characters are all influenced by their Calvinist upbringing, and that upbringing continues in many ways to dictate their adult lives.

Jonas Carex is, of such characters, the one most strongly held by his past. His return to Fribourg is in many ways an attempt to recapture a particularly important part of his youth. When he meets Anne-Marie again, he discovers a whole portion of his earlier life, and he attempts to live that time again. As he moves around Fribourg with Anne-Marie, their words to each other, their rediscovery of certain parts of the city, all vividly recall events from a time when he was younger and happier. During his return to Fribourg, he finds what he calls 'l'origine dont j'avais été privé tant d'années' (*Jonas*, 104). Suddenly, he feels that 'le temps n'est pas. Trois fois dix ans n'existent plus' (115). It takes only the sound of vespers bells for him to remember intact the words of the services that he once attended every day. The sea monster that he continually evokes may be seen as symbolic of this past that now begins to swallow and protect him. This is particularly suggested in the passage in which he calls himself

'Mémoire-Jonas avalée par les années, ensevelie dans le ventre de l'énorme temps' (210).

Only Maître Mange among the other characters relives his earlier years so intensely as Jonas. His most resistant recollections are those of his daughter when she was a child, but he also relives moments of his past that concern his marriage, and he has only to look at paintings in a gallery or images in a book for memories of other incidents to come to his mind. He is fascinated by this process, and he is led to exclaim: 'Que les êtres ont de ressources au fond de leur mémoire' (*Ardent*, 89).

Much of Chessex's poetry is also the product of memory. The poems of *Le Jour proche* are particularly full of reminiscences of loved ones. 'Ecoute cette voix monter de ta mémoire' (34) the poet tells himself as the wind, the sun and the hills bring back the faces of those he once knew. Throughout this volume, to use the poet's own words, 'je reprends sans cesse le chemin de mes visages' (49). *Une Voix la nuit*, as the title suggests, is another such volume of poems in which the poet listens to voices, among them being those of his past and his deceased friends and companions. *Reste avec nous* likewise constitutes an attempt to make old times remain in poems and passages of prose that remember loved ones and the history of a land that is also loved.

Many passages in works such as *Carabas* and *Portrait des Vaudois* consist of memories of Chessex's own past, and others evoke the history of a land that has formed him. The chapter in *Portrait des Vaudois* entitled 'Contes pour la nuit' is one long evocation of Chessex's earlier life, in which memories of a loved one, of his relationship with that person, and of the countryside that served as a background, are all mingled. Some of the short fiction in *Où vont mourir les oiseaux* and *Le Séjour des morts* is based on characters' reminiscences, and several passages in *Feux d'orée* recall memories associated with certain places and features of the countryside. Even the myths and biblical tales to which Chessex constantly alludes may be seen as cultural memories that form part of the collective psyche of a people to whom he belongs.

The land inhabited by that people has its role to play in the preserving of memories. It is seen as a kind of ancestor going back for generations and maintaining customs and traditions for hundreds of years. The Vaud still holds some of the distant past, and Chessex writes with obvious nostalgia: 'Et puis un pays vieillit plus lentement qu'un homme: les visages de la terre, les arbres, les maisons, les odeurs parlent longtemps des jours anciens.'[1]

But of all the memories recalled in the pages of Chessex's texts, it is those concerning his father that are the most persistent. His father's image recurs obsessively, provoking pain, nostalgia, and a resurgence of love. In *Bréviaire*, he explains that his father's shade accompanies him everywhere, and that 'l'ombre appelle, l'ombre insiste, l'ombre est debout devant la porte, l'ombre marche sur la route ... timide, audacieuse pourtant dans son insistance' (67). It is as though his father is constantly attempting to speak to him, and he writes: 'Je vois, je revois ton zèle à me rejoindre' (69). His father's image, at various stages in his life, at those moments that remain particularly in Chessex's mind, comes unbidden into his consciousness. At any moment, at any street corner, his father might appear: 'Il passe dans cette rue. Je le rencontre. Il ouvre les bras' (86). Everything in the world around him is a reminder of his father and seems to carry the dead man's presence. Places such as La Broye and Le Momont, that his father both loved and wrote about in his books on the Vaud, are forever linked to him in his son's mind. The whole countryside of the Vaud is identified with him, and Chessex addresses his memory: 'Tu es là, dans ce mur en ruines, tu es sur ce sentier, tu hantes le rosier sauvage qui penche au vent et rien ne peut faire taire ta voix' (77).

The dead live through such memories, and Chessex's father still lives in his son's texts because he is remembered in them. As he listens to the rain and remembers, the poet seems to see the dead rise from their graves: 'Mes morts se lèvent sous la pluie' (*Le Jour*, 54). It is sufficient to remember and to listen, and 'du fond du sol nous vient la voix des morts' (*Une Voix*, 14). The living and the dead commune through memory. Writing of 'cette cohue de trépassés' that we all carry within us, Chessex says: 'Vivre, c'est les retrouver, les reconnaître à chaque instant autour de soi, en soi, comme de fidèles et infatigables compagnons' (*Saintes*, 90–1).

Because memory seems to overcome death, it is often evoked in the presence of death. In *Reste avec nous*, Chessex describes a wake during which the narrator's mind turns to the past and relives moments associated with the dead man, and some that are simply from his own past, but that seem to exorcise the presence of death. A character in 'Un Moment donné' whose daughter has just been killed sits alone and remembers his child. He realizes that for him these recollections are a poor substitute for the child he has lost, and that 'la mémoire pourtant ne compense pas les dernières pertes' (*Le Séjour*, 250). Yet, instinctively he has recourse to memories that bring back the débris of what was. As he puts it: 'On va d'un îlôt de mémoire à l'autre, on sauve des déchets, des rognures de journées, des copeaux, des tessons ci et là jetés, une espèce de poussière lumineuse, poudre du temps' (249).

The living become witnesses of the dead, the latters' only slim chance of a precarious survival. For Chessex's father, the only way to continue living is through his son and others who remember him. He becomes 'cette ombre acharnée à ne pas nous quitter, nous, ses élus, ses bien-aimés, ses témoins' (*Bréviaire*, 68). Alexandre Dumur regrets bitterly that he never paid more attention to his mother and did not listen to her words while she was alive. Now his memories of her are dim, while a friend of his who sat at his mother's deathbed for days, listening to her reminiscences, is still able to evoke her, to witness to her, and to bring her alive. The dead seem to implore this service from the living. As one character in 'Octobre est le plus beau des mois' says: '[Les morts] appellent du fond de l'air et du désordre de leur tombe: "Ne m'oublie pas, je t'en conjure. Je ne vis que par ta mémoire"' (*Où*, 247).

Memory is, therefore, a kind of barrier against death. At the approach of autumn and the death that it represents, recollection of summer and of life serves as protection: 'Les vignes ont lentement rouillé: seuls aujourd'hui mes souvenirs / les peuplent d'hommes lents et de grives' (*Le Jour*, 29). Memory becomes a womblike shelter for Jonas, who realizes that his recollections of the religious ceremonies that he once attended in Fribourg are all the more attractive because they are 'cave, antre, coque, abri enfoui' (*Jonas*, 29). The evocation of childhood is, Chessex admits, a means of denying death and of protecting himself against it: 'Enfance ô miel à peine goûté, lumière de miel / ... / Que tes bienfaisants fantômes m'aident à nier l'heure mortelle' (*Le Calviniste*, 65).

But this protection is at best fragile. As he thinks of his childhood, the poet realizes that the eternity it promises is precarious: 'Mon éternité vacille comme la flamme d'une petite bougie / à la fenêtre hivernale' (*Comme*, 52). The dead live on only as long as they are remembered, and such remembrance is soon overcome by life itself. Real death does not come with the physical extinction of life, but when one is forgotten; real oblivion comes with the forgetfulness of the living. Chessex pictures the dead struggling to bring themselves to the attention of the living. 'Mais contre quoi se battent-ils,' he asks, 'sinon contre l'oubli qui sera pour eux la seule mort définitive?' (*Bréviaire*, 78). The dead are thus entirely dependent on 'nous les témoins, les garants, nous qui sommes, quelques années encore, leurs seuls *répondants* sur ce sol' (78; italics in original).

It is at this point that literary creation plays a role. For Chessex, literature and memory are bound together. He argues that inspiration and careful observation of the world are essential components of literary creation. Imagination must also take a hand, transforming observation in the text. None of these, however, is sufficient without the participation of memory. He writes: 'A l'observation forcenée des choses doit s'ajouter une profonde faculté de mémoire. J'ai cette mémoire.'[2] It is this memory that selects from the artist's experience what is significant and can be transformed in the text. The writer thus seizes the past and uses it; he takes over the dead and puts them in his work. He needs the past and the dead who inhabit it. Chessex says of memory: 'Qu'elle me gorge ... ! Qu'elle irrigue à chaque instant toute ma pensée, chaque poème!' (*Bréviaire*, 82).

But although memory nourishes the text and is an essential component of literary creation, the contrary is also true: literature also serves memory. The text fixes the past and gives stability to what exists only fleetingly in memory. Commenting on Catherine Colomb's *Le Temps des anges*, Chessex says that the writer seizes on tiny fragments of the past, gestures and words that she brings alive on the page: 'Des pans entiers du passé surgissent soudain sous sa plume, rayonnent d'une vive chaleur.'[3] Colomb then fixes them in words so that they remain for the reader to grasp. In a world in which all is unstable and carried away by the flow of time, this is the only permanence that memory can achieve. The poet holds a moment that he wishes to convey, and 'l'unique délivrance est cette seconde de grâce, qui, par la vertu du poème, devient chant durable' (*Saintes*, 68). In *Bréviaire*, the poet imagines his dead father telling him to grasp a living moment of the past and to hold it in a poem, where it may go on living: 'Dis cette heure à jamais suspendue entre la vie et la mort' (93).

In the text that is fed by memory, the past comes alive and achieves a measure of victory over time and death. The text thus becomes a kind of revenge, 'juste revanche du poète sur le temps voleur d'espérance.'[4] Indeed, the written text may often seem to abolish time completely. For example, as he holds in his hand a copy of Rimbaud's *Poésies* that Georg Trakl had in his pocket when he was killed during the First World War, Chessex seems to hold the very past, too (*Bréviaire*, 43). In much the same way, as he hears children singing nursery rhymes, he suddenly feels the past come alive. Time ceases as these rhymes, sung by children for a hundred years or more, join the centuries together. 'La comptine avait aboli le temps,' he writes (*Portrait*, 154).

Often it is specific individuals, especially loved ones, who are revived in the text. By fixing memories of individuals, it becomes a means of giving life to the dead. Catherine Colomb, for example, evokes the dead in her texts in such a way that we feel them living among us: 'Oui, les trépassés existent parmi nous: prennent place à notre table' (*Saintes*, 89). Marcel Raymond's poems are for him a means of bringing back the woman he once loved and who is now dead, and they are best described as 'l'appel et la résurrection de la compagne disparue' (*Saintes*, 107).

In Chessex's case, it is most of all his father whom he attempts to restore to life in his writing. Shortly after his father's death, he tried to defend the dead man against calumny by physical violence, but he then found a better way of doing this. As he acquired a reputation through his writing, he found it more effective to defend him in his texts. 'Autour de mon père, j'ai élevé une citadelle,' is his comment on these texts (Garcin, 70). However, he began to realize that his writing was not just a defence against lies, but also a means of bringing his father to life again. 'Une entreprise allait te rendre vie à travers moi, te restituer, te ressusciter dans ton pouvoir intègre: mes livres,' he tells his father (*Bréviaire*, 72). He now sees himself as the recreator of his father, a kind of father to his father: 'C'est le fils à son tour qui nourrit la mémoire du père, qui la protège, qui la défend' (Garcin, 70).[5]

The writer inspired by memory becomes a witness to the dead, who live through him and his words. In one of his poems, Chessex imagines his father appealing to him to keep him alive in his texts: 'O mon fils, demeure et témoigne' (*Bréviaire*, 91). But what of the writer himself after his death? According to Chessex, the writer, too, continues to speak after death, and the text becomes his witness. As he reads Georges Nicole's poetry, Chessex feels Nicole's presence in what he reads: 'Le miracle, c'est que du fond de la tombe cette voix nous presse, cette parole trouve notre coeur, nous enseigne les secrets de l'amour et de la mémoire, nous montre les chemins de la mort' (*Saintes*, 85). But the survival of the writer in the text is best conveyed by the ending of *Les Yeux jaunes*. The novel ends with Alexandre's words: 'Alors, tristement, je pressai sur la détente et je me tuai' (189). This sentence, which one critic describes as 'phrase étonnante et détonante,'[6] does seem very strange. How can Alexandre have told the story in the previous pages if he commits suicide? The only answer can be that this ending is a symbolic representation of the writer's survival in the text after death. Chessex indicates by this ending that, although Alexandre is dead, he is still alive in the preceding pages.

After death, the text remains, filling the void left by death. Hence, Edmond de Goncourt, after the demise of his beloved brother, continued to write and to keep his brother alive in what he wrote (*Maupassant*, 100). Flaubert, too, sets up the text as a response to death and the absurdity of existence. He is, in Chessex's eyes, 'l'homme qui essentiellement, profondément, comble par l'écriture le vide du monde, qui dresse l'écrit contre ce vide – exactement: qui substitue à ce vide, mot à mot, page par page, le texte serré, irremplaçable, unique, de l'oeuvre achevée' (*Maupassant*, 36).

Literature *can* outlast death, overcome time, and constitute a principle of permanence and order in a world of flux; it *can* restore memory and the past; it *can* bring the dead to life. In short, the text *can* represent a kind of victory over the absurd. But Chessex is not proposing a simplistic view of literature as immortality. He knows that the victory is not certain, that memories fade, that the text is not always able to survive the dead, and that writers and their texts are forgotten. He is aware of all the vicissitudes that may destroy the text, and these risks are conveyed in 'S'effraie le voeu' (*Où*, 37–41). In this story, the family of a dead man finds among his effects a notebook containing two enigmatic lines of verse. Although unable to understand the verse, they keep the notebook, but they destroy a photograph of the dead man. The reader is left with a strong impression that it could easily have been the verse that was destroyed, and the survival of that rather than something else was largely a matter of chance. In any case, how long, the reader wonders, will the verse be kept before it, too, is destroyed?

Chessex admits that, when he was younger, he saw the written text as 'citadelle contre la mort,' and he thought that 'il demeurera toujours cette *chose*, notre trace sur la terre, parce qu'il y a des livres'

(Garcin, 114; italics in original). Now he is not so sure that traces will remain, and he is even inclined to think that 'quelques journées après ma propre disparition ... le soleil ou le vent ou d'autres traces les recouvriront très vite ou les feront fondre' (Garcin, 114). He suggests elsewhere that the text is, at best, just a brief moment of resistance, an instant of stability in the flux of life. His own texts are momentary victories, for 'rien n'est fixé, rien n'est dit, vous voyez, il s'agirait plutôt de quelques haltes entre la lumière et les ombres.'[7]

Even some of Chessex's early poems suggest that he was aware that the text gave no assurances of victory over death. One poem in *Batailles dans l'air* states clearly that the poet may not find immortality in his verse: 'Mais dans la nuit se perdra l'homme / Qui croyait fonder sa victoire / Sur l'or et les paroles sûres' (44). A more recent poem in *Comme l'os* takes up the idea that the text may, in the end, be a useless arm against oblivion, and the poet concludes: 'Je chante un chant inutile' (91). In 'Le Pain des forts' he depicts a house fallen into ruin, and he sees in it an image of the poem. The ruined house is 'comme du poème qui se voulait dressé contre la mort / Maintenant défait / Retombé gravat et poussière à l'inutile (*Le Calviniste*, 34).

Jonas Carex illustrates in his life that art and the written word may not necessarily stand as a barrier to death and the absurd. Jonas is an art critic and novelist who has abandoned his interest in art and has ceased to write because these activities cannot fill the emptiness in his life or guarantee his survival. He no longer believes that immortality of any kind can be assured through art and writing, and the fact that his son has died represents symbolically that he will leave no posterity, no creation that can provide a measure of survival. Standing before his son's tomb, he says: 'Tu es mort? Je suis plus mort que toi, Etienne' (*Jonas*, 177).

There can be no certainty, then, that the text will provide a means of overcoming death, although the possibility that it will do so is always there. The only thing the writer can do, Chessex suggests, is to go on writing. By so doing, he does at least provide some chance that his texts will survive. In any case, the true writer cannot prevent himself writing and putting into texts those things that obsess him. As he points out in one of his poems, Chessex himself, faced by the disasters and defeats of existence, is haunted by them to the point that he has to write about them: 'Je suis épris de ce désastre et de cette gloire' (*Elégie*, 89). These very obsessions, he says, may become so strong that the question of whether the text will survive becomes secondary: 'Cette fascination et cet enchantement de la mort sont devenus si constants chez moi qu'ils m'empêchent de songer au sort posthume de mes livres' (Garcin, 115).

Obliged to write almost despite himself, Chessex goes on producing texts that are concerned very much with death. This constant contemplation of death in the text becomes in itself a form of victory since it helps him rid himself of some of his obsessions. By concentrating on this theme in his writing, by bringing it before his reader on page after page, the writer makes himself and his readers familiar with it, and it loses some of its power over both of them. Both reader and writer become like the narrator of 'Le Séjour des morts' (*Le Séjour*, 255–66), who knows he is to die soon, and who spends what time he has left familiarizing himself with death. To this end, he frequently goes to the cemetery to meditate on death and the dead, until he comes to treat the dead almost as his neighbours. The idea that he will soon die finally holds no terror for him, and it even seems preferable to a life of suffering.

Most of Chessex's writing may be seen as an attempt to become familiar with death, but this is particularly true of *Le Séjour des morts*, with its emphasis on the presence of the dead among the living. *Le Séjour des morts* constitutes an effort to imagine what it is to die, and to accept that this is inevitable. The story entitled 'Paroles de la petite morte' sums up this aspect of the work. This tale imagines the reactions of a little girl who has just died, and who gradually realizes that she exists in a new dimension. Slowly, she adapts to the reality of her situation and comes to accept it as irremediable. The reader senses in this story an effort to imagine what death is and to grow accustomed to it.

Familiarity with death itself is extended to the dead. Chessex and his characters live all the time with memories of the departed, and they constantly evoke loved ones who have passed away. In the case of Jean Calmet, his dead father is so much a part of his life that his image seems to accompany Jean at certain times. The dead live with other characters, too, and unlike Dr Calmet, they become trusted friends. Hence, Alexandre frequently conjures up memories of his parents, thinking of how they would judge his actions, and seeing his deeds through their eyes. Although he never knew his son, Jonas begins to live with images of him, and he imagines what his son's life might have been. Chessex himself recounts memories of deceased friends, of other writers who have died, and, above all, of his father.

So familiar do Chessex and his characters become with these shadows that they often seem to speak with them. Chessex claims to have lain on the tomb of the poet Auberjonois and to have spoken with him in a kind of wordless communion. On another occasion, he slept on a grave, and '... il y avait tout un nuage de paroles qui montait à travers la tombe' (Garcin, 62). It is no surprise, then, to find Jonas Carex walking in the deserted streets and suddenly feeling as though he has died and that all around him are other dead, whom he can hear talking among themselves. The narrator of *La Tête ouverte* likewise senses the dead around him, and believes that they are trying to communicate with him. David Seligmann in 'Te Deum' is equally aware of these ghosts, and he walks in the streets, looking up in the air, 'car il ne fait pas de doute pour lui que les disparus reviennent peupler l'air qui leur a été familier' (*Le Séjour*, 178).

It is clear that the presence of the dead does not always cause distress. They can, in fact, be familiar companions whose presence is welcomed. One poem says: 'J'aime les morts / Je suis entré dans leur enclos' (*Elégie*, 59). Texts such as this show a kind of tenderness towards the dead. The same is true of many stories in *Le Séjour des morts*, and Chessex says that, while he was writing this book, it was as though he were again talking with the dead: 'Et tout autour de moi les morts parlent, qui s'appellent de tombe en tombe' (Garcin, 18).

Simply to recognize and to write about the dead and the horror of death is a step towards accepting and overcoming the fear that they inspire. Chessex says of René Char: 'Mais l'énumération des scandales et des douleurs est une première reconquête.'[8] Paradoxically, this acceptance holds death at bay to some extent and becomes a barrier against it. Chessex argues that a writer like Jean Brouillaud talks of death in his fiction in order to keep his distance from it. He comments on one collection of this writer's work: 'De son repaire, le menacé s'adresse au monde, il conjure ainsi le progrès du mal. "Si tu dînes avec le diable, sers-toi d'une longue cuiller," dit un aimable précepte anglais. J'ai le sentiment que tous les textes ici réunis sont des cuillers à très long manche.'[9] In this sense, many of Chessex's own texts are best described as spoons with which to sup with the devil.

Acknowledgment of death produces a serenity that robs it of its sting. As one critic remarks, the serenity with which Chessex approaches the theme of death in *Le Séjour des morts* contrasts strongly with the anguish of earlier works.[10] It is as though the contemplation of death through volume after volume of prose and verse has rendered it almost incapable of inspiring fear. The text is not a means of avoiding death, but of rendering it harmless. In the poem 'Ruse et mélancolie,' the poet says he will not attempt to flee the shadows of death, but will cunningly greet them and treat them with familiarity. By so doing, he robs them of their terror. 'J'échapperai aux ombres hâtives par la ruse,' he promises (*Le Calviniste*, 120).

Literature thus becomes a form of exorcism that tames death. 'Poème, que tu sois prière ou souffle / Ta lumière exorcise l'esprit des ruines,' says one poem.[11] He admits that poetry for him is 'le chant qui tente d'exorciser, de désenchanter, et d'enchanter la mort' (Garcin, 65). The act of writing assumes an almost magic power: 'Devant la mort, le livre, la phrase, le texte, le poème sont les magiciens qui se servent d'elle, qui se savent mortels, mais en même temps qui élèvent un rempart mélodieux pour la mieux montrer, pour la mieux manifester' (Garcin, 113–14). Hence, Alexandre Dumur uses the text, in his words, 'pour exorciser mes fantômes' (*Les Yeux*, 19). The constant, obsessive presence of death in all its grotesque forms in Delessert's work likewise constitutes 'toute la ruse primitive, la conjuration, les exorcismes' (*Les Dessins*, 18).

As it exorcises death, the text may even restore a taste for life. When he is particularly depressed, Alexandre Dumur writes a poem about an old bone that he finds in his garden. After contemplating it in the text, he suddenly feels his pleasure in life restored. Chessex points to the example of Gustave Roud as a poet who wrote of death and suffering in order to celebrate the pleasures of living: 'Pourtant, dans l'instant presque indicible où a lieu la rencontre du poète et du monde, la mort recule, le temps s'abolit, une lumière singulière baigne la scène et pour toujours la figure ou la voix élues se trouvent sauvées de la nuit' (*Saintes*, 67). In his *Requiem*, Roud evokes death, but also the pleasure of life, and the text becomes a protection against death because it passes beyond recognition of its importance to celebration of life. Arnem Lubin is another writer whom Chessex treats almost as a hero because, although ill and confined to hospital, he wrote about his experience of suffering and created texts that also express joy in life.[12]

On the other hand, it sometimes happens that death itself assumes a kind of attraction that makes it more interesting than life. Paradoxically, death renders life pointless and is the ultimate proof of the absurd, yet it is the only certainty in life. Because of this, it offers the same sense of certitude and order that the Calvinist finds in his religion, and the poet is able to talk of 'exactitude de la mort' (*Le Calviniste*, 77). It is because life can no longer offer the finality and protection of death that characters like Jean Calmet, Alexandre Dumur, and Raphaël Turner seek the solution to their problems in suicide. They might say, with the poet: 'L'affamé un instant a pu chanter / Ta blancheur, cette lumière, la mort' (*Le Calviniste*, 78).

In a life marked by agitation, pain, and sorrow, death offers calm and rest. Jean Calmet seeks peace in death because life has become unbearably confused and unsettled, his father's memory will give him no rest, he is tormented by jealousy, and he is more and more tempted to give in to the evil urges represented by Mollendruz and his crack-brained Naziism. When Raphaël Turner hangs himself, he is not just repeating the rôle of Judas, who hanged himself after his act of betrayal. He is turning away from the passions and urges that have always possessed him. He finds respite from his passions in this act, for 'Il avait tout oublié des figures, des corps, des désirs, de toutes les enveloppes où se cache le diable' (*Judas*, 217). As he walks to his death, he takes off his clothes and throws his watch in the river, symbolically abandoning all that attaches him to a life that no longer holds any attraction for him. It is equally a final rejection of a society and a culture obsessed with time, agitation, and the hurly-burly associated with the search for 'success.' It is an act of revolt against values that he despises.

The narrator of 'Le Séjour des morts,' knowing that he is soon to die, looks on the prospect with relief, for it will provide him with protection against the vicissitudes of life. With an evident sense of longing, he evokes his own demise: 'Je serai couché dans la terre, seul comme j'étais seul dans la mère que je n'ai pas connue, dehors il pleuvra, il gèlera, moi je serai à l'abri du vieillissement, du froid, des cris des autres, bien couché dans le ventre de la terre qui me portera et me réchauffera comme un enfant' (*Le Séjour*, 264). The sea monster that serves in *Jonas*, on one of its symbolic levels, as an image of death, also carries this connotation of womblike protection and 'touffeur humide' (38), implying that, for Jonas too, death is felt at times as a refuge. Similar desires for death and weariness with life are expressed by the narrator of 'Où vont mourir les oiseaux' as he thinks of the birds who die at the beginning of winter and he wishes 'Ah ... à mon tour disparaître, me défaire avec les oiseaux' (*Où*, 16).

At times these texts express almost a feeling of envy for the dead, who have finally acquired the peace and security that cannot be found in life. In a poem called 'Le Cloître' (the very title of which has connotations of peace and protection), are these lines: 'Quand nous serons morts à notre tour / Puissions-nous sereins nous dissoudre / Devenir en paix cendre et poudre' (*Comme*, 13). Elsewhere, Chessex imagines the poet Gustave Roud telling the living to leave him and his tomb in peace, for he has lost interest in their vain agitation. Roud asks the person who walks above him: 'Ne sais-tu pas qu'ici reposent / Les restes terrestres de ma créature / Peu habitués dès lors à ton arroi?' (Garcin, 117).[13]

Even the nothingness and the sense of emptiness that lies at the heart of much of what Chessex has written can become something that attracts. On occasion, there is a distinct longing for an emptiness that is seen as the final peace, a love of nothingness that is described as 'amour du vide cette volupté' (*Comme*, 30). Another poem says: 'La soif du vide sans cesse appelle' (*Le Calviniste*, 77). In Jean Calmet's attraction to death there is also a feeling for the emptiness and the blessed void that it represents, and when he imagines the ashes of the dead scattered in the wind or on the water, he longs for 'la légèreté d'une semaison sur les eaux, sa fuite entre des rives ombreuses' (*L'Ogre*, 16).

While being principally an object of fear, death obviously has its attractive side. It is the approach of death, which has already set its mark on her, that renders Jean's pupil so alluring. With her pale skin and emaciated face, she becomes 'Isabelle-qui-va-mourir. Et qui le sait. Et qui fascine ses camarades' (*L'Ogre*, 21). When Herbert Cormier in 'Chemin noir' (*Où*, 145–9), runs over a cat with his car, he too is fascinated by its appoaching end as he observes its death throes. Alexandre Dumur is so drawn to the presence of death and the pomp that often surrounds it that he sometimes attends funeral services for complete strangers. On the occasion when he is asked to substitute for a pastor who is late for the service, he accepts with relish. His acceptance is due not just to the residual attraction of a religion whose minister he now pretends to be, but also to the feeling that he is involved in a ritual in which death is present. The hint of necrophilia that appears in some texts, not to mention the actual necrophilia that occurs in others, is linked to the idea that death is attractive. When Alexandre admits to his wife: 'J'eusse aimé ... faire l'amour à une morte bien comestible' (*Les Yeux*, 153), and when he speaks of his pleasure in imagining the dead body of the pastor's wife, this link is very apparent.

Fascination with death is evident in Louis' love of Schubert's music, his taste for Gustave Roud's poem 'Requiem,' and in his sudden emotion on seeing the poet's grave. Chessex explains his own father's suicide, not so much as being the result of despair or as an attempt to escape the horrors of life, but as the result of the attraction exercised by death. 'Tu t'es laissé fasciner par elle. Tu as cédé, violemment, à son feu noir,' he says to his father's memory (*Portrait*, 255). Mingled with such fascination is the desire to know, a curiosity about death and what it means to die. Jonas gives voice to this curiosity when he says: 'Et je ne cesse d'imaginer l'heure de ma mort pour connaître enfin les mystérieuses lois qui excerceront leur pouvoir à mon entrée dans le Cycle' (*Jonas*, 190).

Whether an object of fear, an old friend, an incentive to live, or an alluring presence, death for Chessex is an essential part of the text itself. Much of literary creation is a response to death, an attempt to face it, tame it, and become familiar with it. The text is a response to death, yet it is also dependent on it. It is death that provides the impetus and inspiration for the text, and it is absolutely necessary for its genesis. The work of a writer like Crisinel, for example, could not exist without the misfortunes of the poet's life, the death of his friends, and the presence of suffering (*Saintes*, 61). Baudelaire, too, needed the presence of death and the absurd for the creation of his poetry: 'Et c'est de ces ténèbres, c'est de l'horreur de mourir si hâtivement que cet artiste tire la nécessité de ses propres *Paradis artificiels*' (*Maupassant*, 79). At times, Chessex says, it seems as though the very stuff of poetry is the horrors of life: 'Il m'arrive parfois d'imaginer que le seul sujet de la poésie naît de notre pauvre destin.'[14] As the voice in one of Chessex's poems says: 'Je me couvre encore de blessures / Parfois ces plaies se font mots' (*Chant*, 32).

Alexandre Dumur is an excellent example of a writer whose texts are the product of his contemplation of death. On the anniversary of Gustave Roud's death, Alexandre feels particularly depressed by the presence of death, but this very depression drives him to create a poem about Roud. As he approaches the moment when he has decided to commit suicide, the imminence of his demise spurs him to create another poem. In his own life, Chessex sees the text as a response to and a product of his intense awareness of death, and he has said: 'J'écris parce que j'ai peur de la mort. J'écris contre cette peur, contre la mort. C'est un frêle rempart. Je sais. Mais curieusement la mort nourrit mes livres en même temps qu'ils la combattent.

De ce compagnonnage avec la mort sont sortis la plupart de mes poèmes et presque tout ce que j'ai fait.'[15] In this, as in so many other things, Chessex is a true descendant of Maupassant, Flaubert, and Zola, those naturalists who wrote of death and found inspiration in it. Speaking of Chessex's relationship to these masters, one critic says: 'Le ... Chessex de l'angoisse de vivre, celui qui affronte ses propres hantises et les exacerbe pour en extirper l'essence même de sa création, est bien le fils spirituel de cette famille lucide et tourmentée.'[16]

Chessex attempts to use death against itself in his writing, to do as Roud did, for he says, 'le poème de Roud ... n'est plus brisé par la mort, il se nourrit d'elle, il la porte comme une arme aiguë et musicale' (*Saintes*, 72). The text, and the poem in particular, become a form of protection against death and a reflection of its presence. Paradoxically, they bear traces of the power of death while being a record of the possibility of overcoming it. They are 'à la fois rempart contre le désastre et discours déchiqueté de notre condition.'[17]

The human condition also has its social and political implications, however. As we have seen, metaphysical and social concerns are often closely linked in Chessex's writing, and this is also true of his conception of the text. He believes that the text is a protection against the death of the individual and of man in general, but also against the death imposed on the Vaud and on the countryside by a particular kind of society. The text may also be used as a weapon against that urbanization and commercial exploitation of which he frequently writes. He believes in a certain 'pouvoir sociologique et politique de l'écriture' (Garcin, 113).

The tactic of 'les justes,' who are behind the destruction of nature, is to maintain silence about it. One way of opposing their silence is in political action and in journalism, but Chessex does not believe these methods to be particularly effective. By associating his protests with a political line, the writer risks being represented by 'les justes' as just another politician whose motive is the desire for political influence and power. The best way to oppose the death of nature, he says, is to write about it in texts that are accepted as having literary ambitions. This kind of text has a 'seriousness' that raises it above normal political considerations and makes it particularly effective. This is the kind of text that Chessex has attempted to create, and in 1979 he was able to say: 'Or, depuis dix ans, sans cesse, j'ai montré cette faille, dénoncé un certain nombre de tares, d'hypocrisies et d'horreurs' (Garcin, 40).

The writer becomes a defender of nature merely by writing about it. By depicting the beauties of the Vaud in his texts, Chessex produces an inventory of them that helps preserve them. The public has to see this beauty before it can be defended, and it is often the writer who first reveals it. The writer becomes 'tabellion et sceautier ... archiviste cantonal, protecteur des cailloux et des fleurs rares' (*Portrait*, 18). For this reason, many of Chessex's texts are a defence against the death that threatens the countryside, and especially that of the Vaud.

Chessex compares the writer to Joshua and the text to the trumpet call that destroyed Jericho. He says that the writer must reveal the hypocrisy of 'les justes' and show how they exploit and destroy the countryside. By so doing, he may bring down the whole edifice of deceit and silence that they have constructed. To those who argue that this is to overestimate the power of the text, he responds: 'Un livre ne peut rien, il peut tout, ça dépend de la confiance et de l'endurance, ça dépend de la force et de la rigueur' (*Carabas*, 251). Like a trumpet call, it may not seem to be effective, but in time, it can destroy what appears to be more powerful.

One may find these claims about the power of the text somewhat exaggerated, despite Chessex's comparison of the text to Joshua's trumpet. One may also doubt that the kind of text he has in mind can really be considered nonpolitical. Indeed, there is an argument that says *any* text is political, and that even the one that claims not to be is making a political claim. But, whatever the effect of Chessex's texts in their opposition to 'les justes,' they do serve a purpose on a personal level. Writing about 'les justes,' like writing about death, is a means of exorcism. Chessex frees himself from these forces by revealing them. According to a critic, a work like *Carabas* represents 'La Suisse, Lausanne exorcisés.'[18] In fact, very early in his career, when he discovered the example of Crisinel, Chessex decided that his texts would be a means of freeing himself from a society that he hated and despised. He describes his decision thus: 'Je commençais à comprendre que ... j'écrirais pour être libre. Que je ne me laisserais pas bousculer par les tétrarques, que je chérirais la sauvagerie du rapace ... les excès' (*Carabas*, 89).

Chessex treats the text, therefore, as a form of revolt. But it is revolt on both the metaphysical and the social levels. On the social level, it is rejection of a particular society and its values, and it is in direct line of descent from the naturalists and such texts as *Les*

Soirées de Médan, which, Chessex says with evident approval, 'pensent mal' (*Maupassant*, 87). For him, the text should be what it was for Flaubert: a form of 'printanière révolte' (*Maupassant*, 91), or what it was for Edmond de Goncourt: 'la révolte d'un homme libre' (*Maupassant*, 100). Chessex's ideal writer is, like Jean Burg, someone who upsets, annoys, constantly unsettles, and who can say, 'je gênai: on me détesta' (*La Confession*, 15).

But the text should also be revolt on the metaphysical level, revolt against man's condition and his subservience to death. The text as Chessex conceives it is a protest against the absurd, and he particularly admires Georges Haldas for treating it as 'un défi devant l'indistinct, les maux sournois' (*Saintes*, 172). Writers like Huysmans and Baudelaire, with their insistence on the artificial, are also praised because Chessex sees this as a form of metaphysical revolt. It represents rejection of the natural order of things, of a reality in which 'la loi commune de vivre et de mourir' reigns supreme (*Maupassant*, 80). Huysmans' hero Des Esseintes, by his life of dandyism and artificiality, attempts to replace the ugly reality he can no longer bear with a more satisfactory one: 'C'est contre l'ordre du monde que ce dandy s'est dressé. Lui substituant son ordre propre, avec ses lois esthétiques, ses codes moraux, ses condamnations, ses intransigeances, ses finalités, sa religion' (*Maupassant*, 80).

Chessex clearly has an exalted and somewhat romantic conception of the writer and the text. He believes that the writer should be a *révolté* who stands against the ills of a society and of the human condition. This makes the artist's role a difficult one, for he soon becomes an outcast from the society that he opposes. Like Henri Calet, a writer who rejected the social values of his day, he is forced to live and to write in solitude. Calet is particularly praised by Chessex because he refused to join political parties or to espouse any political line. This made him doubly an outcast, since the revolutionaries of his day rejected him, too (*Maupassant*, 171). Chessex sees himself as being another Calet, who has attacked social ills, written of the importance of death and the absurd, but who has refused to join political parties. The fact that some of his writing has provoked violent opposition from all political parties would suggest that he has had some success, and that his opponents at least suspect that his writing may have some practical effect.

13

Conclusion: Religion and the Text

Jacques Chessex is a literary critic of some distinction who has written extensively about both contemporary writers and masters of the past. His articles have appeared in such highly regarded journals as the *Nouvelle Revue Française*, and several have been collected and published in the volume called *Les Saintes Ecritures*. His critical writing covers appreciation of contemporary writers, book reviews, articles on such Swiss masters as Gustave Roud and Ramuz, the collection of articles on the naturalists published as *Maupassant et les autres*, and a book devoted to Flaubert called *Flaubert ou le désert en abîme*. Chessex has also taught literature and is, of course, the author of fiction and poetry. He has thought extensively about literature, and one might say that his life has been largely devoted to it.

Amid all these texts, there are naturally many comments and analyses of the art of writing. However, there is one aspect of literary creation that, by his own admission, baffles him considerably, and that is the question of the origin or birth of the literary text. He is not sure what impulse produces the text, what drives the process of literary creation. He recounts in *Carabas* that, when he was once asked how he created his books, the only answer he could find concerned the physical apparatus that he preferred: a certain type of paper, a specific kind of ink, his favourite sort of notebook. No answer about the mysterious process of actually writing was forthcoming.

When speaking to Jérôme Garcin, he tries to go a little further than this and to examine in more detail why he writes. However, the explanation still remains somewhat vague. He merely says that he has no overall plan, no organized scheme when he begins to create a text. He imagines a character, and once that character is formed, the events that produce his or her destiny seem to fall into place. Some of these events are dictated by his own experience, others are pure invention. Often the process of writing is a struggle, but sometimes it all comes quite easily. In the end, there is simply a combination of character, events, and style that he can explain only by saying: 'Il y a une rencontre de la fiction et du vrai. Rien n'est préparé, mais tout se destinait à cette rencontre' (Garcin, 159).

It is as though Chessex's writing just 'happens.' This is particularly the case of his fiction, which suggests he is a born storyteller with a great facility for narrating. He is, critics agree, 'un extraordinaire conteur' and one of the best 'raconteurs d'histoires.'[1] Bertil Galland says that, when he first read *La Tête ouverte*, he was immediately aware that 'un conteur superbe s'était révélé.'[2] One might say of Chessex, as he himself has said of Georges-Emmanuel Clancier: 'Simplement, il raconte.'[3]

He can find no logical reason why the desire to tell stories should take possession of him. 'Quelle nécéssité d'écrire des récits? ... Justement, c'est le mystère,' he says.[4] The need to write poetry (which he often refuses to distinguish from fiction) is equally mysterious, for poetry has 'un caractère préservé et mystérieusement nécessaire.'[5] In the end, he does not try to explain a phenomenon that he cannot understand. One critic says that 'il y a en Chessex un grand respect du mystère poétique, qui est reçu et montré comme tel, avec naturel et simplicité.'[6]

The moment when the need to write seizes him is described by Chessex in terms that are clearly drawn from his Calvinist background. Even as he discusses his activity as a writer, the activity that is his main defence against this particular religion, the images and vocabulary that spontaneously occur have obvious Calvinist overtones. He describes this moment as one of inspiration during which he is used by that inspiration. The poet seems to play no active role in this process, but is simply 'chosen' by whatever power breathes on him. The writer's intelligence and organizing ability may contribute to the creation of fictional works, but a poem seems to select the poet: 'La science intervient dans l'écriture de la prose. Mais au moment où le poème *s'écrit*, et j'ai bien dit *s'écrit*, je n'ai pas dit "au moment où j'écris un poème," il se passe un phénomène étrange. C'est lui, le poème, qui décide' (Garcin, 118; italics in original). In the story 'Tu sacerdos eris' (*Où*, 45–6), Chessex shows the blank and despairing side of this picture. He depicts a poet in whose mind the opening lines of a poem keep recurring, but who is *not* inspired to finish the poem. Every time he sits before a sheet of blank paper, inspiration fails. Among poets whom Chessex has known personally, Crisinel is one such who is intensely aware of the fragility of poetic inspiration. 'Et l'élu connaît la précarité de ses chants!' Chessex comments on this poet (*Saintes*, 57).

When the grace of inspiration does come, the writer is transformed into a medium or an instrument for some mysterious power. 'Moi, je n'ai qu'à m'offrir comme un simple intermédiaire, une main, une encre, une plume qui porte l'encre, un point c'est tout,' is how Chessex describes his part in the process (Garcin, 118). At such times, he feels that he is at the centre of forces linking him to circumstances and to other people, and providing him with intuitions that help him create plots and characters. He says that 'il m'arrive de plus en plus de me représenter, de me figurer les visages et l'existence des autres à travers cette intuition, à travers la médiumnité qui non suelement me porte, mais qui éclaire les livres que je suis en train de penser, d'imaginer, de vouloir faire' (Garcin, 168).

As a medium, the poet is in contact with a power that emanates from somewhere beyond the immediately and physically apparent: 'Mais cadeau des dieux ou insufflation plus diffuse, je dois reconnaître que je n'ai jamais écrit de poème sans songer, à un moment *donné* à quelque intervention de l'autre ou de l'ailleurs.'[7] This 'elsewhere' appears to enter the poet when he writes, filling him with a power that is not evident in other circumstances. 'L'ailleurs est en moi,' says a line in one of Chessex's poems (*Le Calviniste*, 48).

The writing of poetry requires a total emptying of the self so that there is room for inspiration. It demands a kind of 'dénudation' (Garcin, 119) akin to that of the believer who seeks communion with God or with some form of the absolute. Chessex says: 'C'est dans cette simplicité que je découvre ma complexité ... le poème étant le révélateur de l'abrupt, parfois de l'abrupt conçu comme Dieu, qui existe ou n'existe pas, je ne sais pas, en tout cas comme l'absolu' (Garcin, 119). The creation of the text thus becomes 'une opération sacrée [qui] révèle naturellement l'absolu parce qu'il est en communication avec le suprême, avec le supérieur' (Garcin, 119).

Sometimes Chessex links these forces explicitly with the divine. 'Mais l'intuition, c'est une façon de deviner, de *diviner* l'instance dans toutes les circonstances, dans tous les avatars possibles,' he argues (Garcin, 169; italics in original). When he writes that, for Crisinel, the poem is 'le privilège d'origine divine' (*Saintes*, 56), he is clearly describing something of what it means to him too. In this view of things, the poet becomes a vehicle for divine energies, a kind of prophet who reveals these energies to man. In 'Poète aux lèvres sales,' Chessex depicts the poet as a kind of 'poète maudit' whom others would prefer to ignore. 'Tu nous cornes l'invisible, poète aux lèvres sales,' the poem begins, but the poet goes on to point out that he has messages for humanity that come from a divine source and that men ignore them at their own peril: 'Mais dans ma voix dérive un peu du seul Souffle' (*Comme*, 33).

As well as being a prophet, the writer is also a kind of priest who interprets the will of the divine. The story already mentioned, in which the poet seeks inspiration in order to complete his poem, is entitled, significantly, 'Tu sacerdos eris.' The writer, like the priest, is called to take up a vocation that cannot be refused. Consequently, Alexandre Dumur pictures himself as a priest. This is partly because he believes his mission is to look into the souls of others and to be 'pêcheur d'âmes, scrutateur d'âmes' (*Les Yeux*, 19). Most of all, however, it is because, like the minister of God, he is chosen. He feels an instinctive brotherhood with the priest, and it is this that drives him, when he is mistaken for a minister at a funeral, to preach a sermon and to conduct the service. Those who mistake Alexandre for a minister sense something in him that makes him akin to one, while Alexandre himself accepts this role quite naturally.

Since the text puts the writer in touch with the divine, it may be compared to prayer: a communion with the divine power. It also requires that emptying of the self, that sense of awe and reverence in the presence of the mysterious, that is required in prayer. Jonas Carex, who has also been a writer, says: 'J'ai souvent comparé ... l'écriture et la prière. L'une et l'autre s'exercent sous le signe de la transcendance' (*Jonas*, 14).

However, although, like prayer, the text orients the writer towards powers beyond this world, it must also be securely rooted in the world. We have seen how important physical reality is to Chessex's conception of writing. He believes that the writer must always maintain awareness of the world and of the people around him, must see the totality of what surrounds him, and must never abandon this, however powerful the forces from 'beyond.' This constant, almost reverent, awareness of the world is in itself a kind of prayer: 'Pensant au poème et à la poésie, je me souviens immédiatement d'un commandement d'Origène: il faut prier sans cesse. C'est le conseil que je me donne en poésie: il faut être poète sans cesse. Il faut que l'oeil, l'esprit, le coeur, le corps demeurent ouverts sans cesse à l'innombrable beauté, à sa signification totale en moi et dans la clarté variée des êtres.'[8] The poem in particular is tied to the real world, and risks falling into artificiality and untruth if it abandons the real. Chessex argues that 'la poésie est le réel absolu, parce que si l'on devait mentir, par la voie du poème ... , on ne serait plus dans le réel, on serait dans le fabriqué' (Garcin, 119).

This is not a call for rigorously 'realistic' writing that faithfully 'captures' reality, as a glance at any of Chessex's texts will readily reveal. He believes that reality is the point of departure for the text, which then transforms the real. The text must possess 'ce pouvoir de métamorphoser le réel le plus banal en oeuvre forte' (*Saintes*, 119) that the best 'realistic' fiction displays. It must be 'révélation d'un autre lieu en ce monde, d'un lieu autrement plus riche – la vraie vie sans cesse pressentie et conjurée' (*Saintes*, 95).

Chessex sometimes refers to this other reality, this possibility of other worlds hidden in this one, as 'the fantastic.' The fantastic is 'l'au-delà du là, le surgissement de l'ailleurs dans le simple et le plat' and he discovers it particularly in the work of Delessert (*Les Dessins*, 15). Georges-Olivier Châteaureynaud also possesses the power to see the fantastic, a power born of 'une observation très rigoureuse du réel et à la fois d'une imagination magnifiquement extravagante.'[9] André Pieyre de Mandiargues likewise transports his readers from a minutely described 'real' world into 'un cadre second.'[10] In most of these cases, the appearance of the fantastic is born of close observation of physical reality, which is seen to contain another reality: 'Plus on est dans le vrai, plus le fantastique surgit. A serrer le réel, à dire la réalité, on dit aussi l'indicible, on ouvre des gouffres.'[11]

The reality behind appearances may also take the form of dreams, and Chessex approves fully of that literature that reveals men's and women's dreams and their importance in the transformation of the real. He praises, for example, Alexandre Voisard's novel *Louve* because it shows how a poet may change reality by dreams, and 'le récit donne au rêve sa revanche' (*Saintes*, 205). The power of dreams is compared in *Carabas* to the seventh trumpet of Jericho that destroyed the walls of that city. Joshua pitted his dreams of creating a new nation against the apparently immovable reality of the city, and won. Chessex, too, hopes that his dream of creating a land free of the power of 'les justes' and of the influence of the Calvinism they represent may come true through the agency of what he writes. No wonder he says, 'Josué est un héros selon mon coeur. Il rêve, il croit à son rêve et à ses visions' (*Carabas*, 249).

Dream and the fantastic – these means of transforming reality – are accessible through the imagination. The writer is like Carabas' cat in the fairy tale. The cat imagines his poor, starving master as the marquis de Carabas, a rich landowner and husband of a princess. He makes others see this picture, too, and he turns his dream into reality. Chessex sums up this story: 'Le pouvoir de l'imaginaire! Le garçon ne possédait rien, le chat le rend riche, l'imaginaire a suscité des terres, un château' (Garcin, 52).

These ideas of art and the text are, of course, very imprecise, relying as they do on ill-defined terms such as *inspiration*, *the absolute*, and *the fantastic*. Nor are they particularly new. The whole idea of inspiration that 'chooses' the writer, who thus becomes a kind of seer or prophet, is reminiscent of the romantics. The heirs to romanticism, the symbolists and 'poètes maudits,' held some ideas that are also similar to Chessex's. The symbolists, and particularly Rimbaud, saw the poet as a 'voyant' or magician, who perceived what others were unable to see. They believed in a kind of 'beyond' that is accessible to the poet by careful use of words. Even the desire to shock that motivated the lives and work of the 'poètes maudits' bears some similarity to Chessex's wish to create a literature of excess that will shock 'les justes.'

Many other opinions expressed by Chessex remind one of the surrealists. The belief that the artist reveals another reality behind appearances is close to the surrealists' belief that the true poet communicates the 'latent content' behind the 'manifest content' of the world around him. Many surrealists argued, as does Chessex, that it is through strict realism and attention to detail that the 'marvellous' is revealed. They likewise saw the artist as a medium for mysterious forces, and they attempted to release these forces through such techniques as automatic writing. Woman, who becomes a privileged being in Chessex's texts, is treated by the surrealists as very special because it is often she who is an instrument of the 'marvellous.' Even the emphasis that Chessex places on literature of excess may be seen as reminiscent of the surrealists' iconoclasm and will to shock. They too opposed a satisfied, respectable bourgeoisie that held a safe and conventional idea of what art should be, as Chessex opposes a similar conception of art held by 'les justes.'

The most significant aspect of these similarities between Chessex's ideas and those held by certain predecessors, is that, in most cases, they concern the 'mystical' or 'religious' properties of art. The romantics, the symbolists, and even the surrealists (despite the latters' attacks on established religion) all sought in art something that mankind has frequently looked for in religion. They all attempted, through art, to commune with some superior power, to lift themselves above banal reality into a kind of 'beyond.' Chessex himself recognizes that this aspect of his theories has religious connotations. He says that when he produces a poem, he is in a special state in which he is the instrument of what he calls 'l'enchantement poétique' and in which 'le mystère triomphe' (Garcin, 120). This, he agrees, is a fundamentally religious conception of the artist's role: 'Il y a une opération religieuse au sens étymologique, car le poème nous relie à des phénomènes que nous ne voyons pas sans lui' (Garcin, 120).

The comparison of this process to prayer, and of the poet to a priest or a medium, also has obvious religious implications. As for the forces with which the poet communes, although Chessex hesitates to link them directly to God, he does use such words as *the divine* and *the absolute*. The use of the word *souffle* to describe poetic inspiration conjures up images of this inspiration as a divinely inspired breath of life, imparted to the poet, just as, according to Genesis, 'the lord God formed man of the dust of the ground and breathed into his nostrils the breath of life' (Genesis 2: 7). It also suggests poetic inspiration as a kind of Holy Ghost or Spirit that blows on the faithful – in this case, the poet – and serves as his inspiration and link to God.

The way in which inspiration is believed to 'choose' the poet is reminiscent of the particular religion that has always preoccupied Chessex. For him, poetic inspiration cannot be commanded by an effort of the will or earned by earnest endeavour. It selects the individual for no apparent reason, falling on him like grace and making him one of the elect. The widespread view of Calvinism is that it, too, represents the individual as predestined. He or she cannot earn salvation through good works alone, or by individual effort, but is singled out by God's grace for reasons known only to God. The text frequently used to justify this view of Calvinism might apply (with some such term as 'the absolute' instead of 'God') to Chessex's view of poetic inspiration: 'Or si c'est chose évidente, que cela se fait par le vouloir de Dieu, que le salut soit offert aux uns, et les autres en soient forcloz.'[12]

Less limited to a particular form of religion, but still 'religious' in its essence, is the view of art as something that reveals hidden realities and transforms the apparent world. This idea of art reminds one of religion as a means of penetrating appearances and revealing the mystery of Creation. Just as the text gives access to the 'beyond' or the 'marvellous' in the world, so religion reveals the hand of God in Creation, the Maker behind the manifest world. Both the text and religion see the essence, the 'real' in appearances, and, by describing them, they transfigure the world of appearances.

It is a short step from seeing the text in these somewhat religious terms to treating it as a substitute for God and for the religion that he rejects. For Chessex, as for Flaubert, the text is often approached as a possible means of replacing God, of filling the void left by the absence of God. It is something that will exist on its own, independent of any deity and of any meaning or finality that a divine presence might lend to life, 'un défi tassé, concentré sur sa compacité – seule apparition, seule densité, seul poids dressé verticalement comme un dolmen, un totem, un monument dans ce vide: *hors de toute catégorie*, donc sans aucune finalité, sans aucun sens, sans aucune nomination possible, sans plus de substance, sans horizontal, sans verticalité – et sans Dieu' (*Flaubert*, 12; italics in original). It is something created from the absence, the nothingness, and absurdity that is life, and that stands, self-sufficient, in that nothingness. Chessex, like Flaubert and Joyce, is tempted to treat the literary work as 'née de sa propre nécessité, et se suffisant à elle-même' (*Flaubert*, 243).

Chessex writes movingly and with admiration of Flaubert's desire to create the Text – a work that is itself a dense, solid, absolute creation, 'le Lieu primaire et universel de toutes les écritures possibles' (214). Flaubert tried to create what Chessex calls 'le livre en soi' (226), that is, something that would be 'unité complexe mais close sur elle-même' (247), a kind of monolithic work that is 'délégation du texte à des pouvoirs supérieurs à sa fonction simplement signifiante' (234). This logocentric view of the text sees it as encapsulating some stable, immutable 'essence.' It begs the issue of whether language is even capable of holding such a stable centre of meaning.

As has been noted before, many modern theorists would argue that it can refer only to an essentially unstable self, because it consists of a regressive series of signifiers that refer to other signifiers.

One must, however, again make the point raised in chapter 11: that Chessex is aware that the world outside the text resists capture by the text. In fact, he never refers to his own writings as the Text, and he never claims to set it up as a self-sufficient entity that will fill the void of existence. But it is also clear that he is very attracted to this concept in Flaubert's writing. Like Flaubert, he examines writing as a means of creating something stable and self-sufficient. This is seen in his exploration of the text as a possible way of overcoming time and of fixing it in a kind of static, everlasting present. He sees it as a possible means of imposing the writer's time on the flux of life. It is also a means of imposing order on chaos through style, of establishing '*le* style, avec ses lois à lui, son fonctionnement interne et son pouvoir d'agression, d'oppression, de conviction' (148). Style in the text is for Chessex, as for Flaubert, 'un système autonome qui lui confère une unité et une densité inaliénable' (218).

In Chessex's practice of the text, it also imposes order by reconciling opposites. It brings together such apparently irreconcilable aspects of existence as life and death, good and evil, freedom and constraint. In this, too, it has religious connotations, for religion is the ultimate unifier, the mysterious power in which all is reconciled and explained. It promises the final explanation, the harmony of all things in God. It is the force that opens eyes that now 'see through a glass darkly' (1 Corinthians 13: 12) and reveals what lies behind the apparently inexplicable.

In all these views of the text, one may easily discern the same longing for stability and a system of authority that is evident in Chessex's nostalgia for the Calvinism that he has rejected. The idea of the text as a self-sufficient entity, the hope that style may impose order, even the practice of the text as reconciliation of opposites, all betray the same desire for a principle of organization. The text is explored as something that will replace Calvinism by affording the same protection and stability in a world that is otherwise experienced as chaos and evanescence.

Yet, while being a possible substitute for Calvinism, and while having religious connotations, the text, style in the text, the text's ability to create unity, and artistic creation in general all become a kind of revolt against the absurd and against a God who does not exist. As in the case of Flaubert, the will to create becomes the supreme form of revolt. The writer takes the place of God, creating, through the Word, his own reality. Chessex points out that, according to the Gospel of Saint John, 'in the beginning was the Word, and the Word was with God, and the Word was God' (*Flaubert*, 270; John 1: 1). God thus uses the word to create, and is revealed in it. The writer, by creating through the word, usurps the function of God. Like Alexandre Dumur in *Les Yeux jaunes*, he engages in a satanic revolt against God and attempts to replace Him.

However, Chessex is aware that this revolt cannot succeed. The Text, that absolute and self-sufficient entity erected to replace God, cannot be achieved because it represents a perfection beyond our grasp. He recognizes that this is an imperfect world in which such an absolute is unattainable. Although he treats words as instruments that can sometimes grasp a reality beyond themselves, their very ability to do this is a sign of their imperfection. Because they are connected to the world outside themselves, and are, in fact, a part of that world, they share its limitations. Both Chessex and Flaubert treat the text as something created from and a reflection of the void and chaos that is existence. It is made of the same stuff as the void that it tries to fill, and it therefore partakes of it. He says in *Flaubert ou le désert en abîme* that the text is 'surgi et constitué dans le désert et sur le désert' (14). It thus leads us back to the despairing emptiness and imperfection of being. It is 'le livre provenu du rien, sur rien, la profération du désert, le retour à un autre désert immense et inconnaissable' (20). The text as Flaubert and Chessex conceive of it is a product of 'cet élan, cette pulsion, cette tension vers le parfait, et qui retombe dans l'imparfait' (271).

The text thus becomes an attempt to use language and style to fill a void and to impose order in the full knowledge that such an attempt must fail. Chessex accepts that words are empty because they seize the emptiness of being. Like Flaubert and Proust, he realizes that 'le mot, le rien et le temps sont associés dans le sentiment d'une même vanité' (135). But, like these two, he goes on writing. He uses style and words *as though* they could replace God, even though he knows they cannot. The text becomes 'la rhétorique de Dieu se substituant à Dieu même' (29), but it is an empty rhetoric. The writer creates *as though* he could create the Text, but his rhetorical devices are used in the knowledge that they cannot fill the void. His task is 'Signifier ce monde où rien jamais n'a de sens ni de signe dans le langage usurpateur' (133). All the writer can do is go on writing and attempting to create, knowing that he merely illustrates the imperfection and the void of existence: 'Car enfin que tenter contre le mal, sinon de porter le livre à sa perfection: au Livre par excellence, au livre sur rien – né du rien, c'est-à-dire dans le sentiment satanique ou âcre du néant de l'ennui – au texte du désert en abîme?' (115)

Chessex and Flaubert both know that they cannot really impose their own time on the fleeting instant and that they will never create an eternal moment. Chessex says of Proust (and he might be speaking of himself): 'Il tente de se reconstituer dans la durée perdue *à partir d'une durée en train de se perdre*' (137; italics in original). The writer's work is, therefore, 'une expérience de pure perte, garantie par sa seule qualité d'oeuvre d'art' (137). The work of art can hold memories and halt time for a while, but it will probably be destroyed by time, says Chessex, and even Proust was aware of that (137). Even style fails to impose order for long on the flux of experience, and is no final remedy against 'la mort, l'ennui, la solitude existentielle, la perte perpétuelle du temps et l'éparpillement de soi' (137). Yet Proust, like all true artists, chooses nevertheless to go on creating 'une oeuvre que l'on sait condamnée à ne pas atteindre son propre accomplissement' (137).

The writer who attempts to be the rival of God is thus constantly reminded that there is no God, no absolute, no eternal moment. He can say: 'Absent de Dieu, et Dieu de toute façon absent, je suis le substitut et le rappel de ce Dieu possible et impossible' (117). He can draw from this fruitless task a kind of pride, for, 'l'Homme-Dieu sort enrichi, même alourdi de sombre orgueil, du mauvais repas où l'a convié sa forcénerie' (119). Speaking of Flaubert's attempt to go on writing despite his awareness of the futility of doing so, Chessex compares this to his own father's suicide in the face of the same futility. He approves Flaubert for maintaining the rhetorical order of the text, for holding to a system of order, knowing that it could not triumph over the disasters of the real world. He says: 'Je vois que Flaubert a conduit son existence par le *système*, qui est une rhétorique de l'indistinct et du non-dit, quand mon père a laissé crouler sa rhétorique hors de toute structure, de tout système, de toute décision syntaxique, puisqu'ici la syntaxe c'est aussi bien le texte intelligible qui constitue l'être, sa *morale*, de façon classique, et c'est à cette morale que mon père a manqué pour accomplir rhétoriquement son *discours*' (163; italics in original).

Conclusion: Religion and the Text 175

Despite the futility of the text, Chessex thrills to the attempt to create an absolute, self-sufficient literary work. He writes lyrically and with intense feeling of the moment when a writer like Flaubert starts to create a text. This moment is 'la poussée élémentaire de la syntaxe et du son' (271), and the writers who create this moment 'défient la mort du texte' (272). Although they know that they cannot succeed, they provoke a magnificent movement of revolt and creative energy. Chessex concludes: 'Or, c'est à cette origine ... qu'il est nécessaire de remonter pour garantir la chance de la Phrase et permettre son accomplissement dans la reconnaissance stupéfiant du texte neuf' (273).

It is clear from all this evidence that Chessex does use the text in an essentially religious manner, and that literature is to some extent a means of replacing the religion that he rejects. But at the same time, he knows that this attempt will achieve little of lasting value and provide no solutions to the problems created by abandonment of religion. He is a religious individual whose preoccupations are always metaphysical. Indeed, he recounts in *Carabas* how, when he fell one day to the very depths of degradation and sexual excess, and when he felt sullied and utterly hopeless, he was suddenly seized by the intuition of 'Dieu, ou l'absolu, ou l'éclair, la totalité de la vie et de la mort, l'extrême, l'inimaginable' (*Carabas*, 211–12). His texts, with their constant metaphysical preoccupations, may be seen as the more usual means employed by him to gain access to the absolute and to satisfy the religious longings that he never attempts to hide. But this is done in the knowledge that they can provide no lasting or totally satisfactory access to any such absolute.

In view of the religious element in all of Chessex's texts, one has to ask the question: Does he really escape the harsh and hated religion that he sees as his heritage? Is the text a successful means of solving the problems posed by this religion and by his rejection of it?

The answer is a qualified 'yes.' The spectre of Calvinism haunts Chessex's texts. He carries over into his writing the obsession with death, sin, and constraint for which he condemns Calvinism. In the sense that his texts are driven by attempts to come to terms with or to escape these things, he can never really evade the grasp of Calvinism. It is unavoidable that the impulse to flee any feared or hated enemy must contain that enemy within it as its motive force. It is equally unavoidable that the void left by the abandonment of a religion, especially in a religious sensibility like Chessex's, should drive him to seek substitutes.

Yet, although the text appears to have a broadly religious function for Chessex, it does at least provide an alternative to that form of religion that he particularly wishes to escape. This is best seen in the way it approaches the presence of death. It affirms life in the face of the obsession with death that Chessex believes to be one of the most destructive legacies of Calvinism. But, alongside the presence of death in his texts is the counterbalancing presence of life and the will to enjoy it. The balance between life and death that Calvinism does not even attempt to maintain is restored by the text.

It is, in the long run, the sense of balance and moderation that is Chessex's best answer to Calvinism. He learns that the text gives only partial solutions to the presence of death, to the absurd, to the passage of time, and to the undoubted suffering encountered in life. But he also learns that partial solutions are the only ones possible, and that it is necessary to struggle on knowing that ultimate and totally satisfactory answers are not possible. Through his exploration of these problems in the text, he comes to realize that the Calvinist desire for total and irrefutable solutions, for definite answers, can never be satisfied. He learns to settle for the partial and incomplete, and this in itself is a victory over Calvinism.

The text as a means of going beyond the Calvinist obsession with clear-cut, black-and-white distinctions is best seen in the way that Chessex uses it as a unifying principle. Whereas Calvinism represents the world as being divided between opposite forces such as good and evil, God and the devil, or the saved and the damned, the text becomes a means of bringing together all such apparent opposites in a fundamental unity. In place of a divisive, maniohean religion, it is proposed as an instrument of reconciliation and harmony. In this way, it remains a fundamentally religious instrument, but it suggests a different religious solution from the one represented by Calvinism. The text is religious in a much broader sense, in the sense in which most religions propose a final harmony and reconciliation. At the same time, it becomes a place in which individuals can also meet to commune with the author. However imperfect that communion may be, it at least emphasizes the text as a meeting place rather than as a divisive force. This victory over division and opposition, incomplete and limited though it may be, represents Chessex's escape from Calvinism. The text becomes his victory over the oppressive force that drives it.

Notes

CHAPTER 1

1 This brief biographical sketch is based on Gilbert Salem, 'Une Esquisse Biographique,' Jérôme Garcin et Gilbert Salem, eds., *Jacques Chessex*, 11–31, and on Eric Lestrient, 'Gros plan sur Chessex,' 7 and 14.
2 Gérard Guégan, '*Les Yeux jaunes*,' Garcin et Salem, 120; Jacqueline Piatier, 'Un Certain Vaudois nommé Chessex,' 13; François Nourissier, 'Lisez romand,' 67.
3 Jean Vuilleumier, '*Le Calviniste*,' Garcin et Salem, 156.
4 Pierre de Boisdeffre, 'Chronique du mois,' 671.
5 Lionel Mirisch, 'Un Goncourt attachant,' 6; Robert Kanters, 'Jacques Chessex entre la mort et la vie,' 10; Jean Devaud, 'Jacques Chessex: *L'Ogre*,' 293.
6 Kanters, 10; Devaud, 293; Ursula Schoeni, 'Chessex, Jacques (1934–),' 160.
7 Jérôme Garcin, *Entretiens avec Jacques Chessex*, 157. Subsequent references to this work are in parentheses in the text.
8 Catherine Belsey, *Critical Practice*, 4.
9 Ferdinand de Saussure, *Cours de linguistique générale*, 100.
10 Christopher Prendergast, *The Order of Mimesis*, 2.
11 Gérard Genette, *Figures II*, 55.
12 Jacques Derrida, *Positions*, 23.
13 Howard Felperin, *Beyond Deconstruction*, 91.
14 Robert Scholes, *Semiotics and Interpretation*, 32.
15 Christopher Butler, *Interpretation, Deconstruction, and Ideology*, 52.
16 Jonathan Culler, *Structuralist Poetics*, viii.
17 Wayne C. Booth, *The Company We Keep*, x.

18 At least one other critic of Chessex's work has also explicitly done this. In a footnote to his excellent article on Chessex's fiction, Henri-Dominique Paratte notes that 'dans la mesure où les modèles de Jacques Chessex ne relèvent pas de la nouvelle critique, une approche sémiotique de son oeuvre nous semble, de toute évidence, devoir éviter le jargon aussi bien que la schématisation excessive' ('L'homme, le pays, le monde, 151–2).
19 Booth, *The Company We Keep*, 254.
20 Jean-Louis Ezine, 'Jacques Chessex: vingt ans après,' 3.
21 François Nourissier, 'Le Maupassant de Ropraz,' Garcin et Salem, 89.
22 Chessex, 'Jacques Brenner: *La Fête au village*,' (1963), 521.
23 Wayne C. Booth, *The Rhetoric of Fiction*, 67–86, 211–38, 395–6 and *The Company We Keep*, 125–9.
24 Y.F., 'La Magie sombre de Jacques Chessex,' 22. On the way that Chessex mingles poetry and prose, creating something that partakes of both, see Marianne Ghirelli, 'Jacques Chessex, poète et romancier,' Garcin et Salem, 52; Garcin, '*Elegie soleil du regret*,' Garcin et Salem, 105; Bernard Christoff, '*Reste avec nous*, de Jacques Chessex,' 23.
25 Garcin, '*Les Yeux jaunes*,' Garcin et Salem, 121; Patrick Grainville, '*Judas le transparent*,' Garcin et Salem, 142; Salem, '*Feux d'orée*,' Garcin et Salem, 172.
26 For more on the effect of Ponge and Paulhan on Chessex's work, see chapter 12 and Garcin, *Entretiens avec Jacques Chessex*, 128–9.
27 Claude-Michel Cluny, 'Un Homme des cantons suisses,' 6; Alain Clerval, 'Jacques Chessex: *La Confession du pasteur Burg*,' 526; Philippe Sénart, 'Autour des romans,' 132; Bertil Galland, 'Jacques Chessex en 1970,' Garcin et Salem, 43; Schoeni, 160.
28 Alain Bosquet, 'Jacques Chessex: *Le Jeûne de huit nuits*,' viii.
29 '*Où vont mourir les oiseaux*, par Jacques Chessex,' 146; italics in original.
30 Georges Anex, 'Jacques Chessex,' 86; Piatier, 13; Anex, '*Portrait des Vaudois*,' Garcin et Salem, 79.
31 There are many other such lists in *Carabas*. For some examples from another text, see *Portrait des Vaudois*, 122, 162, 172, 232.
32 The question of Chessex's style may be related to the strictness of this Calvinist background. He argues that Jaccottet's concise, spare style is due in some measure to his 'goût austère hérité de la tradition protestante' (*Saintes*, 138). May not Chessex's early style have the same source? And, if it does, may not the later luxuriant style be seen as part of his reaction against the severity of Calvinism?

CHAPTER 2

1 Jérôme Garcin, '*Le Séjour des morts*,' Garcin et Salem, 112.
2 Garcin, 'Jacques Chessex: *Le Séjour des morts*,' 93.
3 Alain Bosquet, 'Jacques Chessex: *L'Ardent Royaume*,' 99.
4 Chessex, 'Lettre à un ami sur les poèmes retrouvés,' (1976), 2.
5 Bosquet, '*Le Calviniste*,' Garcin et Salem, 144.
6 Gilbert Salem, 'Une Esquisse biographique,' Garcin et Salem, 13.
7 David Bevan, *Ecrivains d'aujourd'hui*, 58. Subsequent references to the work are in parentheses in the text.
8 Josée-Flore Tappy, '*Le Calviniste*, ou dire la blessure première,' Garcin et Salem, 145. For other references to Chessex's work as mythical, see Henri-Dominique Paratte, 'L'homme, le pays, le monde, 154; Bertil Galland, 'Jacques Chessex en 1970,' Garcin et Salem, 42.
9 Jean-Louis Ezine, 'Jacques Chessex: vingt ans après,' 3.
10 Robert Kanters, 'Comment manger son enfant,' iii.

CHAPTER 3

1 For a brief examination of the differences between what Calvin wrote and the usual interpretation of his writing as harsh and uncharitable, see Basil Hall, 'The Calvin Legend,' in *John Calvin*, ed. G.E. Duffield, 1–18.
2 *A New Dictionary of Theology*, ed. Sinclair B. Ferguson, David B. Wright, and J.I. Packer, 570.
3 Hall, 'Calvin against the Calvinists,' in *John Calvin*, 22.
4 Chessex, 'Pasteurs et dimanches,' *Portrait des Vaudois* (1982), 133–43.
5 François Nourissier, 'Jacques Chessex entre Dieu et Diable,' 65.
6 The linking of Dr Calmet to the sun is also significant since in many myths the Deity (particularly if it is a male deity) is a solar figure. See Joseph Campbell, *The Hero with a Thousand Faces*, 42–3, 69–71.
7 Garcin, '*Les Yeux jaunes*,' Garcin et Salem, 121.
8 Garcin, '*Judas le transparent*,' Garcin et Salem, 139.
9 Henri-Charles Tauxe, '*Les Yeux jaunes*,' Garcin et Salem, 114.
10 Josée-Flore Tappy, '*Le Calviniste*, ou dire la blessure première,' Garcin et Salem, 145.
11 Chessex, 'Reconnaissance à Giono,' (1971), 7–8.
12 On the subject of writing viewed as sin in *Les Yeux jaunes*, see my article '*Les Yeux jaunes* de Jacques Chessex,' 55–61.

CHAPTER 4

1 Chessex, 'Ode à Gustave Roud,' (1976), 18.
2 Chessex, 'Anne Perrier: *Le Temps est mort*,' (1968), 916.
3 Pierre Hugli, 'Pour une mise à mort,' Garcin et Salem, 65–70.
4 See, for example, Philippe Sénart, 'Autour des romans,' 132.
5 Claude-Michel Cluny, 'Un Homme des cantons suisses,' 6; Alain Clerval, 'Jacques Chessex: *La Confession du pasteur Burg*,' 526; Garcin, 'Daniel Boulanger et Jacques Chessex: l'art du raccourci,' 49.
6 Georges Anex, 'Portrait des Vaudois,' Garcin et Salem, 81; Max-Pol Fouchet, '*Les Yeux jaunes*,' Garcin et Salem, 118; Jacqueline Piatier, 'Un certain Vaudois nommé Chessex,' 14; Jean Freustié, 'Croisade contre les puritains,' 93.
7 Eric Lestrient, 'Gros plan sur Chessex,' 14.
8 For a fuller examination of Jean Calmet's ambiguities than there is room for here, see my 'Jacques Chessex: The Ogre Within,' 109–112.
9 It is also an obvious castration symbol. For an examination of *L'Ogre* as demonstrating a classic Oedipus complex, see Robert Deschamps, '*L'Ogre* de Jacques Chessex,' 153–161.

CHAPTER 5

1 Chessex, 'Ramuz élémentaire,' (1967), 17.
2 François Nourissier, 'Le Maupassant de Ropraz,' Garcin et Salem, 90.
3 Louis-Ferdinand Céline, *Voyage au bout de la nuit*, 421.
4 Georges Bataille, *L'Erotisme*, 289.
5 Chessex, 'Le Temps chez Jean Cayrol,' (1966), 864.
6 Chessex, 'Les Cavernes, les oiseaux, la mort ...,' (1965), 698.
7 Chessex, 'Raymond Queneau, sage et savant,' (1965), 475.
8 Christiane Baroche, '*Où vont mourir les oiseaux*, par Jacques Chessex,' (1980), 146.
9 Chessex, 'Singulier Plaideur,' (1969), 785.
10 Guy Rohou, 'Jacques Chessex: *Reste avec nous*,' 1089.
11 Chessex, 'René Pons: *L'Après-midi*,' (1963), 145.
12 Chessex, 'Ode à Gustave Roud,' (1976), 16.

CHAPTER 6

1 This whip is, like the razor in *L'Ogre*, another Freudian symbol.
2 The fact that Jean is a teacher, and that he is a teacher of Latin, indi-

cates that as well as feeling oppressed by authority and power, he is also attracted to them. On the ambiguities of his attitude, see my 'Jacques Chessex: The Ogre Within,' 109–12.
3 Claude Bonnefoy, 'Occasion manquée,' 4.
4 Jérôme Garcin, 'La Célébration du réel,' Garcin et Salem, 73.
5 See ibid.
6 See Georges Anex, 'Jacques Chessex,' 86–7.
7 Much of Swiss literature in German would also appear to be written in opposition to those whom Chessex calls 'les justes.' See Wilfred Schiltknecht, 'Suisse: Zorn et ses frères,' 59–61.
8 François Nourissier, 'Le Maupassant de Ropraz,' Garcin et Salem, 93.

CHAPTER 7

1 Pol Charles, 'Un Sauvage sous la terreur,' 45.
2 Chessex, 'Pierre Gascar: *Le Meilleur de la vie*,' (1964), 144.
3 François Nourissier, '*Portrait des Vaudois*,' 2; Alfred Eibel, 'Jacques Chessex ou la septième trompette de Jéricho,' 1; Georges Anex, 'Jacques Chessex,' 86; Jacques Vandenschrick, 'Pourquoi ces quelques Suisses?' 212.
4 Marianne Ghirelli, 'Jacques Chessex, poète et romancier,' Garcin et Salem, 47–53.
5 Eric Lestrient, 'Gros plan sur Chessex,' *Matulu*, 3, no. 30 (1974), 14.
6 Ibid., 7.
7 Chessex, 'Pierre Gascar: *Le Meilleur de la vie*,' (1964), 143.
8 Nourissier, 'Le Lauréat de la Suisse réelle,' 106.
9 Chessex, 'André Guex: *De l'eau, du vent, des pierres*,' (1970), 313.
10 Robert Kanters, 'Jacques Chessex entre la mort et la vie,' 10.
11 Chessex, 'Notes à propos de René Char,' (1965), 687.
12 Jean Devaud, 'Chessex, Jacques: *Les Yeux jaunes*,' 765.

CHAPTER 8

1 François Nourissier, '*Carabas* de Jacques Chessex,' 4.
2 Although certain of the traits in Vaudois society that Chessex attacks are typical of Switzerland as a whole, he believes that the Vaud is in many ways different from the rest of the country. He points out that the Vaud was linked to Savoy until 1536, that it has a different history from the rest of Switzerland, that it has its own language and customs, and that its religion was imposed on it by Berne. See Garcin, 80.

3 Franck Jotterand, ed. *Pourquoi J'écris*, 38. Subsequent references to this work are in parentheses in the text.
4 Chessex, 'Le Pays où l'on revient toujours,' (1966), 930; italics in original. For a fuller examination of the role of Chessex's father and his native region in the genesis of his texts, see my 'Jacques Chessex and the Origins of Literary Creation.'

CHAPTER 9

1 Ursula Schoeni, 'Chessex, Jacques (1934–),' 160; Yves Velan, 'Lecture pour le Jeûne,' 40.
2 Josée-Flore Tappy, '*Le Calviniste*, ou dire la blessure première,' Garcin et Salem, 145.
3 Jean Vuilleumier, '*Le Calviniste*,' Garcin et Salem, 155.
4 Henri-Dominique Paratte, 'L'homme, le pays, le monde,' 154.
5 Pierre Hugli, 'Pour une mise à mort,' Garcin et Salem, 70.
6 Georges Anex, '*Où vont mourir les oiseaux*,' Garcin et Salem, 127.
7 Velan, 'Lecture pour le Jeûne,' 40.
8 Philippe Nadal, '*Le Calviniste*,' Garcin et Salem, 152.
9 Paratte, 154.
10 Joseph Campbell, *The Hero with a Thousand Faces*, 115.
11 Paratte, 154.
12 Bertil Galland, 'Jacques Chessex en 1970,' Garcin et Salem, 42.
13 Chessex, 'Roger Judrin: *Le Balancier*,' (1963), 1107.

CHAPTER 10

1 On the intertextual presence of Rousseau in French-Swiss letters, see Bevan, 'Ecrivains d'aujourd'hui,' 7.
2 Eric Lestrient, 'Gros plan sur Chessex,' 7.
3 Patricia Serex, '*Comme l'os* de Jacques Chessex,' 59; Gérard Valbert, '*Le Calviniste*,' Garcin et Salem, 143; Jérôme Garcin, '*Le Calviniste*,' Garcin et Salem, 158; Jean Devaud, 'Chessex, Jacques: *Les Yeux jaunes*,' 765.
4 Gérard Guégan, '*Les Yeux jaunes*,' Garcin et Salem, 119.
5 On the awareness of this threat among francophone Swiss writers, see Bevan, 8.
6 Jean-Louis Ezine, 'Jacques Chessex: vingt ans après,' 3.
7 Ibid.
8 Ibid.

9 Chessex, 'Reconnaissance à Giono,' (1971), 9.
10 Garcin, *Entretiens avec Jacques Chessex*, 156 and Chessex, 'Lettre à un ami sur les poèmes retrouvés,' (1976), 6.
11 Chessex, 'Proême pour Nioque,' Garcin et Salem, 196.
12 Ezine, 3.
13 François Nourissier, 'Dis-moi qui tu hantes,' 41; Josyane Pfeiffer, 'Jacques Chessex: *Maupassant et les autres*,' 134; Alain Bosquet, 'Jacques Chessex: *L'Ardent royaume*,' 100.
14 Nourissier, 'Dis-moi,' 41.
15 Nourissier, 'Le Maupassant de Ropraz,' Garcin et Salem, 92.
16 Bertil Galland, 'Jacques Chessex en 1970,' Garcin et Salem, 41.
17 Robert Kanters, 'Comment manger son enfant,' iii.
18 Bosquet, 'Henri Thomas: *Les Tours de Notre Dame*. Roger Grenier: *La Salle de rédaction*. Jacques Chessex: *Le Séjour des morts*. Noël Devaulx: *Le Lézard d'immortalité*,' 130.
19 Chessex, 'Alexandre Voisard: *La Nuit en miettes*,' (1976), 72.
20 Chessex, '*La Grande Année*, ou quelques remarques sur Pierre Oster,' (1964), 1071.
21 Christophe Gallez, 'La Corneille et l'oeuf poché,' Garcin et Salem, 174.
22 Robert Deschamps, '*L'Ogre* de Jacques Chessex: la poésie au service de la psychanalyse,' 156.

CHAPTER 11

1 Bernard Christoff, '*Reste avec nous*, de Jacques Chessex,' 22.
2 Jérôme Garcin, 'La Célébration du réel,' Garcin et Salem, 71–4.
3 Chessex, '*La Grande Année*, ou quelques remarques sur Pierre Oster,' (1964), 1070.
4 Chessex, 'Georges-Emmanuel Clancier: *L'Eternité plus un jour*,' (1970), 138.
5 Chessex, 'G.-O. Châteaureynaud: *La Belle Charbonnière*,' (1976), 101.
6 Chessex, 'L'Inattendu,' (1977), 126–8.
7 Alain Bosquet, 'Jacques Chessex: *Le Jeûne de huit nuits*,' viii.
8 Marianne Ghirelli, 'Jacques Chessex, poète et romancier,' Garcin et Salem, 50.
9 Chessex, 'Lettre à un ami sur les poèmes retrouvés,' (1976), 4.
10 Chessex, 'Le Spectateur passionné,' (1964), 686.
11 See also Jotterand, *Pourquoi J'écris*, 37.
12 Robert Kanters, 'Jacques Chessex entre la mort et la vie,' 10.
13 Henri-Dominique Paratte, 'L'homme, le pays, le monde,' 161.

14 Chessex, 'Monstres et merveilles,' (1965), 1067.
15 See also Chessex, 'A la mémoire de Paul Gadenne,' (1966), 673–7.
16 Chessex, 'Autour d'un anniversaire,' (1967), 729.
17 Philippe Sollers, *L'Ecriture et l'expérience des limites* 72; italics in original.
18 Chessex, 'Lettre à un ami sur les poèmes retrouvés,' 1.
19 Ibid.

CHAPTER 12

1 Chessex, 'Marc Michel: *Pierre qui roule*,' (1962), 138.
2 Chessex, 'Lettre à un ami sur les poèmes retrouvés,' (1976), 3.
3 Chessex, 'Catherine Colomb: *Le Temps des anges*,' (1962), 913.
4 Chessex, 'Georges-Emmanuel Clancier: *L'Eternité plus un jour*,' (1970), 139.
5 See also *Portrait des Vaudois*, 264.
6 Jean Muno, 'Les Fagnes intérieures,' 99.
7 Chessex, 'Lettre à un ami,' 14.
8 Chessex, 'Notes à propos de René Char,' (1965), 691.
9 Chessex, 'Les Cavernes, les oiseaux, la mort ...,' (1965), 697.
10 Jérôme Garcin, 'Jacques Chessex: *Le Séjour des morts*,' 93–4.
11 Chessex, 'Lettre à un ami,' 9.
12 Chessex, 'Dans Les Demeures d'Arnem Lubin,' (1968), 652–8.
13 This poem may also be found in *Les Yeux jaunes*, 158–9.
14 Chessex, 'Lettre à un ami,' 12.
15 Jotterand, *Pourquoi J'écris*, 37. See also Chessex, *Carabas*, 82 and 'Lettre à un ami,' 11–12.
16 Josyane Pfeiffer, 'Jacques Chessex: *Maupassant et les autres*,' 136.
17 Chessex, 'Peines et combats d'André Frénaud,' (1966), 1070.
18 Alfred Eibel, 'Jacques Chessex ou la septième trompette de Jéricho,' 1.

CHAPTER 13

1 Yves Velan, '*Carabas*,' Garcin et Salem, 84; Gérard Guégan, '*Les Yeux jaunes*,' Garcin et Salem, 120.
2 Bertil Galland, 'Jacques Chessex en 1970,' Garcin et Salem, 39.
3 Chessex, 'Georges-Emmanuel Clancier: *L'Eternité plus un jour*,' (1970), 138.
4 Chessex, 'Lettre à un ami sur les poèmes retrouvés,' (1976), 6.
5 Ibid., 7.

6 André Ughetto, '*Le Calviniste*, poèmes de Jacques Chessex,' 150.
7 Chessex, 'Lettre à un ami,' 7–8; italics in original.
8 Ibid., 9.
9 Chessex, 'G.-O. Châteaureynaud: *La Belle Charbonnière*,' (1976), 101.
10 Chessex, 'Monstres et merveilles,' (1965), 1064.
11 Jean-Louis Ezine, 'Jacques Chessex: vingt ans après,' 3.
12 Jean Calvin, *Institution de la religion chrestienne*, 467.

It may be argued that predestination is not as important an element of Calvin's doctrines as it is generally believed to be and that the view of it as the very basis of his theology is a misrepresentation. This may be so, but what we are dealing with in Chessex's work is the commonly perceived and practised form of Calvinism. It is this form of the doctrine that influences his texts and against which he reacts.

On the idea that Calvin did not really make predestination the basis of his doctrines, see François Wendel, *Calvin: Sources et évolution de sa pensée religieuse*, 119–216.

Bibliography

A: WORKS BY CHESSEX

Books

The following list shows the original date of publication and original publisher. When I have used a different edition for this study, it is indicated after the first entry for that title. I have not included here certain translations, exhibition catalogues, and collaborative works.

Le Jour proche. Lausanne: Aux Miroirs Partagés, 1954.
Chant de printemps. Geneva: Jeune Poésie, 1955.
Une Voix la nuit. Lausanne: Mermod, 1957.
Batailles dans l'air. Lausanne: Mermod, 1959.
La Tête ouverte. Paris: Gallimard, 1962.
Le Jeûne de huit nuits. Lausanne: Payot, 1966.
Charles-Albert Cingria. Paris: Seghers, 1967.
La Confession du pasteur Burg. Paris: Christian Bourgois, 1967. (I have used the edition published by L'Age d'Homme, Lausanne, 1982.)
L'Ouvert obscur. Lausanne: L'Age d'Homme, 1967.
Reste avec nous, précédé de Carnet de terre. Lausanne: Cahiers de la Renaissance Vaudoise, 1967.
Portrait des Vaudois. Lausanne: Cahiers de la Renaissance Vaudoise, 1969. (I have used the edition by Editions de L'Aire, Lausanne, 1982.)
Carabas. Paris: Grasset, 1971.
Les Saintes Ecritures. Lausanne: Galland, 1972. (I have used the edition published by L'Age d'Homme, Lausanne, 1985.)

L'Ogre. Paris: Grasset, 1973. (I have used the Livre de Poche edition, 1975).
Les Dessins d'Etienne Delessert. Lausanne: Galland, 1974.
Le Renard qui disait non à la lune. Illustrations de Danièle Bour. Paris: Grassset, 1974.
L'Ardent Royaume. Paris: Grasset, 1975. (I have used the Livre de Poche edition, 1980).
Bréviaire. Lausanne: Galland, 1976.
Elégie soleil du regret. Lausanne: Galland, 1976.
Le Séjour des morts. Paris: Grasset, 1977.
Marie et le chat sauvage. Illustrations de Danièle Bour. Paris: Grasset, 1979.
Les Yeux jaunes. Paris: Grasset, 1979. (I have used the Livre de Poche edition, 1981.)
Où vont mourir les oiseaux. Paris: Grasset, 1980.
Maupassant et les autres. Paris: Editions Ramsay, 1981.
Judas le transparent. Paris: Grasset, 1982.
Le Calviniste. Paris: Grasset, 1983.
Feux d'orée. Lausanne: Editions de L'Aire, 1984.
Comme L'os. Paris: Grasset, 1988.
Morgane Madrigal. Paris: Grasset, 1990.
Neuf, l'oeuf. Illustrations de Danièle Bour. Paris: Grasset, 1990.
Flaubert ou le désert en abîme. Paris: Grasset, 1991.
Les Aveugles du seul regard. Paris: Editions de la Différence, 1992.
La Trinité. Paris: Grasset, 1992.

Articles

'Marc Michel: *Pierre qui roule*.' *La Nouvelle Revue Française*, 19, no. 109 (1962), 138–9.
'Catherine Colomb: *Le Temps des anges*.' *NRF* 20, no. 120 (1962), 911–13.
'René Pons: *L'Après-midi*.' *NRF* 21, no. 121 (1963), 145.
'Roger Judrin: *Le Balancier*.' *NRF* 21, no. 126 (1963), 1105–7.
'Jacques Brenner: *La Fête au village*.' *NRF* 22, no. 129 (1963), 521–2.
'Pierre Gascar: *Le Meilleur de la vie*.' *NRF* 24, no. 139 (1964), 143–4.
'Le Spectateur passionné.' *NRF* 24, no. 142 (1964), 686–91.
'Michel Planchon. D'ombres et de pierres.' *NRF* 24, no. 143 (1964), 919–20.
'*La Grande Année*, ou quelques remarques sur Pierre Oster.' *NRF* 24, no. 144 (1964), 1068–72.
'Henry Bauchau: *L'Escalier bleu*.' *NRF* 24, no. 144 (1964), 1108–9.

'Notes à propos de René Char.' *NRF* 25, no. 148 (1965), 687–93
'Monstres et merveilles.' *NRF* 25, no. 150 (1965), 1063–8.
'Raymond Queneau, sage et savant.' *NRF* 26, no. 153 (1965), 475–9.
'Les Cavernes, les oiseaux, la mort ... ' *NRF* 26, no. 154 (1965), 693–9.
'Le Temps chez Jean Cayrol.' *NRF* 27, no. 161 (1966), 863–7.
'Peines et combats d'André Frénaud.' *NRF* 27, no. 162 (1966), 1067–71.
'A la mémoire de Paul Gadenne.' *NRF* 28, no. 166 (1966), 673–7.
'Le Pays où l'on revient toujours.' *NRF* 28, no. 167 (1966), 929–31.
'Ramuz élémentaire.' *NRF* 30, no. 175 (1967), 12–19.
'Pierre-Alain Taché: *Ventre des fontaines*.' *NRF* 30, no. 178 (1967), 693–4.
'Autour d'un anniversaire.' *NRF* 30, no. 178 (1967), 728–9.
'Anne Perrier: *Le Temps est mort*.' *NRF* 31, no. 185 (1968), 916–17.
'Dans Les Demeures d'Arnem Lubin.' *NRF* 32, no. 191 (1968), 652–8.
'Singulier Plaideur.' *NRF* 33, no. 197 (1969), 782–6.
'Georges-Emmanuel Clancier: *L'Eternité plus un jour*.' *NRF* 35, no. 205 (1970), 137–9.
'André Guex: *De l'eau, du vent, des pierres*.' *NRF* 35, no. 206 (1970), 313.
'Reconnaissance à Giono.' *NRF* 37, no. 218 (1971), 7–9.
'Alexandre Voisard: *La Nuit en miettes*.' *NRF* 47, no. 277 (1976), 71–2.
'G.-O. Châteaureynaud: *La Belle Charbonnière*.' *NRF* 47, no. 281 (1976), 100–1.
'Lettre à un ami sur les poèmes retrouvés.' *NRF* 48, no. 283 (1976), 1–14.
'Ode à Gustave Roud.' *NRF* 48, no. 283 (1976), 15–19.
'L'Inattendu.' *NRF* 50, no. 295 (1977), 126–8.
'Proême pour Nioque.' In *Jacques Chessex. Un Dossier de Lectures*, ed. Jérôme Garcin et Gilbert Salem. Lausanne: Editions de l'Aire, 1985, 196–8.

Interviews

Jotterand, Franck, ed. *Pourquoi J'écris*. n.p.: La Gazette Littéraire, 1971.
Ezine, Jean-Louis. 'Jacques Chessex: vingt ans après.' *Les Nouvelles Littéraires*, 24–30 décembre 1973, 3.
Lestrient, Eric. 'Gros plan sur Chessex.' *Matulu* 3, no. 30 (1974), 7, 14.
Garcin, Jérôme. *Entretiens avec Jacques Chessex*. Paris: Editions de la Différence, 1979.
Bevan, David. *Ecrivains d'aujourd'hui. La Littérature romande en vingt entretiens*. Lausanne: Editions 24 Heures, 1986.

B: WORKS ON CHESSEX

Anex, Georges. 'Jacques Chessex.' *Le Magazine Littéraire*, octobre 1978, 86–7.
Baroche, Christiane. '*Où vont mourir les oiseaux*, par Jacques Chessex.' *Sud* nos. 34–5 (1980), 146–7.
Boisdeffre, Pierre de. 'Chronique du mois.' *La Nouvelle Revue des Deux Mondes* (décembre 1973), 667–7.
Bond, David J. 'The Dualistic Vision of Jacques Chessex's Fiction.' *Swiss-French Studies Etudes Romandes* 2, no. 2 (1981), 74–90.
– 'Jacques Chessex: La Conscience calviniste.' *Bulletin de la Société des Professeurs Français en Amérique.* (1987–8), 173–84.
– 'Jacques Chessex: The Ogre Within.' *International Fiction Review* 16, no. 2 (Summer 1989), 109–12.
– '*Les Yeux Jaunes* de Jacques Chessex: L'écriture et le diable.' *LittéRéalité* 3, no. 1 (printemps 1991), 55–61.
– 'Jacques Chessex and the Origins of Literary Creation.' *Romance Quarterly* 39, no. 2 (May 1992), 167–77.
Bonnefoy, Claude. 'Occasion manquée.' *Les Nouvelles Littéraires*, 30 juin–6 juillet 1976, 4.
Bosquet, Alain. 'Jacques Chessex: *Le Jeûne de huit nuits*.' *Le Monde [des Livres]* 26 avril 1967, viii.
– 'Jacques Chessex: *L'Ardent Royaume*.' *NRF* 46, no. 275 (1975), 99–100.
– 'Henri Thomas: *Les Tours de Notre Dame*. Roger Grenier: *La Salle de rédaction*. Jacques Chessex: *Le Séjour des morts*. Noël Devaulx: *Le Lézard d'immortalité*.' *NRF* 50, no. 296 (1977), 127–31.
Charles, Pol. 'Un Sauvage sous la terreur.' *Marginales* 143 (1972), 44–45.
Christoff, Bernard. '*Reste avec nous*, de Jacques Chessex.' *Revue des Belles-Lettres* no. 3 (novembre 1964), 21–3.
Clerval, Alain. 'Jacques Chessex: *La Confession du pasteur Burg*.' *NRF* 30, no. 177 (1967), 526–8.
Cluny, Claude-Michel. 'Un Homme des cantons suisses.' *La Quinzaine Littéraire* 32, 15–31 juillet (1967), 6.
Deschamps, Robert. '*L'Ogre* de Jacques Chessex: la poésie au service de la psychanalyse.' *Présence Francophone* no. 16 (printemps 1978), 153–61.
Devaud, Jean. 'Jacques Chessex: *L'Ogre*.' *French Review* 49, no. 2 (December 1975), 292–3.
– 'Chessex, Jacques: *Les Yeux jaunes*.' *French Review* 53, no. 5 (April 1980), 765–6.

Eibel, Alfred. 'Jacques Chessex ou la septième trompette de Jéricho.' *Matulu*, no. 8 (novembre 1971), 1, 5.
F., Y. 'La Magie sombre de Jacques Chessex.' *Le Monde [des Livres]*, 30 mai 1980, 22.
Freustié, Jean. 'Croisade contre les puritains.' *Le Nouvel Observateur*, 21-7 juillet 1977, 93.
Garcin, Jérôme. 'Jacques Chessex: *Le Séjour des morts*.' *Le Magazine Littéraire*, septembre 1977, 93-4.
– 'Daniel Boulanger et Jacques Chessex: l'art du raccourci.' *Les Nouvelles Littéraires*, 19-26 novembre 1981, 49.
Garcin, Jérôme et Gilbert Salem, eds. *Jacques Chessex. Un Dossier de Lectures*. Lausanne: Editions de l'Aire, 1985.
Kanters, Robert. 'Comment manger son enfant.' *Le Figaro Littéraire*, 3 novembre 1973, iii.
– 'Jacques Chessex entre la mort et la vie.' *Le Figaro Littéraire*, 28 mai 1977, 10.
Mirisch, Lionel. 'Un Goncourt attachant.' *La Quinzaine Littéraire*, 1er-15 décembre 1973, 5-6.
Muno, Jean. 'Les Fagnes intérieures.' *La Revue Générale* no. 6/7 (juin-juillet 1979), 97-101.
Nourissier, François. '*Portrait des Vaudois*.' *Les Nouvelles Littéraires*, 25 décembre 1969, 2.
– '*Carabas* de Jacques Chessex.' *Les Nouvelles Littéraires*, 10 septembre 1971, 4.
– 'Lisez romand.' *Le Point* 16 (8 janvier 1973), 67.
– 'Le Lauréat de la Suisse réelle.' *Le Point* 62 (26 novembre 1973), 106.
– 'Dis-moi qui tu hantes.' *Le Figaro Magazine* 111 (21-7 mars 1981), 41.
– 'Jacques Chessex entre Dieu et Diable.' *Le Figaro Magazine* 161, 15-21 mai 1982, 65.
Paratte, Henri-Dominique. 'L'homme, le pays, le monde: engagement existentiel de Jacques Chessex.' *Présence Francophone*, no. 12 (printemps 1976), 149-64.
Pfeiffer, Josyane. 'Jacques Chessex: *Maupassant et les autres*.' *Repères* no. 1 (1981), 134-6.
Piatier, Jacqueline. 'Un Certain Vaudois nommé Chessex.' *Le Monde [des Livres]* 1er novembre 1973, 13-14.
Rohou, Guy. 'Jacques Chessex: *Reste avec nous*.' *NRF* 31, nos. 186-7 (1968), 1089-90.
Schoeni, Ursula. 'Chessex, Jacques (1934-).' *Columbia Dictionary of Modern European Literature*. 2nd. rev. ed. New York: Columbia U.P., 1980, 160.

Sénart, Philippe. 'Autour des romans.' *La Revue de Paris*, juillet–décembre 1967, 127–32.
Serex, Patricia. '*Comme L'os* de Jacques Chessex.' *Le Magazine Littéraire*, janvier 1989, 59–60.
Ughetto, André. '*Le Calviniste*, poèmes de Jacques Chessex.' *Sud* 68 (1987), 150–1.
Vandenschrick, Jacques. 'Pourquoi ces quelques Suisses?' *La Revue Nouvelle* 67, no. 2 (février 1978), 207–14.
Velan, Yves. 'Lecture pour le Jeûne.' *La Revue Neuchâteloise* 11, no. 39 (été 1967), 39–41.

C: GENERAL WORKS

Bataille, Georges. *L'Erotisme*. Paris: Editions de Minuit, 1957.
Booth, Wayne C. *The Rhetoric of Fiction*. Chicago: U. of Chicago P., 1967.
– *The Company We Keep: An Ethics of Fiction*. Berkeley and London: U. of California P., 1988.
Belsey, Catherine. *Critical Practice*. London: Methuen, 1980.
Butler, Christopher. *Interpretation, Deconstruction, and Ideology*. New York: Oxford U.P., 1987.
Calvin, Jean. *Institution de la religion chrestienne*. Ed. Henri Chatelain, Jacques Pannier, et Abel Lefranc. Paris: Honoré Champion, 1911.
Campbell, Joseph. *The Hero with a Thousand Faces*. Princeton: Princeton U.P., 1972.
Céline, Louis-Ferdinand. *Voyage au bout de la nuit*. Paris: Gallimard/Livre de Poche, 1952.
Culler, Jonathan. *Structuralist Poetics*. London: Routledge and Kegan Paul, 1975.
Derrida, Jacques. *Positions*. Paris: Editions de Minuit, 1972.
Duffield, G. E., ed. *John Calvin*. Appleford, Berks.: Sutton Courtenay Press, 1966.
Felperin, Howard. *Beyond Deconstruction: The Uses and Abuses of Literary Theory*. New York: Oxford U.P., 1985.
Ferguson, Sinclair B., David B. Wright, J.I. Packer, eds. *A New Dictionary of Theology*. Leicester: Inter-Varsity Press, 1988.
Genette, Gérard. *Figures II*. Paris: Editions du Seuil, 1969.
Prendergast, Christopher. *The Order of Mimesis: Balzac, Stendhal, Nerval, Flaubert*. Cambridge: Cambridge U.P., 1986.
Saussure, Ferdinand de. *Cours de linguistique générale*. Paris: Payot, 1969.

Schiltknecht, Wilfred. 'Suisse: Zorn et ses frères.' *Le Magazine Littéraire*, mai 1989, 59–61.

Scholes, Robert. *Semiotics and Interpretation*. New Haven: Yale U.P., 1982.

Sollers, Philippe. *L'Ecriture et l'expérience des limites*. Paris: Editions du Seuil, 1968.

Wendel, François. *Calvin: Sources et évolution de sa pensée religieuse*. Paris: Presses Universitaires de France, 1950.

Index

absurd, the, 22, 62–4, 153, 171, 176
ambiguity: in Chessex's attitude to Calvinism, 46–9, 97, 99, 100–1, 102–3, 104, 180 n. 8, 180–1 n. 2; in Chessex's attitude to God, 46–9, 180 n. 8
Anex, Georges, 109
anguish, as theme in Chessex's texts, 60–1, 79
animals: as representatives of freedom, 93; as representatives of life-forces, 92; as symbols of unity, 111, 131. *See also* Calvinism: and nature
Aragon, Louis, 126
Arland, Marcel, 4, 122
Auberjonois, René, 156
authority. *See under* Calvinism

Baroche, Christiane, 15
Barth, Karl, 26
Bataille, Georges, 57
Baudelaire, Charles, 4, 58, 93, 98, 160, 163
Beckett, Samuel, 63
Belsey, Catherine, 6
Berger, Yves, 4

Bernanos, Georges, 122
Berne, 28, 36, 43, 67
birds, as symbols of freedom, 93
Bodard, Lucien, 107
Booth, Wayne C., 11, 14
Borgeaud, Georges, 120
Bosquet, Alain, 15, 18
Brouillaud, Jean, 156
Budry, Paul, 135

Calet, Henri, 53, 163
Calvin, Jean, 25, 26, 41, 46, 81, 99, 179 n. 1
Calvinism: and authority, 67–70, 73–4, 130; Christocentric element of, 26; and death, 19–20, 38, 50–2, 53–5, 57–8, 63–4, 74, 96, 97, 99, 110; and devil, 29–36, 39, 78, 85, 101, 105, 106, 109, 110, 128, 176; difficulty of escaping, 97–103; disorder as product of, 44–5; dualism in, 29–30, 34, 37, 104, 109, 114–15, 176; excessive nature of, 27, 40, 44–6, 48, 65, 73, 114, 176; God of, 21, 26, 27, 28, 29–30, 34, 38–9, 46, 47–8, 68, 69, 78, 84, 86–7, 88, 99–100,

105, 109, 115, 132; and guilt, 28–9, 34–9, 40–1, 50–1, 78, 84, 88, 96, 118; hypocrisy as product of, 45, 73, 75–6, 162; influence on Chessex's life, 3, 16, 20–4, 25, 29–30, 36, 40–1, 43, 103, 106, 118, 125, 127; influence on Chessex's texts, 7, 16–17, 20–4, 25–39, 40–9, 115, 130, 165–8, 170–1, 175–6; kinds of, 25–6, 179 nn. 1, 2, 3; liberal tradition in, 25–6; and 'moderation,' 65–6, 81; and nature, 30, 33–4, 39, 92; nostalgia for, 40–4, 46, 106, 172; as order, 41–4, 48–9, 67–8, 172; and predestination, 53–4, 63, 170–1, 185 n. 12; as protection, 42–4, 46, 48, 105, 172; and punishment, 16, 27, 35, 36–9, 50–1, 62, 64, 68, 99; rejection by Chessex, 16–17, 22, 40, 41, 46, 78–96, 97–103, 105, 106, 175–6; and sin, 16, 19, 27, 28–9, 34–5, 36, 37–8, 40, 41, 43–4, 50–1, 57, 62, 64, 65, 101, 106, 109, 110, 118–19; solitude as product of, 61–2, 105, 106; in the Vaud, 13, 16, 19–24, 26, 34–5, 36, 43, 45, 47, 51–2, 62, 65–6, 67, 76–7, 86, 97, 105, 169; violence as product of, 30, 45, 51–2, 53, 74–5, 77, 112–13, 139; and women, 32–3, 57–8, 101, 106, 110; and writing, 37–8, 179 n. 12. *See also under* Catholicism; fox

Camus, Albert, 22, 63, 67, 142

cat: as symbol of devil, 33; as symbol of freedom, 93

Catholicism: as earlier religion of the Vaud, 111–12; as happier religion than Calvinism, 52, 105, 106; as more liberal than Calvinism, 99; as order, 43

Cayrol, Jean, 58

Céline, Louis-Ferdinand, 6, 54

cemeteries, 55–6, 108, 124, 155

Cendrars, Blaise, 6

Chappaz, Maurice, 34, 53, 71, 72, 73, 105

Char, René, 91, 156

characters, literary: Chessex's creation of, 165; as projections of author, 12–14; as representations of 'real' people, 11, 131–2

Châteaureynaud, Georges-Olivier, 135, 168

Chessex, Jacques: biography, 3–4
WORKS:
– 'Allons, allons,' 59
– 'L'Après-midi,' 134
– *L'Ardent Royaume*, 13, 20, 23, 26–7, 33, 44–5, 46, 55, 66, 69–70, 75, 81, 82–3, 84, 85, 88, 105, 119, 121, 124, 134, 136, 137, 138, 140, 148
– *Batailles dans l'air*, 56–7, 154
– *Bréviaire*, 38, 61, 90, 95, 130, 133, 134, 136, 149, 150, 151, 152
– *Le Calviniste*, 21, 22, 27, 39, 50, 54, 55, 58, 59, 62, 66, 78–9, 89, 95, 100, 115, 118, 150, 154, 157, 158, 159, 166
– *Carabas*, 5, 6, 7, 12, 13, 14, 15, 20, 23, 29, 30, 38, 45, 47, 51, 54, 58, 60, 65, 66, 70, 71, 72, 73, 76, 80, 81, 82, 83, 84, 85, 86, 90, 92, 96, 97, 98, 105, 106, 117, 118, 119, 120, 121, 122, 123, 124, 125, 128, 135, 139, 144, 145, 148, 162, 164, 168, 169, 175

- *Chant de printemps*, 59, 80, 94, 143, 160
- *Charles-Albert Cingria*, 5, 14, 46, 52, 71, 105, 114, 129, 130, 135
- 'La Clairière,' 57, 95
- 'Le Cloître,' 159
- *Comme l'os*, 22, 30, 32, 40, 41, 50, 61, 82, 109, 118, 150, 154, 159, 167
- *La Confession du pasteur Burg*, 14, 15, 20, 23, 27, 35, 41–2, 44, 45, 46, 50, 51, 73, 75, 87, 88, 92, 94, 118, 119, 121, 123, 144, 163
- 'Un Coq à Esculape,' 61
- 'Cueillir des pommes,' 134
- 'Cul et chemise,' 57
- *Les Dessins d'Etienne Delessert*, 19, 51, 53, 57–8, 63, 157, 168
- *Elégie soleil du regret*, 21, 22, 54, 55, 57, 88, 89, 93, 123, 140, 154, 156
- 'La Femme cernée,' 137
- 'Une Fête-Dieu qui finit mal,' 55
- *Feux d'orée*, 56, 79, 90, 134, 148
- *Flaubert ou le désert en abîme*, 21, 144, 164, 171–2
- 'Foins,' 134
- 'Le Fort,' 56
- 'La Fosse,' 50
- 'Le Génie du lieu,' 55
- *Le Jeûne de huit nuits*, 55, 59, 61, 79, 127, 144
- *Jonas*, 13, 23, 27, 29, 36, 39, 41, 42, 43, 64, 81, 83, 84, 85, 87, 88, 89–90, 99, 106, 111, 113, 117, 118, 134, 147–8, 150, 154, 158, 160, 167
- *Le Jour proche*, 3, 59, 62, 89, 148, 149, 150
- *Judas le transparent*, 13, 23, 27, 30, 31, 32, 35–6, 41, 45, 75, 95, 109, 110, 134, 138, 139, 158
- 'Juke-Box ou le contrôle des terres,' 56
- 'Le Mage,' 29, 39
- 'Le Mal retourne au mal,' 95
- 'La Mamelle des morts,' 50, 53, 67
- *Marie et le chat sauvage*, 93
- *Maupassant et les autres*, 53, 56, 59, 124, 129, 134, 135, 136, 141, 142, 153, 160, 162, 163, 164
- 'Le Miroir de Dylan Thomas,' 62
- 'Un Moment donné,' 149
- *Morgane Madrigal*, 13, 32–3, 58, 83, 86, 87, 94, 95, 110, 137
- 'Octobre est le plus beau des mois,' 150
- 'L'Oeuf,' 32
- *L'Ogre*, 4, 12, 13, 20, 23, 24, 26, 27–8, 29, 33, 38, 42, 46, 48–9, 53, 56, 57, 67–9, 73–4, 82, 85, 91, 92, 93, 94, 106, 107–8, 112, 121, 126, 131, 134, 159
- *L'Ouvert obscur*, 50, 55
- *Où vont mourir les oiseaux*, 15, 29, 50, 53, 55, 57, 60, 83, 95, 104, 109, 137, 148, 150, 153, 158, 159, 165–6
- 'Paroles de la petite morte,' 155
- 'Un Petit Vent frais,' 83
- *Portrait des Vaudois*, 12, 13, 15, 21, 26, 30, 36, 37, 46, 51–2, 56, 59, 62, 67, 73, 74, 76, 77, 79, 80, 82, 84, 86, 88–9, 90, 92, 94, 97, 98, 107, 111, 112, 113, 119, 120, 129, 133, 134, 148, 152, 160, 162
- 'Repose en paix,' 56
- *Reste avec nous*, 30, 33, 53, 55,

56, 58, 72, 74, 76, 91–2, 93, 108, 111, 133, 134, 148, 149
- 'Les Restes de la nuit,' 57
- *Les Saintes Ecritures*, 19, 22, 23, 27, 28, 34, 35, 38, 47, 51, 53, 54, 57, 59, 60, 61, 62, 72, 87, 92, 94, 105, 113, 114, 118, 129, 130, 134, 135, 149, 151, 152, 153, 157, 160, 161, 163, 164, 166, 168
- 'Secret de la colline,' 95, 137
- 'S'effraie le voeu,' 153
- *Le Séjour des morts*, 18, 32, 50, 51, 52, 53, 55, 56, 57, 59, 61, 62, 95, 126, 129, 134, 148, 150, 155, 156, 158
- 'Le Séjour des morts,' 55, 57, 155, 158
- 'Sur toutes les coutures,' 137
- 'Te Deum,' 55, 156
- *La Tête ouverte*, 4, 14–15, 33, 53, 55, 58, 66, 72–3, 84, 93, 117, 118, 119, 123, 144, 156, 165
- *La Trinité*, 20, 22, 23, 38, 53, 55, 56, 57, 85, 87, 102, 118, 140
- 'Tu sacerdos eris,' 167
- 'La Voie abandonnée,' 52
- *Une Voix la nuit*, 50, 59, 62, 80, 88, 89, 103, 148, 149
- *Les Yeux jaunes*, 13, 20, 22, 23, 26, 29, 30, 31–2, 33–4, 35, 37, 38, 39, 43–4, 46, 51, 59, 75, 81, 83–4, 85–6, 94, 102, 118, 119, 128, 134, 139, 153, 159, 167, 173

Chessex, Pierre (father of Jacques), 3, 79, 143–4, 149, 150, 152, 155
childhood: nostalgia for, 119; theme in Chessex's texts, 147–8
Christianity, unity in, 111–12
Cingria, Charles-Albert, 52, 71, 72, 73, 105, 114, 120, 128–9, 130

Clancier, Georges-Emmanuel, 135, 165
Colomb, Catherine, 151, 152
communication model of literature, 9–10, 145–6, 176
confession, in Chessex's texts, 12–13, 118–19, 144
Constant, Benjamin, 3–4
Corinthians, First Epistle to, 172
Crisinel, Edmond-Henri, 34, 51, 57, 72, 73, 160, 162, 166, 167
criticism, literary. *See* theory, literary
critics, literary: praise of Chessex's texts by, 14–15, 165; support for Chessex in France by, 121
curiosity: towards other people, 136–41; towards physical world, 135–6
Cuttat, Jean, 53, 60

Dari, the, 30
Daumier, Honoré, 66
Da Vinci, Leonardo, 141
day, as symbol of life, 89
dead, the: as companions of the living, 155–6, 160
death: attraction of, 157–60; as calm, 158–9; as incentive to live, 157, 160; in nature, 54–5, 106, 111, 131; as only certainty, 157–8; linked to sex, 57–8, 108; text as exorcism of, 155–7; text as response to, 160–2; as theme in Chessex's texts, 19, 50–9, 60, 61–2, 64, 78–80, 83–4, 87, 102, 103, 104–5, 106, 113, 131, 132, 150–63, 176. *See also* rabies, *and under* Calvinism; unity

decay, as theme in Chessex's texts, 59, 64
Delessert, Etienne, 51, 53, 57–8, 157, 168
Derrida, Jacques, 8, 10
desire: for other people, 136–40; for physical world, 135–6, 143
devil: and Calvinism, 29–36, 39, 78, 85, 101, 105, 106, 109, 110; cat as symbol of, 33; linked to disorder, 128; linked to fox, 33–4; in nature, 110–11, 131; owl as symbol of, 33; snake as symbol of, 33
Dionysus, 91, 92, 95, 112
disorder: linked to devil, 128; linked to sin, 43–4. *See also under* Calvinism
dreams, in literary creation, 168–9
dualism, in Chessex's texts, 16, 104–7, 114–15, 116. *See also under* Calvinism
Du Bouchet, André, 126
Duras, Marguerite, 7

Easter, as symbol of life, 88–9, 111
Ecclesiastes, Book of, 66
Echallens, 112
Emonet, Father, 46–7
Evian, 122
evil. *See* Calvinism: and sin
excess: praise of, 65–6, 80–2, 101, 139, 169–70; sexual, 35, 36, 44–5, 75, 115. *See also under* Calvinism

fantastic, the, in literary creation, 168–9
Felperin, Howard, 9–10
first-person narrative, in Chessex's texts, 12, 118

fish: as symbol of Christ, 90; as symbol of unity, 111
Flaubert, Gustave, 4, 7, 9, 12, 14, 21, 124, 139, 141, 144, 153, 161, 163, 164, 171–5
Florence, 38
food, as symbol of life, 82
fox, 38; linked to devil, 33–4; as symbol of Calvinism, 39; as symbol of fate of man, 63, 113; as symbol of freedom, 93; as symbol of unity, 111, 114, 131
France, Chessex's attachment to, 98, 122, 125
freedom: animals as representatives of, 93; birds as symbols of, 93; cat as symbol of, 93; in nature, 93; sea as symbol of, 93; women as symbols of, 84
French literary tradition: influence on Chessex, 116, 120–1, 122–6; universality in, 125–7
Fribourg, 3, 27, 46, 47, 52, 63, 78, 99, 105, 106, 107, 117, 134, 147
funerals, 56, 108

Galland, Bertil, 106, 114, 124, 165
Garcin, Jérôme, 18, 21, 32, 73, 129, 164
Gascar, Pierre, 80, 91
Genesis, Book of, 170
Genette, Gérard, 8
Ghirelli, Marianne, 136
Gide, André, 122–3
Giono, Jean, 37, 122
God: as loving being, 46–7, 78–9, 88, 99, 105, 110; rejection by Chessex, 21–2, 46–8, 173–4; as unity, 109, 110. *See also* text,

literary: as substitute for God, *and under* Calvinism; nature
Goncourt, Edmond de, 153, 163
Goncourt Prize. *See* prizes, literary
Grosjean, Jean, 126
Guillevic, Eugène, 126
guilt. *See under* Calvinism; sea monster

Haldas, Georges, 62, 163
hedgehog, as symbol of life, 91, 107-8
hospitals, 56
Hugli, Pierre, 43
Huysmans, Joris-Karl, 163
hypocrisy. *See under* Calvinism

imagination, in literary creation, 169
implied author, 14
inspiration, literary, 165-71
interpretive approach. *See under* theory, literary
Ionesco, Eugène, 67

Jaccottet, Philippe, 5, 23, 60, 62, 87, 120
Jericho, 162, 168
Jonah, 36, 42, 89-90, 99, 111
Jonah, Book of, 89-90
Joshua (biblical character), 162, 168
Joyce, James, 120, 133, 171
Judas, 31, 72, 81, 109, 138, 158
judges, 66, 69
Judrin, Roger, 114, 137
Jura, the, 143
'justes, les,' 65-77, 78, 81, 82, 84, 86, 100, 117, 132, 161-2, 169-70. *See also under* prison

Kafka, Franz, 4
Kanters, Robert, 24, 91, 126, 139
Knox, John, 26
Kristeva, Julia, 10

La Broye, 149
La Côte, 113
Lambrichs, Georges, 4
language: ability to change reality 143-4, 146; and attempt to seize physical world, 135-6, 172, 173; in creation of identity, 143-5; in creation of writer's identity, 144-5; inability to seize non-linguistic phenomena, 139-40, 141-3, 146; as partaking of imperfection, 173-4. *See also* mimeticism, in Chessex's texts
Lausanne, 3, 4, 75-6, 79, 84
Leclerc, Annie, 7
Le Clézio, Jean Marie Gustave, 141
Le Momont, 149
life: affirmation of, 16, 78-96, 97, 99, 100, 101, 104-5, 107-8, 131, 132, 176; animals as representatives of, 92; day as symbol of, 89; Easter as symbol of, 88-9, 111; food as symbol of, 82; hedgehog as symbol of, 91, 107-8; love as affirmation of, 86-8, 90; nature as source of, 88-9, 90-2, 102-3, 106, 110-11; pigs as symbols of, 82; spring as symbol of, 88-9; wine as symbol of, 82; women as symbol of, 83, 100, 101, 102, 110; the young, as representatives of, 82-3
logic, rejection of, 129
logocentrism, in Chessex's texts, 7-8, 130-1, 171-3

loss, sense of. *See* Calvinism: nostalgia for
love, as affirmation of life, 86–8, 90
Lubin, Arnem, 157
Luke, Saint, Gospel of, 31, 46

Malraux, André, 22, 63, 81, 120, 122, 126, 135
mandalas, 86, 110, 137
Manicheism. *See* Calvinism: dualism in
Mann, Thomas, 120
materialism, Chessex's attacks on, 75–6
Matthew, Saint, Gospel of, 36
Matthey, Pierre-Louis, 23, 130, 134
Maupassant, Guy de, 7, 9, 53, 56, 62, 124, 136, 139, 141, 161
May 1968, 82–3
memory: as barrier to death, 149–51; text as preservation of, 151–3, 174; as theme in Chessex's texts, 147–53
Mercanton, Jacques, 23, 120
metaphysical, the: in Chessex's texts, 19, 22–3, 125–7, 163, 175; in literature of the Vaud, 19
mimeticism, in Chessex's texts, 8–9, 132, 133, 143. *See also* language: and attempt to seize physical world
Montaigne, Michel de, 51
Montreux, 76, 135
moon, as symbol of unity, 111
Morand, Paul, 122
mystical, the, in Chessex's texts, 22–3, 106, 170
mythical, the: in Chessex's texts, 23, 137, 148, 179 n. 6; as unity, 113–14

Nadal, Philippe, 110
naturalism, 9, 56, 123–4, 125, 134, 139, 161, 162–3, 164
nature: communion with, 91–2; the devil in, 110–11, 131; as freedom, 93; God in, 110–11; as innocence, 93; love of in Chessex's texts, 90–1, 98, 103, 117, 131, 133–4, 136; linked to sex, 95–6, 110; as source of life, 88–9, 90–2, 102–3, 106, 110–11; as unity, 110–11, 114, 131. *See also under* Calvinism; death; women
necrophilia, 159
Nicole, Georges, 34, 57, 154
Noël, Bernard, 7
Nourissier, François, 4, 52, 73, 97, 123
nouveau roman, 5–6, 10, 11, 130
'nouveaux justes,' les, 70–1
Nouvelle Revue Française, 164
Novalis, 92

order. *See under* Calvinism; religion; style; text, literary
Origen, 168
Oster, Pierre, 129, 134
others: desire to seize, 137–40; impossibility of knowing, 139–41, 145; visual appropriation of, 137–9
Ouchy, 134
owl, as symbol of devil, 33

pagan religions: linked to Christianity, 112; unity in, 112
Pan. *See* Dionysus
Paratte, Henri-Dominique, 114, 141, 178 n. 18
Paris, 4; Chessex's love of, 98, 121–2

texts, 147–53. *See also under* sea monster
Paul, Saint, 87
Paulhan, Jean, 15, 60, 123, 128, 178 n. 26
Payerne, 119
Perrier, Anne, 41
Perros, Georges, 58
persecution mania, 72–3, 118–19
personal element, in Chessex's texts. *See* confession, in Chessex's texts
Philippe, Anne, 7
Pieyre de Mandiargues, André, 57, 95, 168
pigs, as symbols of life, 82
Poètes maudits, 169
poetry, relationship to prose, 14, 165
Ponge, Francis, 3, 15, 123, 128, 129, 136, 142–3, 178 n. 26
Pons, René, 61
predestination. *See under* Calvinism
prison, as symbol of 'les justes,' 69–70
prizes, literary, 4, 121, 126
prose, relationship to poetry, 14, 165
Proust, Marcel, 129, 173
Pully, 3
punishment. *See under* Calvinism

Queneau, Raymond, 60

Rabelais, François, 129
rabies, as symbol of death in nature, 34, 38, 63, 74, 111
Ramuz, Charles-Ferdinand, 34, 51, 114, 119–20, 126, 129, 164
Raymond, Marcel, 152
reality, physical, in Chessex's texts, 133–6, 167–8. *See also* language, and attempt to seize physical world; nature, love of in Chessex's texts; senses
Réda, Jacques, 126
religion: art as, 170–1, 172, 175–6; as order, 43
religious attitude to literature, 130–1
remorse. *See* Calvinism: and guilt
revolt: praise of, 71–3, 82–3, 181 n. 7; text as, 162–3, 172–5
Rifaterre, Michael, 10
Rimbaud, Arthur, 152, 169
Rivaz, Alice, 52–3, 59, 62, 118, 135
Robbe-Grillet, Alain, 138
romanticism, elements of in Chessex's texts, 65, 117, 163, 169–70
Ronsard, Pierre de, 59
Roud, Gustave, 23, 40, 57, 62, 63, 79, 120, 157, 159, 160, 161, 164
Rousseau, Jean-Jacques, 90, 117–19, 182 n. 1

sadness, in Chessex's texts, 61–2
Sartre, Jean-Paul, 6, 22, 67
Satan. *See* devil
Saussure, Ferdinand de, 8, 9–10
Savonarola, Girolamo, 38
scandal, caused by Chessex's texts, 73, 119
Scholes, Robert, 10
Schubert, Franz, 39, 79, 117, 160
sea, as symbol of freedom, 93
sea monster: as symbol of guilt, 36; as symbol of past, 147–8; as symbol of protection, 42, 83, 99, 158; as symbol of resurrection, 88–90; as symbol of unity, 111, 113, 114, 131

seasons, as symbols of life and death, 89, 103, 108, 129
senses, in appropriation of physical world, 136
Sépey, 30
sex. *See* Calvinism: and sin; *and under* death; nature
sin. *See under* Calvinism
snake, as symbol of devil, 33
solitude. *See under* Calvinism
Sollers, Philippe, 144
Soutter, Louis, 43
spring, as symbol of life, 88–9
Steffan, Uve, 89
Steinbeck, John, 133
Stil, André, 121
style: in Calvin's texts, 25; concision in Chessex's texts, 15, 123, 128, 144, 178 n. 32; exuberance in Chessex's texts, 15, 142–3, 144; importance for Chessex, 14, 128–9, 165; as order, 172
Supervielle, Jules, 4
surrealism: elements of, in Chessex's texts, 169–70
Switzerland: dual nature of, 107; French: literary traditions of, as influence on Chessex's texts, 117–121; marginalization of, 121
symbolism, elements in Chessex's texts, 169, 170

Tardieu, Jean, 126
Tauxe, Henri-Charles, 34
Tel Quel group, 10, 144
text, literary: linked to the divine, 166–8, 170; as substitute for God, 170–1, 173; as sharing the imperfections of the world, 173–4; as order, 127–9, 136, 151–2, 153, 154, 172; origins of, 164–71; as prayer, 167–8, 170; as protection, 172; self-sufficient, 171–2, 173, 175; as unity, 125–32, 172, 176. *See also under* death; memory; revolt
theory, literary: Chessex's attacks on, 4–7, 164; interpretive approach, 11; objections to Chessex's attacks on, 6–12
Thomas, Dylan, 62
time, as theme in Chessex's texts, 62, 64, 174, 176
Tournier, Michel, 5, 122
Trakl, Georg, 152

unity: in Chessex's texts, 18–19; in Christianity, 111–12; in Creation, 109–10; fish as symbol of, 111; fox as symbol of, 111, 114, 131; God as, 109, 110; of life and death, 107–8, 129; moon as symbol of, 111; the mythical as, 113–14; nature as, 110–11, 114, 131; in pagan religions, 112; sea monster as symbol of, 111, 113, 114, 131; search for in Chessex's texts, 16, 24, 107–15; in the text, 125–32, 172, 176; in the Vaud, 111–13
universality, in Chessex's texts, 126–7, 133

Valais, the, 143
Valbert, Gérard, 118
Vaud, the: 47, 52, 61, 73, 82, 90, 91, 133, 134, 143, 161, 162; Chessex's origins in, 97–9, 105, 116–17, 125, 148–9, 181 n. 2; dual nature of, 107; linked to

Chessex's father, 98–9, 149, 182 n. 4; literary traditions as influence on Chessex's texts, 117, 124–5, 127; as unity, 111–13. *See also under* Calvinism
Velan, Yves, 37–8, 62, 109
violence, in desire to know others, 139. *See also under* Calvinism
visual, the, in Chessex's texts, 136
Voisard, Alexandre, 62, 94, 127–8, 143, 168
voyeurism, 31–2, 43, 138–9

wine: as symbol of life, 82; compared to literary text, 144
witches, 32–3, 94–5
wolf, 33
women: as literary inspiration, 85–6, 101; as other, 141; as protection, 83; as stability, 86, 128; as symbols of freedom, 84; as symbols of freedom from guilt, 85; as symbols of life, 83, 100, 101, 102, 110; as unity, 110, 114, 131; linked to nature, 16, 94–5; religious awe for, 86, 101; treated as a class, 101–2. *See also under* Calvinism
women characters, individuality of, 101–2
Wordsworth, William, 10
writer: as medium, 166–7, 169; as priest, 170; as prophet, 169

young, the, as representatives of life, 82–3

Ziegler, Jean, 71
Zola, Emile, 4, 136, 141, 142, 161

www.ingramcontent.com/pod-product-compliance
Lightning Source LLC
Chambersburg PA
CBHW051404070526
44584CB00023B/3287